The Concept of Class

An historical introduction

Peter Calvert
Reader in Politics, University of Southampton

Hutchinson
London Melbourne Sydney Auckland Johannesburg

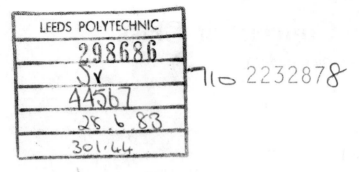
Hutchinson & Co. (Publishers) Ltd
An imprint of the Hutchinson Publishing Group
17–21 Conway Street, London W1P 5HL

Hutchinson Group (Australia) Pty Ltd
30–32 Cremorne Street, Richmond South, Victoria 3121
PO Box 151, Broadway, New South Wales 2007

Hutchinson Group (NZ) Ltd
32–34 View Road, PO Box 40–086, Glenfield, Auckland 10

Hutchinson Group (SA) (Pty) Ltd
PO Box 337, Bergvlei 2012, South Africa

First published 1982

Set in VIP Times by Computape (Pickering) Ltd

Printed in Great Britain by The Anchor Press Ltd
and bound by Wm Brendon & Son Ltd
both of Tiptree, Essex

British Library Cataloguing in Publication Data

Calvert, Peter
  The concept of class.
  1. Social classes
  I. Title
  305.5′01   HT609

ISBN 0 09 146670 9 cased
      0 09 146671 7 paper

The Concept of Class

For Simon

Contents

Acknowledgements

The research for this book was carried out with the aid of a grant from the Department of Politics of the University of Southampton. I should like to express my particular thanks to the two research assistants who aided me, Peter Davies and Frieda Stack, for their unfailing helpfulness and good humour, and to those of my colleagues with whom I discussed specific aspects of the work. I should also like to thank Alison Reeves, Pam Powell and Liz Jones for their hard work in producing the final typescript. Neither they, nor the Department, has any responsibility for what follows.

Introduction

As Max Weber said in his lecture 'Science as a vocation', the conscious discovery of the concept was one of the most important moments in scientific progress. A concept is an abstract entity with a defined meaning, and it represented for the Greek philosophers a standard of absolute value against which all other things were to be measured. But precisely because a concept is an abstract entity, it has no meaning unless it is given a label, a name. The giving of a name to a concept is an act of labelling, in that we may consciously choose a name for any given concept; on the other hand, the existence of the label does not guarantee the contents of the bottle, in that the abstract meaning attached to that name changes over time, as men and women change their preoccupations and focus on different aspects of the same problem.

This book deals with the concept of class. Class is one of the most commonly used of political concepts today. [There are literally hundreds of books devoted to exploring aspects of this subject of class, and huge research programmes are in progress to employ it further in the understanding of modern social entities.] Curiously enough, however, very little academic attention has recently been devoted to elucidating the use of the concept of class as such. By this I mean that in academic writing, as opposed to a great mass of popular literature, the question currently being explored is not 'What is class?' but 'How does class explain such and such a social phenomenon?' The purpose of this book, therefore, is simply to ask again the former of these two questions. It follows, therefore, that the preoccupations of this book are somewhat different from those of other writings today in political science and sociology. It does not seek to explore a wide range of literature which assumes the existence of a defined concept of class, except in so far as individual specimens of such books or articles seem to represent a significant transformation of the concept of class as it is currently used. Hence this book is not a general overview of the literature on class, and readers may well find that aspects of the subject which are of particular interest to them are either only sketchily handled or not noticed at all. They may rest assured that this is not because the author does not consider these works to be of importance, merely that they do not come within the confines of the intention of this book as it has been conceived from the beginning.

Secondly, and on the other hand, a chapter and a half of this book is devoted to discussing and investigating what we may call the 'prehistory' of the concept of class and endeavouring to ascertain, as far as possible, at what point it became a term consciously used and applied to politics and society. This investigation will lead us into the consideration of some rather obscure books and articles, and it involves some detailed consideration of the relationship between words and their meanings. This work, too, has not been undertaken merely out of a pedantic zest for the byways of lexicography; it forms an essential part of the exercise of understanding how concept and label came to evolve and to be brought together. The particular historical circumstances in which they did so was, I shall argue, of crucial significance for the future, and indeed our present, use of the term.

Last, one important lesson of this exercise has been the difficulty – indeed, the impossibility – of confidently translating concepts from one language to another. Class differs from many other political concepts in that it is precisely the universal application that is claimed for it which gives it its powerful role in modern political discourse. The question of how far we can rely upon this term in changing cultural circumstances is one of fundamental interest. It is my conclusion, as will be seen, that we cannot.

Peter Calvert
Southampton

1 The classical concept of class

Academic discussion of class and its significance today commonly takes its point of departure from Marx. Marx regarded classes as the fundamental organizational structures of society. They derived ultimately from the division of labour, but they had evolved away from the infinite number of small social groups that would be created merely by this form of differentiation. Nor were they measures of peoples' wealth or resources; what united individuals within a single class was their relationship to the factors of production. Contemporary capitalist society, with which Marx was principally concerned, had therefore come to be distinguished by a relatively small number of classes, which were sufficient for the purpose of analysis. The exact number is not consistently stated. In the *Communist Manifesto*, published in 1848, Marx and Engels referred principally to two: the bourgeoisie and the proletariat. At the end of his life, in *Capital*, Marx wrote of three:

> The owners merely of labour power, owners of capital, and landowners, whose respective sources of income are wages, profit and groundrent, in other words, wage-labourers, capitalists and landowners, constitute then three big classes of modern society based upon the capitalist mode of production. [Marx 1962, vol. III, p. 862]

Marx did not live to give a final answer to his question 'What constitutes a class?', and it is not my purpose at this point to do it for him. In the course of a long and active literary life Marx spoke of class frequently, and it is possible to give a large number of different answers based on his own work. But we must now distinguish two different ways in which he used the word 'class'. For Marx, class was above all an *analytical* concept, one which he used to explain the course of historical development in the past as well as his historical aspirations for the future. In his historical works, on the other hand, as in *The Eighteenth Brumaire*, he employed it as a *descriptive* term to label divisions in French society as he saw them actually existing at the time.

A concept is an idea, an 'idea of a class of objects' or 'a general notion'. As an abstraction used for analytical purposes it is a fundamental tool of the social sciences. To select a concept for use, however, implies the existence of a label identifying that concept, and it is at this point that problems arise. For it is the normal process of the growth of language to use, in labelling new concepts, words that have already acquired a range – sometimes a very considerable range – of definable meanings. These meanings continue to exist alongside the new concept, becoming confused with it and constantly affecting its interpretation. In tracing the growth of a concept, therefore, we have to begin with a word, and in this case we begin with the word 'class' as we find it in English.

The classics and class

The word 'class' entered the English language at a remarkably apt moment for a word whose use was to cause so much controversy in later ages. It was during the time of the Commonwealth and under the rule of Cromwell that it was first recorded by Thomas Blount (1618–79). Blount, a younger son of an old Herefordshire family, was, as a zealous Catholic, unable to pursue his profession and so turned to literature, the study of foreign languages and the compilation of a dictionary, *Glossographia*, which appeared in 1656. In this, the fourth English dictionary to be printed but the first to cite sources and to give etymologies, he gives the following definition: '*Classe (classis)* a ship, or Navy, an order or distribution of people according to their several Degrees. In Schools, (wherein this word is most used) a Form or Lecture restrained to a certain company of Scholars'.

The Latinate meaning, 'a ship, or Navy', need not detain us, since it did not long survive. More obviously of political significance is the second meaning, 'an order or distribution of people according to their several degrees'. The application of this general meaning to the special conditions of school life give us Blount's third meaning and, incidentally, also that of special significance to students in British universities and colleges who are ranked in first, second and third classes for their honours degree classifications. In the United States, since the early nineteenth century, the term has referred to all the students entering college who study and graduate together in a given year. The common factor, in school or university, is the degree of understanding of the subject matter being studied either manifested by, or to be expected from, the individual in question.

The Latin word *classis* (pl. *classes*) from which the word 'class' is derived, however, has an even more definite, political significance, to which Blount alluded under the word 'classical':

Servius Tullius [an early King of Rome] caused a general valuation of every Citizens estate throughout *Rome*, to be taken upon record, with their age, and according to their estates and age, he divided the *Romans* into six great Armies or Bands which he called *Classes*; The valuation of those in the first *Classe*, was not under two hundred pounds, and they alone by way of excellency, were termed *Classici*: And hence figuratively, are our best, and most approved Authors, *viz.* such as are of good credit and authority in the Schools, termed *Classici Scriptores*, Classical Authors.

Since English writers of the seventeenth century were as familiar with Latin as they were with English, they tended to use the Latin word *classis* as if it were English; hence in the plural it is difficult to tell which sense was intended. The *Oxford English Dictionary* (*OED*) records the use of *classes* in this way by Bishop King as early as 1594 and by the physician Sir Thomas Browne (1605–82) in his *Pseudodoxia Epidemica*: *Enquiries into vulgar Errors* (1646). Though we cannot assume that either of these learned men (addressing, as they were, a learned audience) would necessarily have preferred the English form to the Latin one, their use of the Latin word does suggest that the English word was not yet readily available and that it was domesticated in the decade between 1646 and 1656.

But what exactly did the Latin word mean? According to Lewis and Short, compilers of a standard Latin dictionary, it means literally 'a summoning', from *calo*, *calare* (or *kalare*), meaning 'to call out, proclaim, or summon a religious assembly'. It had two main meanings. The first and more important one was to designate classes of the Roman people, in the sense of the divisions established by the Servian Constitution. The second was that of an armed gathering, in the earlier period a body of armed men either on land or water, but latterly specifically a fleet.

It is tempting to suppose that the appearance of the English equivalent in the period of the English Civil War and the Common-wealth which followed it was associated with its immediate applica-tion to the divisions between different groups of people. There is little evidence for this, however, and it is quite likely that the fact that it was recorded at this particular time merely reflects an improvement in lexicography, for in fact it was not used at this time to describe divisions in English, as opposed to Roman, society.

Throughout the seventeenth century and the first part of the eighteenth, social distinctions in England were expressed in terms of 'rank' or 'station', the former referring to those more specific attributes associated with the granting of particular titles and the latter being a general term for one's position in society, whatever it might be. As Sir Thomas Browne observed in 1682, 'Content may dwell in all stations.' This meaning of the word 'station' seems closely related to the other word commonly used during this period to refer to a person's occupation or employment, and indeed seems to overlap with it; both are in turn derived metaphorically from the root meaning of a specified place or location. It differs clearly from 'class' in being a concept essential to the individual rather than to the collectivity, and when writers of the period wished to refer to occupational groups or ranks as a whole, they tended to use the word 'order', a word used in this sense in England since about the year 1300.

The first public use of the word 'class' in the English language to refer to divisions in *modern* society seems to have been made simultaneously in Scotland and England. It was first used in Scotland by Adam Ferguson in 1767. Ferguson, who was born in 1723 and died in 1816, was one of the leading figures of the Scottish Enlightenment, Professor of Natural Philosophy and subsequently Professor of Pneumatics and Moral Philosophy at the University of Edinburgh. In his *Essay on the History of Civil Society*, published in 1767, he introduces the word in this new sense, with a reference to the established and usual term, in a description of the difference between democracy and aristocracy:

In the second, the sovereignty is lodged in a particular class, or order of men; who, being once named, continue for life; or by the hereditary distinctions of birth and fortune, are advanced to a station of permanent superiority. From this order, and by their nomination, all offices of magistracy are filled; and in the different assemblies which they constitute, whatever relates to the legislation, the execution, or jurisdiction, is finally determined. [Ferguson 1966, p. 66]

No doubt many voices in England and Scotland may have spoken the word earlier in its revived sense, but it is satisfying to give credit where credit is due, and in this case the credit for its first use in England in print, also in 1767, must go to that strange eccentric Jonas Hanway (1712–86). Apprenticed to a merchant in Lisbon at the age of seventeen, he had travelled extensively in Russia and Persia before returning to settle down in England in 1750 as a philanthropist who founded several hospitals and devoted much time and effort to the cause of poor children but at the same time strenuously opposed the naturalization of the Jews. His *Letters on the importance of the rising Generation of the labouring part of our fellow subjects* appeared in 1767, and in the preface, dated December 1766, he used the term 'class'. It was, however, in his *Observations on the Causes of the Dissoluteness which reigns among the Lower Classes of the People* (1772) that he employed the word 'class' in the very title of his work and, incidentally, coupled it, probably for the first but certainly not for the last time, with the word 'lower'. (It is a satisfying irony that it was Hanway who gave the as yet inchoate *middle* classes what was to be their nineteenth-century badge of rank by being the first man to carry and to use an umbrella on the streets of London.)

The revived word was soon to find new users on the other side of the Atlantic, where in the newly independent United States there were men who saw the rise of faction as stemming from the existence of difference classes. In the tenth of *The Federalist Papers* (1788), written to expound the virtues of the new Constitution to the citizens, the pamphleteer James Madison wrote:

the most common and durable source of factions has been the various and unequal distribution of property. Those who hold, and those who are without property, have ever formed distinct interests in society. Those who are creditors, and those who are debtors, fall under a like discrimination. A landed interest, a manufacturing interest, grow up of necessity in civilised nations, and divide them into different classes, actuated by different sentiments and views. The regulation of these various and interfering interests forms the principal task of modern legislation, and involves the spirit of party and faction in the necessary and ordinary operations of government. [Beloff 1948, p. 43; cf. Locke 1960, pp. 14–27]

The influence of the French Enlightenment

The new term, it is reasonable to assume, must have had some very special significance for its users to displace the older words such as 'rank', 'order' and 'station'. It can be no accident that it came into widespread use at a time when the act of classification had, in the natural sciences, proved most dramatically to form the essential foundation for further analysis.

The classification of plant species was already a busy occupation of naturalists in the later seventeenth century as the competing voyages of sailors and explorers from the European nations disclosed an extraordinary range of new plant species. But it was in 1762 that Carl Linnaeus (1707–78) published his *Species Plantarum*, the first universally accepted system of classification and the one which, with extensive revision and modification, remains the basis of scientific nomenclature to this day. Under it the word 'class' denoted one of the highest groups into which the Animal or Vegetable Kingdoms were and are divided, a usage first recorded in English nine years before (*OED*). Jean Baptiste de Lamarck (1744–1829) extended the systematic view of the world to geology with his classification of fossil shells. Building on the work of William Smith (1769–1839), who was the first to assign relative ages to the rocks, the outlines of a new science of geology began to emerge. And in the last years before the French Revolution, the work of Antoine Laurent Lavoisier (1743–94) gave meaning to the discoveries of his contemporaries in the development of a unified view of matter based on the identification of the chemical elements.

In each of these fields, the very possibility of a unified treatment owed much of its philosophical impetus to the new view of the universe advanced by Sir Isaac Newton (1642–1727). It was on this basis that Diderot (1713–84) became the founding editor and guiding spirit of the great *Encyclopédie*, which was to unify the sciences through the construction of a vast compendium of universal knowledge.

The spirit of flexibility and adaptability which the Encyclopédistes brought to their task made its completion in 1766 an event as momentous for the social as for the natural sciences. Whether the *Encyclopédie* was attacked by the Jesuits, suppressed by the state or bowdlerized by the printer Le Breton, such attention was but a further tribute to the work's success. And, as Diderot himself made plain in his introduction, success in this case meant the achievement of its main aim, which was no less than 'to change the normal mode of thought' (*pour changer la façon commune de penser*), as well as its secondary one, 'to gather together the knowledge scattered over the face of the earth' (*rassembler des connaissances eparsées sur la surface de la terre*). Not all knowledge was available in Europe, let alone in the Philosophe's study. If it were, the normal, cultivated man could understand everything. And the end task was to understand the nature of man himself.

Diderot seems to have been the first to realize, and certainly the first to proclaim, that the key to understanding man lay in his works. In the *Encyclopédie* they were revealed in all their marvellous complexity to the *noblesse* of the tottering *ancien régime*. And it is in the *Encyclopédie* that there emerges the first sense of the extension of classification to human social groups, distinguished by common properties or attributes – in short, the emergence of the division of man into classes.

As often happens when terms used in one field of knowledge are borrowed by another, the new term was not borrowed unaltered. In biology, 'class' referred to a number of coequal divisions, to be regarded as being, as it were, on a common (and high) level of generality. And, insofar as the term was originally applied to occupational groups of a relatively small and homogeneous membership, its use appeared at first reasonably similar. The concept of evolution had not then been invented, of course, but there was in the minds of even these early classifiers the notion that all fields of knowledge would turn out in the end to be related, and in particular the plant and animal world on the one hand and the mineral world on the other.

The mineral world, by contrast, was clearly arranged in layers, one on top of another. The realization of this was even then beginning to give rise to the concept of stratification, which in due course was to lead in biology to Darwin's concept of evolution, and in archaeology to the discovery of stages of human social development measured by the prevailing use of tools. From classification to stratification, therefore, was an easy, if potentially misleading, logical step for the theorists of society. In this sense the Encyclopédistes' use of the word was fraught with inconvenient possibilities for the future, even if they did not realize it, and the assumptions thus generated are enshrined in the common but dangerous term used by modern sociologists to embrace the study of all forms of divisions in society, namely 'social stratification'.

Of course, the Encyclopédistes did not regard their achievement, in itself, as being the creation of a finished work. They expected further editions of the *Encyclopédie* in due course to include the results of fresh investigations, each systematizing, testing and evaluating the new knowledge that they contained. If the Enlightenment failed to reveal clearly the outlines of the debates to come, however, it was because its rays fell on the scene of the first moves in what Blanqui in 1837 was to term the industrial revolution (Mathias 1969), and that was to give a very different meaning to the terms which they were in the habit of using.

The economic meaning of class

How then did the word *classe* come to be used in France to denote a division of French society? Where did it come from, and what other meanings did it have? The lexicographers give us fairly clear answers.

Bloch and Wartburg state that the root sense was a borrowing of the Latin *classis* in the sense of 'class of citizens' and was first recorded in the fourteenth century by Bersuire. They add that the other senses were developed in French. That the root sense refers exclusively to the ordering of Roman citizens, however, is indicated by Wartburg himself in his monumental *Französisches Etymologisches Wörterbuch* (Bloch and Wartburg 1964; Wartburg 1940). In this sense it is used by, for example, Montesquieu in 1748 (Montesquieu 1966, vol. I, pp. 10–12) and by Helvétius in 1758 (Helvétius 1909, p. 233).

As a category of pupils it was established at least as early as 1549, and it is from this usage, rather than any more complex one, that appears to be derived the meaning given to it by Rich in 1680 of 'rank in which one puts persons of the same profession according to merit' (*rang auquel on met des personnes de la même profession, d'après leur mérite*) (Wartburg 1940).

Then in 1753 comes its use in the *Encyclopédie* to denote 'each of the great groups of animals, of vegetables' (*chacun des grandes groupes d'animaux, de végétaux*), preceded, most significantly, by the introduction in 1752 of the word *classification* and succeeded in 1756 by the verbal form *classer* ('to class'). This leaves open the question of when it received its final transformation into a term denoting social division and how and why this was achieved. Here Wartburg offers us little or no assistance, finding evidence only from 1792 for the still rather general social sense of 'category of citizens distinguished according to their social condition' (*catégorie de citoyens distingués d'après leur condition sociale*), which still lacks the clear implications of economic qualification which are implied in the mention of the term 'fortune' by Ferguson.

We must look, therefore, to the writings of the Physiocrats or, as they were originally termed, the Economistes, to ascertain whether or not their scientific zeal for the founding of the new science of economics extended to placing human beings themselves into classes.

The origins of the Physiocratic school, the first true school of economists (Higgs 1968), are usually dated to July 1757, on the day when the fateful meeting took place at the Palace of Versailles between François Quesnay, physician to the King and to Madame de Pompadour, and his future ardent disciple, the Marquis de Mirabeau. Quesnay, then 63, was a philosopher in search of just such a disciple, but until then he had published virtually nothing, his articles on corn, men and taxation in the great *Encyclopédie* having appeared under borrowed names for fear of jeopardizing his official position. Under *Grains* (1757) Quesnay had mentioned 'classes' in a general way which echoed Cantillon (Cantillon 1931, pp. 78–9) and like him, prefigured, without establishing, a new usage, when he wrote: 'It is by increasing the revenue of the proprietors and the profit of the farmers that it [i.e., proper cultivation] procures gains for all the other classes and supports a consumption and expenditure by which it is in turn maintained' (Meek 1962, p. 82). Then came the first edition of his *Tableau Economique*, privately printed at Versailles in 1758 with the technical aid of King Louis XV, who worked the press. Here Quesnay makes the new word serve a much more crucial function to distinguish between two 'expenditure classes'. One of these he termed the 'productive expenditure class' (*classe des dépenses productives*); the other, as yet unnamed, was in the third edition (1759) clearly termed the 'sterile expenditure class' (*classe de dépenses stériles*), a term which, since it was used in Quesnay's fashion to refer to manufacturing and commercial expenditure as opposed to investment in agriculture, caused not a little irritation.

Quesnay held, and his disciples came to advocate fervently, that the only true wealth was that procured from the soil by agriculture, and that agriculture alone yielded a net profit. It was, therefore, the secret of the wealth of the nation to promote the growth of agriculture and to remove all obstacles to this, in particular the inefficient and highly detrimental system of tax farming which, they recognized, was responsible for the fact that the country was poverty-stricken and the King constantly in debt. Quesnay sought in the *Tableau Economique* to demonstrate that the product of the land was expended not only in productive but also in what he regarded as unproductive investment or taxation – setting, incidentally, a bad example to later economists by using not only imaginary figures but also arbitrary assumptions about how the profit was divided.

Here we are more interested in the fact that in showing how expenditure varied in its effects on the economy, he found it necessary to distinguish between two broad social groupings, which he terms *classes*, according to their relationship to the process of production, to which in the last version of his work, the *Analyse*, published in June 1766, he had added a third, similarly distinguished. By this time, too, the cumbersome word 'expenditure' had been dropped from their designation. 'The nation is reduced to three classes of citizens: the productive class, the class of proprietors and the sterile class,' he asserted (Meek 1962, p. 150).

The productive class comprised those actually engaged in agriculture, broadly construed, 'that which brings about the regeneration of the nation's annual wealth through the cultivation of its territory, which advances the expenses which agricultural work entails, and which annually pays the revenue of the proprietors of the land'. The class of proprietors included 'the sovereign, the owners of land, and the tithe-owners'. The sterile class was made up of 'all the citizens who are engaged in providing other services or doing other work than that of agriculture, and whose expenses are paid by the productive class, and by the class of proprietors, which itself draws its revenue from the productive class' (ibid., 150–1).

The potentially explosive effect of Quesnay's work was not lost on the authorities, though their wrath actually fell on his disciple, Mirabeau, for the publication in 1760 of his *Théorie de l'Impôt*. Although without imprint, the secret of its authorship soon leaked out and this strident call for a reform of the tax structure created a sensation, and its author was consigned to prison in Vincennes, from which he was freed after eight days through the intercession of Madame de Pompadour herself. After this experience, caution prevailed among the naturally cautious members of what by now was a potentially powerful and well recognized school. Free trade in corn, introduced in 1763, owed as much to the work of theorists who did not describe themselves as Physiocrats, and the moves toward the improvement of the taxation system fell far short of radical reform. Quesnay himself died in the same year as Louis XV and shortly before the accession to office of Turgot, who, though not himself a member of the school, openly sympathized with some of its principal aims and, it was hoped, might realize them.

In his *Réflexions sur la formation et la distribution de richesses*, written in 1766, Turgot also divided society into three classes. Though the book was not published until 1770, in its hundred short paragraphs it seems to have remained virtually unaltered, and in style and expression it is far more telling and effective, as well as more tactful than the writings of Quesnay.

Turgot's analysis was based on the concept of a series of stages in human development, such as had already, to some extent, been understood as applying to economics by the Physiocrats themselves. Thus society had passed through hunting, pastoral and agricultural stages of development, becoming more complex in the process.

So now we have the Society divided into three classes: the class of Husbandmen, for which we may keep the name *productive class*; the class of Artisans and other *stipendiaries* supported by the product of the land; and the class of *Proprietors*, the only one which, not being bound by the need for subsistence to one particular kind of work, may be employed to meet the general needs of the Society, for example in war and the administration of justice, whether through personal service, or through the payment of a part of its revenue with which the State or the Society may hire men to discharge these functions. The name which for this reason suits it best is the disposable class. [Turgot 1973, p. 127]

In the succeeding section, section XVI, Turgot added a significant comment on the resemblance between the 'two industrious or non-disposable classes':

Both also have this in common, that they earn nothing but the price of their labour and of their advances, and this price is almost the same in the two classes. The Proprietor beats down those who cultivate his land in order to give up to them the smallest possible proportion of the product, in the same way as he haggles with his Shoemaker in order to buy his shoes as cheaply as possible.

Thus far, Turgot had much in common with the Physiocrats, but at this point he parted company with them, for he began to introduce the subject of capital, the accumulated surplus, 'whether in the form of revenue from his land, or of wages for his labour or his industry'. Having considered the traditional alternative of buying a landed estate, Turgot proceeded to demonstrate how the use of capital in manufacturing industry had brought about a subdivision of the 'industrial stipendiary class' into entrepreneurs and artisans (section LXI), and a similar division in the class of cultivators (section LXV). Having expounded the way in which capital should be employed for maximum return, he concluded (section XCIV) that the possessors of moveable capital were, by virtue of the fact that they possessed capital, to be understood as belonging, in person, to the disposable class. The wealth they obtained, however, he concluded in true Physiocratic style, came ultimately from the net product of the land.

In Turgot's work the concept of class, as deriving from the relations of the individual to the process of production, is well developed, therefore. The only true producers are those who work the land. Artisans are industrious, but they are not productive. Together with the productive class, however, they receive no remuneration save the cost of their labour, until the time comes when they can employ a surplus in the form of capital to reinvest. The conclusion of the accumulation of capital, however, is to transfer them to the third class, that of the proprietors, who alone are freed from the burden of subsistence and to this extent may be employed by the state for its own purpose.

There is no doubt that Turgot's concept of class derives from Physiocratic thought in the main. But it is of more than passing interest that Meek records a letter from the Scots philosopher David Hume (1711–76), apparently written to Turgot in late September 1766, in which he distinguishes between 'Merchants, properly speaking' and 'all Shop-Keepers and Master Tradesmen of every Species' as being comprehended in one 'class', and in which the English word is employed several months before its appearance in print in Ferguson's work (Turgot 1973, p. 18).

That the term remained, even for a time, only a technical term of economics in French is certainly not likely. It seems to have been loosely used even by those for whom it should have had the greatest precision, so that we find Mirabeau himself employing it quite rhetorically in his *Essai sur le Despotisme* (1776), when he writes scornfully of the Ordonnances of Louis X and Philip V, 1318: 'These benefactors of the fourteenth century believed that they were doing a kindness to the greatest part of men (for in all countries SLAVES or VILLAINS were the most numerous class) by allowing them the right to live and breathe for themselves' (Mirabeau 1776, p. 33).

In one respect at least, Mirabeau makes evident what Turgot did no more than imply, that the division of society into classes might not be accounted just or inevitable. Before going on to consider these implications, however, it would be helpful to consider two points. Were the English and the French senses of the word in fact the same? Did they influence one another, and if so, how?

The evidence of Hume's letter is inconclusive, for Hume had lived in Paris from 1763 to 1766 and could reasonably be expected to be fully conversant with the Physiocrats' use of the term. If the term had indeed originated in Scotland, then it would be natural to expect it to appear in the works of other figures of the Scots Enlightenment, and above all in the works of Adam Smith (1723–90). Smith's letters, however, give no indication that, despite his interest in the origins of civil society, he was ready to adopt the new word to denote divisions of modern society, preferring, as did James Millar, to employ the word 'rank'. In *The Wealth of Nations* (1776) the word 'class', both as a noun and as a verb, is indeed used, but in a strictly classical sense in which, although the basis of occupation is present, it is present in a very non-Physiocratic form. He wrote:

In the republics of ancient Greece and Rome, during the whole period of their existence, and under the feudal governments for a considerable time after their first establishment, the trade of a soldier was not a separate, distinct trade, which constituted the sole or principal occupation of a separate class of citizens. [Smith 1925, vol. II, p. 191]

From the very beginning of the same work, however, Smith has been talking of the division of labour in society (a term which, although it echoes Mandeville, he effectively invented; cf. Mandeville 1728). And when he does so in such a way as to delineate layers of social stratification, he uses the term 'rank'. We find it first in his description of the prime topic of his enquiry: the question of why civilized societies are more productive than their predecessors:

The causes of this improvement in the productive powers of labour, and the order, according to which its produce is naturally distributed among the different ranks and conditions of men in the society, make the subject of the First Book of this Inquiry. [ibid., vol. I, p. 2]

And this cause is to be found, first and foremost, in the division of labour:

It is the great multiplication of the productions of all the different arts, in consequence of the division of labour, which occasions, in a well governed society, that universal opulence which extends itself to the lowest ranks of the people. [ibid., vol. I, p. 12]

This extension is in itself to be valued:

> Is this improvement in the circumstances of the lower ranks of the people to be regarded as an advantage or as an inconveniency to the society? The answer seems at first sight abundantly plain. Servants, labourers and workmen of different kinds make up by far the greater part of every great political society. But what improves the circumstances of the greater part can never be regarded as an inconveniency to the whole. No society can surely be flourishing and happy, of which the greater part of the members are poor and miserable. It is but equity, besides, that they who feed, cloath and lodge the whole body of the people, should have such a share of the produce of their own labour as to be themselves tolerably well fed, cloathed and lodged. [ibid., vol. I, p. 80]

Smith is certainly describing the sort of society that France was at the time. Significantly, however, he is not using the French word, nor its English equivalent, to designate its social divisions. When he uses the word 'class' as a noun he is referring, in the first instance, to the divisions of Roman society.

Even when he uses the word 'rank', he does not use it in the sense that in the same year Turgot was employing the term *classe* – that is, to designate divisions of society in terms of their relationship to the process of production. Smith gives us no precise indication of how many ranks he thinks there might be; nor, despite his early promise, does he relate the economic improvements he describes to precisely and consistently labelled social groups, as Turgot certainly does. It is because of this that what for Turgot was a precise and meaningful term retained in English the imprecision and uncertainties which had always been associated with the older term 'rank'. The economic meaning which the Physiocrats had attached to their new term became diffused in English into yet another word denoting social stratification. The word 'class' in English has resisted every attempt to make it more precise ever since.

This, however, is no reason for not attempting the task. Let us, therefore, at this point recapitulate the development of the senses of the word so far.

Derivation Latin *classis*, meaning 'a summoning', from *calo, –are*.

A a division of the Roman people under the Servian Constitution;

A(i) an armed gathering, earlier an army, later a fleet;

AA the top division of the Roman people, the best people, from which 'classical', designating the best.

From sense **A** is derived French *classe*, meaning:

A   (fourteenth century) a division of the Roman people (sense still current in late eighteenth century;

B   (1549) category of pupils in schools;

B(i) (1680) ranks in which one puts people of the same profession according to merit;

C   (1753) a category or sort of animal or plant.

In English the order of development appears to differ noticeably (cf. Onions 1966). Sense **B** is established in Elizabethan times. By 1646, however, there has already emerged from sense **A** a new general meaning:

D   (1646) an order or distribution of people according to their several degrees; in this sense it is used by Mandeville in 1723 and by Hume in 1766 in his letter to Turgot, by which time the Physiocrats have borrowed sense C and given it their own meaning;

E   (1758) a division of society according to relations to the process of production.

Though this last sense is fully established by Turgot in 1776 in French, its sharper and more precise connotations tended not to follow it into English, where, from the time of Ferguson in Scotland and Hanway in England, we see it being absorbed in the older, vaguer and less analytical sense D. This, however, has implications which go far beyond mere looseness of usage. For it was in English that the new term absorbed the political connotations of subordination and superordination which had previously been designated habitually by the term 'rank' but which in French were reserved for the distinct concept of 'estate', which we shall examine in chapter 2. It is from this very confusion of economic and political overtones that the word has acquired so much of its popularity since.

2   Class as balance

The world of the ancient Greeks

We have already seen how the adoption of the term *classe* by the Physiocrats was accompanied only gradually by the realization that there might be two or more views about its desirability. Eighteenth-century writers, for whom the question of classes was on the whole a marginal, technical point, easily proceeded from the view that the emergence of classes was associated with the intensification of production to the view that the division of society into classes was both natural and desirable. They did so the more easily because of a long tradition in the Christian world of regarding social divisions as divinely ordained and as the necessary foundation of political order. In turn, this tradition had come to lean heavily for its philosophical amplification on the work of the Greeks, and above all on Aristotle, 'the Philosopher' to the Middle Ages.

They were happily unaware of the full dangers inherent in translating the terminology of the Greek city-state into the very different context of later times. We, however, should not be. It is paradoxical but essentially true to say that there is no real concept of class in Aristotle, and that the various terms in Greek which are rendered as 'class' in English translations have very different senses from those that we have attributed to them. Moreover, translators have often, with the strong awareness of class that forms part of their own political tradition, introduced the word to pad out a sentence in the Greek which involves no such generality. Above all, for the Greeks social divisions have a concreteness and a legal backing which, though present in Roman society, is entirely absent from the world of the eighteenth century and its successors, so though in one sense it is true to say that the Greeks spent much of their time discussing class, in another it is truer to say that they had no concept of class at all.

To understand why this is so we need first of all to know something about the structure of a Greek city-state.

Legally, the residents of such a state comprised three radically different groups. Slaves had no rights and were regarded as property. Metics, that is to say, resident foreigners – even those whose families had resided within the territorial limits of the state for several generations – were free men and did not in general, as might be expected of trading people, suffer from social discrimination. They remained outside the citizen body, nevertheless, and could not take part in its political activities. Citizens alone were entitled to political participation. Their status was attained by birth. The degree of participation to which they were entitled, on the other hand, varied according both to the constitution of the state and to their own place within it.

Generally, the majority of citizens would be farmers and the majority of the remainder artisans or tradesmen. At any one time there were only a very small number of people who had wealth sufficient for all their needs, and in the earlier stages of Greek history a relatively small number of ways were open for them to spend it. Even in the democratic states, the existence of a class of citizens with enough spare time to engage in politics owed little to the division of labour between them and virtually everything to the existence of a separate slave work force. That distinction they took for granted: it was in the nature of things that mankind should be divided into rulers and ruled. As Aristotle put it: 'For he that can foresee with his mind is naturally ruler and naturally master, and one that can do these things with his body is subject and naturally a slave' (*Politics*, Book I, p. 1252a).

It is clear that from an early period most, if not all, of the Greek city-states had a defined class structure; the case of Athens, because of its later importance, may be examined in greater detail. Like the other states, Athens was originally a monarchy, but like them also, though rather earlier than most, it was transformed into an aristocracy by the gradual and progressive attentuation of the royal powers. The title of king (*basileus*) remained, and indeed was to remain until the later days of the Athenian commonwealth, but the powers were assumed by an elected magistracy which was, according to old but doubtful tradition, thrown open to all nobles in 753–752 BC and became an annual office in 683–682 BC. The noble class were known as the *Eupatridai*. Besides them there were two other free classes, the *Georgoi*, or peasants, and the *Demiurgoi*, or traders, who enjoyed some civic rights, particularly that of taking part in the *Ekklesia*, or general meeting. Without civic rights, though free men, were those who tilled the lands of others, the *Hektemoroi*, or sixth-parters, from the fact that they were allowed to retain one-sixth of what they produced by way of fee.

During the seventh century BC the non-noble classes seem to have successfully asserted their rights to a greater share in the government, so that by the end of it there had emerged a formal structure of taxation classes based on wealth, assessed by the annual yield of landed property measured in corn, oil or wine.

The highest class were the *Pentakosiomedimnoi* (Five-Hundred-Measure Men), defined as those whose land produced as many measures of corn and as many measures of oil or wine as together would amount to 500 measures. The second class were the *Hippes* or Horsemen, who produced between 300 and 500 measures and so were adjudged capable of maintaining a horse and riding it to war. Those with between 200 and 300 measures were the *Zeugitai*, or Teamsters, who could till their land with a yoke of oxen. The chief magistracies, the offices of *archon*, *polemarch* and *basileus*, were open to members of the first class only, but with the institution of the *Thesmothetai* six more magistracies were created, giving members of the older classes of the *Georgoi* and *Demiurgoi* representation in the government, so that wealth rather than family became the criterion of political power. Those outside the political circle, now known generically as *Thetes*, or labourers, were, however, increasingly important to the state because of the need to maintain a substantial navy, and, as in other states in Greece the increasing impoverishment of the farm labourers was giving rise to bitterness and unrest. In many other states this was resolved, one way or another, by an upheaval and the emergence of a dictatorship or tyranny.

That this did not happen at once in Athens was due to the legislation of Solon, son of Exkestides, whose name was to become proverbial for later generations as a designation for a wise law-giver. Solon cancelled old debts (*c.* 594 BC) and forbade the enslavement of debtors in future. He then redrafted the Athenian Constitution, probably while holding office as an extraordinary legislator or *nomothetes*, published it on wooden frames in the public hall and made all citizens swear to uphold it.

'And he arranged the constitution in the following way,' wrote Aristotle:

he divided the people by assessment into four classes as they had been divided before, Five-hundred-measure man, Horseman, Teamster and Labourer, and he distributed the other offices to be held from among the Five-hundred-measure men, Horsemen and Teamsters – the Nine Archons, the Treasurers, the Vendors of Contracts, the Eleven and the Paymasters, assigning each office to the several classes in proportion to their assessment; while those who were rated in the Labourer class he admitted to the membership of the assembly and the law-courts alone. [*The Athenian Constitution*, Book VII, p. 3]

The formal disability of the Labourers, whom Solon had thus wisely admitted into the Constitution, remained even when Athens had evolved into a fully fledged democracy, as is evident from Aristotle's parting comment on this subject:

even now when the presiding official asks a man who is about to draw lots for some office what rate he pays, no one whatever would say that he was rated as a Labourer. [ibid., Book VII, p. 7]

The distinctions between classes are the more tellingly shown by the degree of equality observed within them, and here Solon's reforms were no less significant. The principle of selection by lot was introduced in the final choice among the elected candidates for the magistracies and, it appears, also for the membership of the new Council of Four Hundred, whose job it now became to prepare business for the Assembly. The ambitions of the richest class were circumscribed by the introduction of sumptuary laws and the imposition of strict penalties for idleness. Participation, moreover, was not a right to be exercised at will but a duty, as Aristotle makes clear:

And as he saw that the state was often in a condition of party strife, while some of the citizens through slackness were content to let things slide, he laid down a special law to deal with them, enacting that whoever when civil strife prevailed did not join forces with either party was to be disfranchised and not to be a member of the state. [ibid., Book VIII, p. 5]

There could be no more striking example of the Greek belief in the need for balance between all the elements in the state. Each trade and each occupation was seen as contributing its share, and when in the *Republic* Plato wishes to demonstrate unequivocally the need for divisions within the state, he does so by building up his imaginary state according to the order in which its citizens will feel the necessity for new trades to make life itself possible, for each man will do better by keeping to one trade only (*Republic*, Book II, pp. 367–72).

Before considering what use Plato was to make of this fact, however, we must examine carefully what terminology the Greeks used to refer to these various divisions. The fundamental division, that between slaves, metics and citizens, was not really one of class at all, in any sense of the word. It is significant that the Greek word most often given in this sense as an equivalent for 'class' (*genos*) means 'race'.

The division of the people into taxation classes by occupation and wealth was a formally ordered constitutional fact; in other words, taxation classes were determined by law and had political significance only because the law said so. The purpose of these divisions was to establish the principle that the more a citizen contributed to the state, the greater would be his share of civic responsibilities. With the establishment of democracies, the divisions, it seems, simply lost their original significance. When Aristotle talks about taxation classes in the *Politics*, he uses the general word *timematos*, which, perhaps significantly, comes from the same root as the Greek word for 'honour' (as, for example, in *Politics*, Book II, p. 1266a).

Now, as is well-known, Aristotle also has much to say on the subject of the political relationships of such broader social groupings as the 'rich' and the 'poor'. What may well escape a modern reader who approaches the *Politics* only through the medium of translation is that in referring to such generalizations he uses a quite different, and much less specific, vocabulary. Hence an apparently precise and modern-sounding statement, such as 'inasmuch as fortune has brought into existence two component parts of the state, rich and poor, let any resolution passed by both classes, or by a majority of each, be sovereign', loses much of its apparent precision when it is realized that the word here translated as 'classes', *mere*, means no more than 'category' (*Politics*, Book VI, p. 1318a). The same general word is used a little later when he considers whether the so-called 'military class', literally 'the military' (*polemikon*), and the so-called 'class that deliberates about matters of policy and judges questions of justice', literally 'members of the Council' (*boulenomenon*), are to be regarded as identical or distinct (*Politics*, Book VII, p. 1329a). Certainly, there is no sense in which these broader social groupings are to be identified specifically with membership of the legally constituted taxation classes. Time and again the word 'class' creeps into English translations to amplify the terser expressions of the original. And each time it does so, it introduces to the unwary reader a wide range of wholly modern impressions which are, to put it no more strongly, absent from the original.

For the Greeks, moreover, the most concrete social distinctions were those between one trade and another. What gave these distinctions their peculiar significance for the later world was the debate over the special nature of the trade of ruler. It was a debate in which the case for a distinctive body of rulers had been put most memorably by Plato.

A carefully designed class structure was to form the essential social framework of Plato's ideal state. The ideal could not be achieved 'unless either philosophers become kings in their countries or those who are now called kings and rulers come to be sufficiently inspired with a genuine desire to wisdom; unless, that is to say, political power and philosophy meet together'. By philosophy Plato means the desire and search for the knowledge of the whole of truth and reality, this reality being absolute and independent of the world as perceived, knowledge of which is neither wholly true nor wholly false. A ruler can only attain, or strive to attain, such knowledge by rigorous and exacting education, and those who are thus to be trained form the first class, the Guardians of the ideal state or Republic, to whom the care of the state is to be entrusted. Plato shocked his contemporaries, not by his suggestion that philosophers should rule but by his proposal that they should be kings, a word which then had a musty air about it. It seems probable that his use of the term was designed to emphasize that those properly trained for the job must exercise their responsibilities with full authority and without restraint.

At the age of 20, having completed their initial course of training, the trainee Guardians would be divided into two classes, the Rulers, to whom specifically the care of the state was to be given, and the Auxiliaries, who would execute their orders. These would form two of the three classes of the state, the third being made up of the Craftsmen, of whom, once he had dealt with the education of the Guardians, he has little or nothing to say. They would it seems, continue to live in the ideal state much as they did at that time in the real world.

Though the institution of the ideal state is possible, Plato is at pains to argue, it will, like all existing states, become corrupted in time. Central among the forces prompting a steady decline towards timocracy, dominated by the rich, and leading in turn inevitably to oligarchy, democracy and tyranny or despotism, is struggle between classes.

> But the violence of their contention ends in a compromise: they agree to distribute land and houses for private ownership: they enslave their own people who formerly lived as free men under the guardianship and gave them maintenance; and, holding them as serfs and menials, devote themselves to war and to keeping these subjects under watch and ward. [*Republic*, Book VIII, p. 546]

Thus Plato proceeds from the assumption of the necessity of classes, based on his observation of the division of labour in society, towards a total view of the state as a dynamic entity, destined to change and prone to decline. There is in this an important lesson for the modern social scientist. Many now consider that because of their belief in real as opposed to physical entities, Plato and his followers were unconcerned with the physical world and unversed in its ways. Nothing could be further from the truth. Plato himself frequently uses contemporary examples to illustrate the points he is making and was certainly not adverse to trying to put his ideas into practice, as is demonstrated by the fact that he accepted the invitation of the tyrant Dionysius I to come to Italy, and there made one of his most distinguished converts in the person of the tyrant's brother-in-law, Dion. According to one authority, his reward was to be obliged to leave Syracuse in haste, but the dictator's agents caught up with him, and he was for a brief period sold into slavery at Aegina before being ransomed and returning to Athens.

But their awareness of the physical world was not always matched by an equally critical awareness of the value of the data it presented to them. One of a number of examples that occurs in Plato's last work, the *Laws* (probably composed 357–347 BC) is particularly relevant, since it highlights the extent to which the philosopher may, initially or subsequently, have come to be unconsciously influenced by the assumptions of the society in which he himself lived. Plato is here describing the founding not of an ideal state but of a new colony, such as was familiar to all educated Greeks of his period.

The welfare of the state will best be secured if there is equality of wealth. The idea of holding property in common, the foundation of the *Republic*, is here specifically rejected as impracticable. But the greatest possible degree of equality must be attained. Hence the land should be divided equally between the 5040 households of which the new colony is to consist in such a manner that each has two landholdings, one near and one far away from the dwelling and that the quality of land provides, as nearly as possible, an equal livelihood for all (*Laws*, Book V, pp. 737–41). Though the land held may be equal, however, the colonists will undoubtedly arrive with very different degrees of wealth, and they must therefore be divided into property classes, 'so that by a rule of symmetrical inequality they may receive offices and honours as equally as possible, and may have no quarrelling' (ibid., Book V, p. 744). And while no man may have less than the basic allotment, neither may any man be permitted to retain more than four times the value of the allotment in other forms of wealth. He will be subject to denunciation and conviction if he does not choose rather to acquire merit with his fellows by surrendering the surplus voluntarily to the state. And a detailed register of all forms of wealth will be maintained by the Law Wardens of the state to ensure that the laws are upheld.

Plato states specifically that there should be four such classes, and since the passages concerned repeatedly emphasize that these numbers are in no way random but have been selected for their arithmetical and geometrical significance, this number too must have meaning.

For in relation to economics, to politics and to all the arts, no single branch of educational science possesses so great an influence as the study of numbers: its chief advantage is that it wakes up the man who is by nature drowsy and slow of wit, and makes him quick to learn, mindful and sharp-witted, progressing beyond his natural capacity by art divine. [*Laws*, Book V, p. 747]

But what is that meaning in this case? It is not explained. Plato makes use of the division in taxing his classes differentially for the assumption of magisterial office, in organizing voting, in arranging for the provision of priests, market stewards and judges at the athletic contests, in regulating marriage and in apportioning fines for offences. But he does not say why there should be four of them, and one is forced to conclude that the number suggested itself involuntarily, being that current in contemporary Athens. Since the classes are not otherwise considered, there is no question that, for example, they might come into conflict one with another as groups, and it seems strange that Plato does not investigate this possibility and, as Aristotle did later, consider what its implications might be. Inequality is accepted but regulated.

It was during the last twenty years of Plato's life, and specifically during the preparation of the *Laws*, that Aristotle was a member of the Academy. His medical family background and biological training naturally inclined him, it seems, towards the clinical method which he was to apply to politics with such success. It must also have brought home to him how very different from one another individual men and women actually were.

In the *Politics* this is a point which he is at pains to emphasize. 'And not only does a city consist of a multitude of human beings, it consists of human beings differing in kind,' he wrote. 'A collection of persons all alike does not constitute a state' (*Politics*, Book II, p. 1261a). Inequality, it seems, is inherent not in the nature of groups generally but in that of those political organizations which we call states. But there is no escaping from the state. For 'man is by nature a political animal, and so even when men have no need for assurance from each other they none the less desire to live together' (*Politics*, Book III, p. 1278b).

As Aristotle himself observed and reminds us, in many (and originally of the Greek states in most), the large proportion of free men who worked with their hands were not, in fact, regarded as citizens and were ranked with slaves and foreigners. On the other hand, he is emphatic that in a properly constituted state there should be equality between citizens in respect of political authority, though he is critical of Plato's argument in favour of redistributing income within the state, which he regards as potentially disastrous:

It is a bad thing that many citizens who were rich should become poor, for it is difficult for such men not to be advocates of a new order.

Nor can the situation be avoided simply by educating people equally to accept it: 'It is possible for all to have one and the same education,' he concedes,

but for this to be of such a nature as to make them desirous of getting more than their share of money or honour or both; moreover civil strife is caused not only by inequality of property but also by inequality of honours, though the two motives operate in opposite ways – the masses are discontented if possessions are unequally distributed, the upper classes if honours are equally distributed, bringing it about that 'Noble or base in the like honour stand.' [*Iliad*, Book IX, p. 319]

For Aristotle, then, the fundamental division in society is that between the well-off and the propertyless, but there are many other divisions within society, and these polar opposites, which are nowhere defined or delimited, certainly do not include all, and may well not include many, of the total body of citizens. Even if they did, the claim to rule rests not on wealth alone but on various qualities befitting the task.

In politics with good reason men do not claim a right to office on the ground of inequality of every kind ... the claim to office must necessarily be based on superiority in those things which go to the making of the state. [*Politics*, Book III, p. 1283a]

He is noting, in the passage that follows, those things actually recognized in the states of his time as conferring the right to office.

Now it has been said before that all make a claim that is in a manner just, though not all a claim that is absolutely just; the rich ... because they have a larger share of the land ... the free and well-born as being closely connected together (for the better-born are citizens to a greater degree than those of low birth, and good birth is in every community held in honour at home) ... and we shall admit that virtue also makes an equally just claim, for we hold that justice is social virtue, which necessarily brings all the other virtues in its train; but moreover the majority have a just claim as compared with the minority .... [ibid., Book VII, p. 1283a]

Aristotle's acceptance of the pre-eminence of birth was natural for its time and for the essentially agrarian communities to which all Greek city-states so closely related. His assertion of the importance of virtue, a sense of justice and the strength of numerical superiority, however, stemmed from much more profound considerations about the quality of life which a Greek citizen might have and should, indeed, strive to attain.

Given that what we know of Aristotle's own thought comes to us through the unreliable medium of reconstructions by students of their lecture notes, it is, of course, always uncertain whether he was misquoted or misunderstood. In his critique of Plato, for example, he used Plato's own assumptions about the origins of society to identify up to eight distinct groupings which might claim a share in the rule of the state. This is not to say that he necessarily supported any one of these possible claims. Yet of one thing we can be certain: for Aristotle, as for his contemporaries, civic virtue was of prime importance, and virtue in an individual entitled him to pre-eminence, not merely to equality. However, as Aristotle himself notes in a passage that is often misconstrued, it is equality rather than inequality that makes for political stability. 'The ideal of the state', he says, 'is to consist as much as possible of persons who are equal and alike, and this similarity is most found in the middle classes' (*Politics*, Book IV, p. 1295b).

This is not, as is often suggested, Aristotelian authority for the ascendance of the 'middle class' in the sense that that phrase might have been (and, indeed, *was*) understood in Victorian England. Aristotle's 'middle classes' – literally 'the middle part' (*tois mesois*) – are merely those citizens who are neither rich nor destitute. They do not form a distinct group with a permanent existence separate from each of the two extremes. They are not a class in any generally accepted modern sense at all. And it must again be emphasized that they do not correspond to any or all of the taxation classes legally established by the Constitution for the apportioning of civic responsibilities.

It is particularly important to stress this point, since when Aristotle turns his attention to the ordering of the state in the formal sense, he is emphatic about the need for taxation classes. Taxation classes are essential to a stable state, he affirms, as 'has been well-known to students of politics for some time'. Such classes, he claims to have been told, were established in Egypt by Sesostris (*Politics*, Book VII, p. 1329), and this he gives as evidence of their reality and importance. They had, moreover, he believed, been discovered independently on Crete.

There is, of course, no historical evidence of a foundation for Aristotle's belief that taxation classes in the Greek sense had been known in Pharaonic Egypt, still less (though the Ancient Egyptians certainly suffered from taxes) that they had been specifically ordained by the quasi-legendary Sesostris, whom modern Egyptologists identify with Senusert III of the Twelfth Dynasty (1887–1849 BC). It appears that here we are looking at an example of what M. I. Finley (1971) has described as the belief in the historical reality of 'the ancestral constitution', that belief by which custom gains authority in the popular mind from being retroactively fathered by a legendary law-giver. Such a law-giver, for the Greeks themselves, was a Theseus or a Lycurgus.

Though Aristotle differed in many ways from Plato, therefore, in one respect at least they agreed, and that was in holding the essential foundation of political order to be a balance between competing groups. It was an opinion that was to dominate learned views on politics down to the end of the eighteenth century, and to continue long afterwards to provide a contribution to the debate on class in a wholly changed context of meaning. Obviously, there is some parallel to the Greek taxation classes in the qualifications for the franchise in mid-nineteenth-century Europe, but in one respect these were always different: they were not, as they were for the Greeks, associated with a specific act of creation of the political community, new colonies being constituted in the model of their founder state.

Once constituted, the balance between rulers and ruled maintained this class structure, with but slow movements between one class and another. Aristotle rejects Plato's prescription for the transfer of infants as violating the bonds of family loyalty, decency and respect.

Aristotle rejects also Plato's argument about the equalization of property, as much on the grounds of its inherent impossibility as on the grounds that new injustices will be created. Nowhere is this seen more clearly than in his treatment of slaves and women. Whereas Plato in the *Republic* simply assumes the existence of slaves, Aristotle in the *Politics* undertakes a critical examination of slavery as an institution. He does not reject it out of hand as unjust, though he notes that other thinkers of his day in fact do so. Nor does he shun the argument that men who, to all appearances, are naturally born to rule, such as those who have held high office in defeated states, may, in the conditions of the real world, find themselves enslaved. Similarly, men of slavish temperament may and do find themselves in positions of authority. Instead he welcomes the paradox, on the ground that the fact that men perceive it as such indicates that there are indeed qualities that distinguish the man born to rule from the man born to slave. Though not everyone finds himself in the position in which his talents best fit him to serve, the existence of those talents will drive him in the direction for which he is best fitted.

Women he sees as naturally dependent on men; yet they are not slaves. For him it is the household rather than the individual that is the fundamental unit of the society which he terms the state, and it is with the family that he begins his exploration of political life. The education of women is no less important than the education of men, 'for the women are a half of the free population, and the children grow up to be the partners in the government of the state' (*Politics*, Book I, p. 1260b). At the end of the *Politics* he argues in favour of communal meals for women as well as for men.

For Aristotle the ideal life is that lived in accordance with virtue, which is to be found in a middle course of life. This same criterion, he declares, applies to the state and to its constitution, which is its way of life. The wealthy are unwilling to be governed and the poor unable to govern, and if either or both are preponderant in the state, the result is 'a state consisting of slaves and masters, not of free men'. Therefore 'the middle class state will necessarily be best constituted in respect of those elements of which we say the state is by nature composed' (*Politics*, Book IV, p. 1295b). He goes on:

> It is clear therefore also that the political community administered by the middle class is the best, and that it is possible for those states to be well governed that are of the kind in which the middle class is numerous, and preferably stronger than both the other two classes, or at all events than one of them, for by throwing in its weight it sways the balance and prevents the opposite extremes from coming into existence. Hence it is the greatest good fortune if the men that have political power possess a moderate and sufficient substance, since where some own a very great deal of property and others none there comes about either an extreme democracy or an unmixed oligarchy, or a tyranny may result from both of the two extremes.... [*Politics*, Book IV, pp. 1295b, 1296a]

From which it follows that since this is the case in most states, most states are either democracies (in the bad sense of the word) or oligarchies.

Aristotle himself was to live to see these observations rendered null by the rise to supreme power of his former pupil, Alexander of Macedon. In the last year of his life, under the rule of Alexander's successor Antipater, property qualifications were reinstated at Athens and the state returned to the Solonian Constitution, a move with which he would have been in complete agreement. On the other hand, he had lost all sympathy with his former pupil some years before his death, when in 328 BC he had ordered the execution of Callisthenes for his refusal to accept the oriental custom of prostration before the divine monarch, and though in Athens itself the Aristotelian school retained, with some minor interruptions, its philosophical and moral ascendancy, elsewhere in the Greek world the Hellenistic monarchies that followed marked a reversion to an earlier pattern in which monarchical government superseded, and came to dominate, the careful balance between the interests of social groups which had grown up over the centuries. Ultimately these monarchies, in turn, were swallowed up in the great *cosmopolis*, or world state, of the Roman Empire, a universal, divinely ordained monarchy before which other social divisions were levelled.

Even for the classical Greeks, class balance had always been not simply a matter of secular advantage but something divinely ordained. (Plato is as careful, in the division of his city, to balance the twelve gods as the four classes.) The acceptance of Greek thought by the Christian world of the Middle Ages, therefore, was facilitated by the extent to which that thought appeared to support the Christian assumptions, many of them, in turn, the product of the late Hellenistic world of the New Testament and the Hellenized Empire that succeeded it, particularly in the East.

Precisely for this reason, we should note, before turning to those assumptions and to that world, that the Greek 'tradition' was very much more complex in itself than the concentration thus far on the works of Plato and Aristotle would suggest. Certainly, it is relevant that it is the works of these two men, and above all those of the latter, that were to have currency in later ages as if they were the products of those times. But as Havelock (1957) has demonstrated, there were other political theorists and, as he suggests, an entire 'liberal' tradition of Greek thought, which, though familiar to the Greeks themselves, was not inherited but which is not on that account any less desirable or admirable.

Democritus (the inventor of the atomic theory) left a brief set of twenty-three aphorisms which convey the impression of a writer of the Periclean period striving for a rather different balance of classes. Havelock renders his thinking thus:

14   At that time when the powerful [classes] confronting the have-nots take it upon themselves to pay toll to them and to do things for them and to please them: This is the situation in which you get [the phenomenon of] compassion and the end of isolation and the creation of comradeship and mutual defence and then civic consensus and then other goods beyond the capacity of anyone to catalogue in full.
15   It is consensus that makes possible for cities the [execution of] mighty works enabling them to execute and carry through wars. [Havelock 1957, p. 142]

Democritus, who has already declared as axiomatic the need to obey the dictates of justice, then proceeds to draw the conclusion that the man in authority has the obligation to perform well, before proceeding to state that it is equally the duty of the private citizen to neglect neither his public nor his private responsibilities. The private citizen, therefore, cannot be absolved from responsibility for his own condition – a far cry from the static balance striven for by Plato and assumed as a satisfactory, if rather conservative, compromise by Aristotle. It is not sufficient to accept authority.

Havelock further argues that Aristotle's very belief in the efficacy of the city-state vitiated his doctrines as a guide to action in the regional and emerging super-states of his day. Yet the comprehensiveness of his mind and the respect which his work in other fields brought to his political theory protected it. It was the conservative and authoritarian elements in Greek thought that were admired by the shapers of the Roman Empire.

The Christian world

The Christian world of the Early Fathers and of the Middle Ages was itself the heir of the Roman Empire, and to this extent it inherited a conflict of Christian belief with pagan reality as well as with pagan beliefs.

Like the Greeks, the Romans had formally constituted classes, but these had had a rather different origin from those of Athens and rested broadly on the concept of property. The Constitution of Servius Tullius (578–534 BC), which has already been mentioned, established rather than recognized the existence of property classes in Rome, with the deliberate intention of breaking the structure of the clans into which the citizens had previously been exclusively divided, although these survived the reform. At the same time the citizens were also divided for military purposes into centuries, or regiments. It is certainly not a coincidence that this reform is associated with the name of an Etruscan king ruling over an alien people, nor that following the establishment of the Republic (510 BC) the class system seems to have been further modified by the patrician upper class, which thus consolidated its seizure of political power. In response, the lower classes, the plebs, took the dramatic step of seceding to the Aventine Mount, and refused to return until the patricians guaranteed them the protection of officers of their own, called tribunes, who in the course of time acquired a veto power over the action of patrician magistrates (494 BC). Nevertheless, the continued agitation of the plebs for the codification of the law led to the appointment of a commission for the purpose (451 BC), and a series of legal provisions which broke down the boundaries between the classes followed. Ultimately, when the last of the divisions had gone, a new nobility emerged which was even more exclusive than the old patriciate and much harder to break into, as even Cicero was to find in the very last years of the Republic.

What remained from the earlier struggles was the concept of the equal protection of the laws and of legal processes which took no account of the distinction between rich and poor. They did, however, make, as was the custom of the day, a very clear distinction between a free man and a slave, and by the end of the Republic Roman society was, in fact, divided into four layers: the nobles, other citizens, freedmen and slaves. Under the Empire the distinction between the first two rapidly vanished, as proscription after proscription destroyed the small number of old families that might have pretensions to political power, though the elaborate sumptuary laws of earlier periods remained for some time as a useful means of raising revenue through fines and privileged confiscations.

These classes were described not by the term used in the Servian Constitution but by the word *ordo*, which not only corresponds to the English word 'order' and the French *ordre* but also translates as 'rank', as in 'the ranks of the armed forces'. It was therefore ultimately from Roman practice that the eighteenth-century writers derived their habitual use of the words 'rank' and 'order', which 'class' was later to supersede.

The early Christians emerged as a religious sect promising salvation to the poor in a society that otherwise held out little promise of hope or happiness. The Gospels are quite uncompromising on the virtues of poverty. In the Sermon on the Mount Jesus enjoined his followers to reject utterly the necessities of earning a living:

Therefore I say unto you, Take no thought for your life, what ye shall eat, or what ye shall drink: nor yet for your body, what ye shall put on. Is not the life more than meat, and the body than raiment?

Behold the fowls of the air: for they sow not, neither do they reap, nor gather into barns; yet your heavenly Father feedeth them. Are ye not much better than they? [Matthew 6:25–6]

When a young man came to Jesus to ask him what he must do to attain eternal life, he was told:

If thou wilt be perfect, go and sell that thou hast and give to the poor, and thou shalt have treasure in heaven: and come and follow me.

The young man was unwilling to do so, 'for he had great possessions', and he went away.

Then said Jesus unto his disciples, Verily I say unto you, That a rich man shall hardly enter into the kingdom of heaven.

And again I say unto you, It is easier for a camel to go through the eye of a needle, than for a rich man to enter into the kingdom of God.

Modern commentators on this passage have suggested that 'the eye of a needle' was a city gate, and that the phrase did not suggest the total impossibility that it would, taken literally, to a medieval or a modern reader. The following passage, however, makes a very different point, one perhaps no less comforting to the wealthy Christians of a later period:

When his disciples heard it, they were exceedingly amazed, saying, Who then can be saved?

But Jesus beheld them and said unto them, With men this is impossible, but with God all things are possible. [Matthew 19:16–26]

For the message of the Gospels was above all one of brotherhood, a brotherhood transcending not only social grades and distinctions of rank but also differences of race and other distinguishing signs that could provoke discrimination. The widow who offered her 'two mites, which make a farthing' to the Temple treasury contributed, in proportion to her need, more than the rich people who gave large amounts (Mark 12:41–4), and in the kingdom of heaven the terrestrial order of things would be completely reversed, 'For whoever exalteth himself shall be abased; and he that humbleth himself shall be exalted' (Luke 14:11).

The message of the Gospels was not the only influence on the political action of the early Christians. There were, inevitably, many others.

Foremost among these, to begin with, was the fact of the Roman Empire, a vast structure of immense age, created by pagans in flagrant violation of the precepts of the divine law. *Reddite Caesaris Caesari* – 'Render therefore unto Caesar the things which are Caesar's' (Matthew 22:21) – was the injunction of Christ himself, and Caesar commanded obedience in a way that a true Christian could not always accept. Yet with the conversion of Constantine the Great in AD 338, service to the Christian Emperor became in itself the service of God as well as furnishing proof of the rightness of his doctrines. It opened the way for the whole-hearted acceptance of the Empire itself and of the Roman way of life as the model for medieval Christian life. As the Latin language bound together the peoples of the Empire in contemplation of a single book, so Church membership and Roman citizenship came to be seen as spiritual and material aspects of the same life. And as Ullmann points out, the translators of the Vulgate, in rendering the Hebrew original, made use of Roman legal terms which gave the structure of law underlying Christian precepts a strongly Roman cast (Ullmann 1965, p. 21).

In the later years of the unified Empire its rulers strove in vain to make that law even more effective in stitching together the crumbling fabric of civilized urban life. The very transience of Emperors and their dynasties strengthened the hierarchical structure of the Imperial civil service and threw into relief the assumptions of social stratification on which the Empire depended. For if (for example) people would not bake bread for fear of the hard work and penalties attached to giving short measure at absurdly low prices, the remedy was to make the trade of a baker hereditary and the penalty for escape, if he were recaptured, burning alive. Escape to the barbarians, however, became ever easier, and after the Battle of Adrianople (378) the effects of the incursions were severe enough to threaten the lives even of members of the administrative classes.

A century and a half later the unhappy Boethius, in his prison cell, remembered too late that official dignity does not really clothe the individual with honour and romance, and indeed draws the more attention to his indignities on his fall. 'If one who had been many times consul chanced to visit barbaric lands,' he mused, 'would his office win him the reverence of barbarians? And yet if reverence were the natural effect of dignities, they would not forgo their proper function in any part of the world, even as fire never anywhere fails to give off heat' (*Consolation of Philosophy*, p. 83).

All men, then, are equal before God. And yet, because Christians might by this time once again be subjects of a pagan ruler, it became increasingly urgent to determine what degree of obedience they might owe respectively to the temporal and to the spiritual power. St Ambrose of Milan (d. 397) asserted to the Emperor Theodosius that the civil power had authority neither over ecclesiastics nor over the goods of the Church; this view was refined by Pope Gelasius (d. 496) into the doctrine that the spiritual and temporal powers inhabited two separate though interdependent spheres. In between them lay the work of St Augustine, Bishop of Hippo (354–430), who had lived through the period of the disaster of Adrianople and the collapse of civilization that followed.

In his *City of God* Augustine explained the disasters, and indeed the constitution of civil society itself, as the products of man's fallen state. Although naturally social beings, since the Fall men had been incapable of realizing a truly harmonious society under God without the need for government and laws. From the Fall, too, had resulted the division of civil society into masters and servants and the establishment of the institution of private property. Rulers, both good and bad, constituted God's judgement upon his flock, just as in the Church lay the fount of goodness and mercy. That Church was constituted by Christ himself under the leadership and direction of St Peter (*Tu es Petrus* – Matthew 16:18) and his successors, and this fact inevitably gave to the Church's role a significance for later generations that Augustine, perhaps, neither knew nor intended.

From this time on, society in Christian lands would be not only stratified horizontally, between master and servant, but also divided vertically between ecclesiastic and layman, and in due course the ecclesiastics would themselves become rulers, transforming the robes of the poor Roman of the second century into the priestly vestments of a prince of the Church. Before this was achieved, however, many centuries elapsed in which the very survival of the state seemed at times to hang in the balance, and many inchoate states failed to crystallize into permanent foundations. So potent was the memory of the Roman Empire that in a quest for stability the Papacy was ultimately to attempt to reconstitute it in the West to provide the necessary source of temporal power and security when the Holy Land, Africa and Spain had already been overrun by the new and formidable power of Islam.

When the new Empire tried to regain the power of the old, the Papacy was eventually to challenge its creation and, if not to defeat at least to disrupt it sufficiently so that it failed to provide more than a formal apex for the new European political structure. Instead Europe began to coalesce into a set of distinct nations, each distinguished by a common language, which corresponded only roughly to an overlapping set of monarchical states. Within these states there were, apart from the clergy, nobles, serfs or villeins and even slaves. Relations between king and noble, and between noble and villein, were those between master and man, symbolized by the ceremony of homage and the taking of an oath which imposed, in the eyes of his fellows and of the Church, reciprocal obligations upon each party.

The oath taking, or act of homage, was an individual act, however. We cannot regard the nobility of an early medieval state as a class in any recognizable sense: there were too few of them; the distinctions between them were both marked and hierarchically organized; and the relationship between a few of the higher nobility and the king was far closer than the relationship between those few and the lesser nobility. And, as we have already seen, from the earliest period of what became known as the feudal system, a special problem was presented by the towns, whose citizens claimed, with increasing success, special rights and privileges as free men engaging in trade and commerce. It was in the cities of Italy and France, in the course of the twelfth century, that the notion of the political began to reappear. But, as Ullmann (1965) has pointed out, the fact that it did so emerge owed most to the concrete relationship between lord and vassal, and nothing at all to the Church's view of the king as appointed by God.

The legally established divisions between the nobles, the clergy and the rest of the citizens were formalized into categories known as 'estates'. Each was regarded as a necessary part of the social whole, being related to one another 'like the organs or limbs of a body' (Toennies 1931). As the individual limbs or organs had different roles to play, so did the members of each estate, and each estate, accordingly, had a proportionate role in the legal business of government.

The historical origin of the estates in France goes back to the high Middle Ages. The king of France was at the time almost powerless, except within that limited area round Paris known then, and still known today, as the Île de France. At the election of Hugues Capet (987–96) to fill the vacant throne, the great lords of France, who acknowledged him as their nominal superior and suzerain, neither did homage nor rendered service.

Over the next two centuries the monarchy strengthened its base through a regular succession of co-opted successors and through its close relation with the Church within its own holdings. But the rise of Normandy and, subsequently, the loss of Burgundy to the Empire (1032) seemed to threaten the total disintegration of the old Carolingian kingdom. The recovery of the monarchy began with the early discovery by Louis VI (1108–37) of the importance of the rise of towns, which, beginning in Italy, became the most dramatic evidence of the emergence of a new medieval culture. By granting charters to the towns, the king became protector of the townsfolk against the rapacity of local feudal lords and gained the right to intervene, which he did effectively, outside the immediate limits of his own territory, consolidating his own strength in the territory of his vassals south to the Loire. By drawing his royal officers from among the smaller nobles, from the Church and, significantly, from the merchant classes of the towns, he achieved even more, as he built up an administrative machine that he could use as an instrument of his power. The alliance with the towns was always self-interested, and the Capetians did not grant to towns in their own territories the same degree of independence that was enjoyed by those communes in the north, such as Beauvais, which received charters, or the consulates formed in the south with the assistance and support of the local nobles against the influence of their own feudal superiors. Under Philip II Augustus (1180–1223) the new alliance brought tangible and spectacular benefits in the shape of the recovery of Normandy and the Angevin lands north of the Loire; his successors were to carry royal authority south to the shores of the Mediterranean, building on the foundations their predecessors had laid.

Philip's power and pretensions brought him into collision with another rising power, that of the Papacy. It was to support him in his opposition to the extreme claims of Boniface VIII (1294–1303) to secular as well as spiritual rule that in 1302 he summoned the first authenticated meeting of the States General, in which representatives of the towns took part.

In 1614, when the States General had met for the last time, the process through which the nobility came to be dependent on the Crown was already well under way. Apparently, the nobility were still all-powerful, and, as the events of the Fronde were to show, they had in no way suspected that they might lose that power. France was still a feudal country. The noble had rights of feudal justice, the *banalités du moulin, du four et du pressoir* and the sole *droit de chasse*. A peasant had to have a licence from the seigneur to sell land, to pay dues when he bought it, to pay tithes in kind and to pay toll dues when he went to market. Above all, the peasantry felt the full weight of the two great taxes, the *taille* and the *gabelle*, which furnished Louis XIII (1610–43) with the largest revenue in Europe.

However, even if the peasantry was thus burdened, the nobles were not beneficiaries of the system. Every noble, from the lordly *prince du sang* to the despised and impoverished *hobereau*, or country nobleman, lived in a condition of chronic debt. Required by the obligations of their blood and status to maintain the dignity of their position, there were only two legitimate ways in which the nobles could obtain the necessary money. One was to 'regild the family shield' through marriage to the daughter of a well-to-do merchant family, but pride prohibited this except as a last resort. The other was to obtain royal favour. The monarchy, however, sensibly distrusted the pretensions of the nobility to the extent of preferring to use commoners in the royal service who could have no independent illusions of grandeur. These, and those who could afford to purchase from the crown offices that carried with them noble status, in due course swelled the ranks of the nobility, though in a subordinate category of the *noblesse de la robe*, looked down upon by the older *noblesse de l'epée*, which associated its hereditary honours with war and the glory of war.

Though the *noblesse* grew in numbers with each generation, and the more rapidly because in France all the children of a noble marriage were noble, it was still a closed group, entry to which was not within its power to control. The poorest of them, the impoverished *hobereaux*, were often poorer than many rich peasants and clung all the more fiercely to their empty titles and next-to-worthless privileges, since they had nothing else to distinguish them from the majority of their fellow men.

For these, their fellow men, the route to promotion too lay solely through royal service. The office holders, together with the traders and merchants who dwelt in the towns and the notaries and the lawyers who might be found in almost every village, were known as the *bourgeoisie* (those living in towns). Some of the *bourgeois* or peasantry sent their sons into the Church, the Second Estate; the *bourgeoisie* was the Third. But whereas in England a poor boy such as Thomas Wolsey might through hard work rise to become a prince of the Church, in France the bishoprics, of which there were a great many, were reserved exclusively for the *noblesse*. The Roman Catholic rule of celibacy prevented the Church from becoming a self-perpetuating social group like the other two.

The estates of pre-revolutionary France, therefore, were legal constructs. Each was politically divided internally in a manner that prevented the emergence of a common consciousness of membership transcending other closer interests, and it is no accident that among the ranks of the intellectuals of the Enlightenment who prefigured the Revolution many of the *noblesse de la robe* were eager to get 'their own back' on their haughty superiors. The key to the whole system was the monarch. It was he who was the ultimate guarantor of the system of privilege under which the nobility lived and which, characteristically, was manifest throughout the eighteenth century in the construction of their country *châteaux* – a term which, again, has no exact English equivalent. Despite the obvious incongruity of the feature with the architecture then fashionable, each *château*, old or new, continued to sport at least one tower in which the precious documents confirming the rights of feudal privilege were stored. When the revolution came it was to these towers that the peasants advanced to burn the proofs of their bondage and, if they felt like it, the tower, the *château* and the owners too.

With the revolution also vanished the estates, swallowed up in 1789 in the Third Estate, their representative body transformed first into the National Assembly and then into the Convention. The revolutionary governments took as their motto the epigram *Liberté, Egalité, Fraternité* and sought to obliterate the old divisions, both social and regional, in the common concept of 'citizen' of what was soon to become the French Republic. The novelty did not lie in the concept of a republic, for there had been republics before, but in the abolition which accompanied it (and which the American Constitution of 1787 had just heralded) of formal titles and badges of distinction.

The French Revolution, therefore, suppressed the concept of 'estate' as a legally formalized division within society and did so, moreover, not only within the traditional territories of France but in the Netherlands and Germany as well. In England the concept had disappeared much earlier, the nobles and clergy having both been granted political membership of the House of Lords, and though the estates of the Scottish Parliament retained their separate identity longer, they lost it altogether at the Union of 1707.

Given the existence of these legally defined categories, it was inevitable that medieval thinkers would have seen as distinctions of estate those divisions which today men see as those of class. Those thinkers, however, being members of the clergy and not secular writers, stressed not their distinctions but their common humanity. 'Just as one man is a member of a family, so a household forms part of a city: but a city is a perfect community, as is shown in the first book of the *Politics*' (Aquinas 1959, p. 43).

Aquinas (1224–74), the leading figure in the intellectual life of his day and one who has, whether known to us or not, continued to exert a profound influence on political thought to this day, especially (but not exclusively) in Roman Catholic countries, was no stranger to the idea of inequality, in its economic as well as its political forms. In his *Summa Theologica* (qu. 92, pt. I) he distinguishes clearly between two sorts of subjection: the servile and the political. The existence of each derives from the interaction between three types of natural inequality among mankind. The first is that between the sexes, which results from the necessity of procreation. The second, man's peculiar distinction, follows from the fact that he had been given free will. The third is differentiation in respect of bodily powers. 'This, however, would not constitute any defect or shortcoming in those less favoured either in body or in soul' (Aquinas 1959, p. 103).

As the quotation from the *Politics* shows, Aquinas had the advantage of being able to write after the rediscovery of Aristotle's political writings. The *Politics* itself was translated into Latin in the year 1260 and was eagerly read by the schoolmen. Aquinas noted that Aristotle's advocacy of the mixed constitution ran parallel to his own interpretation of the structure of God's constitution for the Jews, as set out in Deuteronomy 1. Each involved specified rights and duties for king, nobles and people, to use the terms of his own time. In this respect, at least, there was no conflict in his mind between the works of the Philosopher and the word of God.

The mixed constitution, establishing a unified state through the elements of monarchy, aristocracy and democracy, was not, however, universally regarded by medieval thinkers as just, since it rested on the institution of private property. That institution was a social and political fact, but it was not wholly evident that it was in accordance with the divine will, at least not in so far as that will was expressed through the New Testament. Some writers argued that private property, which, as far as the Church was concerned, was entirely absent from the monastic tradition in which so many of them had been brought up, was in fact wrong. Aquinas dealt with this thorny problem. In his opinion, 'Private property is not opposed to natural law, but is an addition to it, devised by the human reason.' Thus in establishing the institution civil law complemented, and did not contradict, divine law. The institution itself involved the obligation both to use it and to share it for the common good. The possession of property imposed on its holder the duty of charity to those less fortunate. By performing this duty, the well-to-do could acquire merit; equally, by not performing it, they earned opprobrium, since the fact that they were not subject to the dictates of necessity imposed on them standards of behaviour that were higher than those expected of the less fortunate, as is shown by the fact that Aquinas was prepared to allow that a man might steal food if his privation were severe, even though he did not have a right to it in terms of human law. This, in turn, can be seen as a special case of his view that civil laws could be unjust 'if the burdens, even though they are concerned with the common welfare, are distributed in an inequitable manner throughout the community' (ibid., pp. 171, 137).

Aquinas, who had followed Augustine in taking the city as the model for his ideal state, did not neglect to say something about the chief function of actual cities as they were then emerging. For the evident purpose of the medieval city was to trade, and here too biblical guidance was less than wholly consistent. Aquinas's writings expressed a view which was to prevail throughout the Middle Ages. Trade was morally right if it was engaged in to provide necessities for other people. It was wrong to engage in it purely for profit or to obtain more than a moderate return for the amount of labour expended. Making an excessively high return on trade, as on loans at interest, was usury and a sin. Aquinas did not distinguish merchants as a class, however; he was concerned only with the welfare of the individual souls of those who engaged in trade, as, indeed, in his discourse on private property he had been concerned primarily with the moral welfare of the man who held it or who aspired to it. It was this concern for the welfare of the individual soul, which neatly characterizes medieval thought, that prevented medieval thinkers, despite their interest in universals, from arriving at a theory of class and of class behaviour. In so far as there is evidence of the concept of classes in the work of Aquinas, it is clear that he sees them as collections of individuals within the life of the city, participating as a perfect family under an equitable system of laws by which the burdens are equally and fairly distributed. The fact that property is to be shared creates an evident balance of interest between the members of his society, which is reinforced by the view that in economic terms the interaction between them, that of trade, is to be for the common good and not for the benefit or aggrandizement of any one individual or group of individuals.

In Dante's (1265–1321) essay on *Monarchy* we find a very similar set of arguments to support the position that the only proper form of government is monarchy. Dante is aware that one of the principal pitfalls of any argument for monarchy, is the objection that if unity is so excellent, why has God created so many human beings? In his view, the reason is that the specific capacity of mankind is an intellectual capacity or potentiality. And because that potentiality cannot wholly and at once be translated into action by one man, or by any one of the particular communities listed above, mankind has to be composed of a multitude through which this entire potentiality can be actualized. [Dante 1954, pp. 7, 8]

From this, he argues, defending his position with a quotation from the *Politics*, 'men of superior intellect naturally rule over others.' They do so whether in the home, in the city or in a kingdom.

But the purpose of this rule is to maintain a balance. Under a monarchy 'the citizens do not exist for the sake of the consuls, nor the people for the sake of the king; on the contrary, the king is for the sake of the people, and the consuls for the citizen' (Dante 1954, p. 20). In short, the government was the servant of all (*Minister Omnium*), and, significantly, when Dante spoke of all he spoke of mankind as a whole, Christian and Muslim and Jew, for his concept of universality extended far beyond anything that had been known since the days of the first Roman Empire, which in ideal form he sought to recreate.

On the other side, the influence of Aristotle is equally evident on the writings of Marsiglio of Padua (1270–1342), whose *Defensor Pacis* (1324) used the same authority to uphold an essentially democratic concept of human society. For Marsiglio the authority for human laws, or the legislator, was the body of the whole citizens (*universitas civium*). This was the human as opposed to the divine legislator; the government was the instrument of the popular world, and the laws made by it were human laws, created by the society and not simply the expression of divine law. All citizens, moreover, formed part of the community, so that in human terms the clergy had no power over other members of the society, and the breach between spiritual and temporal authority was absolute. It is scarcely surprising, therefore, that Marsiglio's book was almost immediately the subject of Inquisitorial proceedings. Declared a heretic by the Pope at Avignon in 1327, he fled for protection to the Imperial court; all attempts to extradite him failed.

Times were changing, and such heretical views were much more easily accepted than they would have been fifty years before. Partly this was due to the new thinking since the rediscovery of Aristotle; partly, on the other hand, it was due to the increasingly self-contradictory position of the Papacy itself and to the secularization of clerical life as the Church became an increasingly wealthy and powerful institution; and partly it was due to a returning confidence in the nature of man's ability and reason in the conduct of secular affairs. This is confirmed by the fact that very similar conclusions were reached, through an entirely different process of reasoning, by Marsiglio's contemporary, Bartolus of Sassoferrato (1309–52). Bartolus, a Roman lawyer from Perugia, also concluded that government and law arose from the will of the citizen body, but he did so on the basis of the Roman law, which was familiar to all. As in the opposing case of Dante, we note that the humanistic aspects of his thinking developed with greater ease because the nature and construction of the Italian city-states in the fourteenth century were very different from those of great national monarchies of northern Europe.

Bartolus argued that because the people could create customary law, as was universally accepted at that time, there was no reason to suppose that the people could not also make statutory law, which had every bit as much validity as the customary law which was universally acknowledged. Sovereignty, for Bartolus, rested in the people; the citizenry itself was its own prince (*civitas sibi princeps*). Bartolus went even further in identifying a council as the governing body of the citizens, elected by them and representing them. It was for the people to determine how much or how little power this council should have, and the people themselves were to judge how they were to be ruled. Bartolus, however, fell short of the position of Marsiglio by excluding from citizenship not only the Aristotelian classifications of slaves, foreigners, women and children but also clerics, holding that laity and clergy formed two separate sections of the community, which, from the point of view of government, were in no way related.

In the works of these two thinkers we see the reconstruction of the ideal of the Aristotelian state in medieval terms. Neither is primarily concerned with the reality of the bitter struggles for power which make up the history of the European states at that time, and in particular the great struggle between the king on the one hand and the estate of the nobles on the other. It is this, after all, that constitutes the principal theme of the history of England, France, Spain and the Empire during precisely those years that the theorists were stressing the uniformity ànd interdependent nature of the state, and one can only conclude that for them this interrelationship transcended the actual divisions and struggles which they saw before them. Paradoxically, the increasing popularity of what Ullmann (1965) calls the 'ascending thesis' of government was to

frighten the later medieval monarchs into a reassertion of monarchical supremacy and the nobles into a degree of acceptance of it
which their earlier predecessors would have been unwilling to
make. The balance and harmony which could not be provided by
good example was in the end created by fear, and men accepted
the authority of the monarch as God's representative on earth
because they were alarmed by the evils that might be unleashed if
they did not.

In a long diminuendo writers between the fifteenth and the
eighteenth centuries continued to offer a simplistic version of the
monarchical thesis, which slowly degenerated into a form of social
quietism. The duty to serve in whatever social position one had been
assigned to, to undertake the task that was set and not to question
the will of God in assigning more power, wealth or authority to
others, was repeatedly expressed by the clergy as well as by lay
writers. Here, for example, is an extract from a late eighteen-
century review in the *Gentleman's Magazine* of a work entitled 'On
the advantages which result from Christianity, and on the influence
of Christian principles on the Mind and Conduct', by the Reverend
James Cowe, MA, vicar of Sunbury in Middlesex:

Though a distinction of rank is essential to the existence of society, yet, let it
ever be remembered, that you are all equally responsible to Providence for
the blessings you enjoy; that the Governor of the world is attentive to the
part you are now acting; and that the condition of the virtuous peasant, or
industrious mechanick, is more respectable, and more happy, than that of
the man, however wealthy, or however elevated his station, who is enslaved
to sensual appetites and criminal luxury, and inattentive to religious and
moral obligation. By frugal industry, peaceable manners, conjugal fidelity,
and the influence of religion, you and your families live contented and
happy in your cottages, and are useful to the world; but you may be assured,
that this would far from being the case, if you neglected the proper duties of
your station, if you degraded your nature by immoral practices, and if you
were not humble, benevolent and upright, in private life. Even then,
cultivate innocence, virtuous simplicity of manners and godly sincerity, and
guard against drunkenness, sourness of temper, and party-disputes.
Remember, that Christianity inculcates supreme love for God, and cheerful
contentment with your lot; represses undue solicitude respecting earthly
treasures; and directs you to aspire after the splendours of another world,
designed for you in the realms of eternal light and peace. [*Gentleman's
Magazine*, August 1799]

Class as balance

There are three principal reasons why we have to be aware of this long prehistory of the concept of 'class as balance': first of all, because of the obvious strength these ideas have had, measured in terms of the length of time they have been current, as an explanation of the stability of society; second, because their intrinsic interest can be easily overlooked by modern social scientists, many of whom are too easily convinced that no book written before the eighteenth century can have any bearing on the important preoccupations of their own day; third, because without knowledge of this background, it would be impossible to place in perspective the position of Marx, his contribution to the theory of class, and the extent to which we should regard it as original or merely as a restatement, in new terms, of problems which were much older.

This long history of both society and ideas which has been so briefly outlined here is dominated by the theme of the organic unity of state and society, in which each individual and each group had its proper and necessary role to play. Only at the end of the period does the word 'class' itself appear, and in the meanwhile we have encountered three related but distinct concepts, the features of which it will be helpful to set out here again:

Category   A category is a grouping imposed ad hoc by an observer in order to make sense of the world as he sees it. Terms like 'the rich', 'the poor', 'a rich man', 'a poor man' are categories and not classes, in that they have no exact criteria for membership and no defined boundaries in relation to one another. But at least since Greek times they have been seen as distinctions useful in the interpretation of politics, normally in the sense that a well ordered society implies and requires a balance between the interests of each.

Taxation classes   The Greeks and the Romans both divided society into taxation classes. Members of each class, distinguished principally according to their wealth, were required to contribute an appropriate share to the running of the state, in terms both of taxation and of military and political service. Taxation classes were of great importance under monarchical or aristocratic governments; their gradual disappearance as effective divisions in society was an essential part of the transition towards democracy in Athens. Since the divisions between them were arbitrary, however, their formal abolition was not an essential part of this process.

Estates In the medieval and early modern world estates were legal divisions of society, again requiring their members to contribute differential shares to the running of the state. Three estates were normally distinguished: the nobles, the clergy and the commoners, or Third Estate. Representatives of each met in the Estates, or assembly of notables, to make laws and agree to taxes. Originally there was an economic division between the nobles and the commoners, but in time this division disappeared as commoners became richer and nobles poorer. Nobles, however, were liable to contribute personal military service, something which – ironically – they came to value as an honour. The distinction between the clergy and the other two estates, however, was one of position before the law and not a matter of economics. Some of the clergy were very rich; many were required by their vows to live in a state of poverty seldom endured by the most needy peasant. The abolition of the power and privileges of the first two estates was both the major target and the major achievement of the French Revolution.

After the dissolution of estates, however, there remained the concept of *status*. Originally a legal term designating any mark of distinction placing an individual in a defined position in society in relation to others (for example, marriage), this word was already in use in eighteenth-century England in a much more general sense; today we understand status to be something that can be either claimed or ascribed by others, although a successful claim can be ratified, as it were, only by wider recognition. Its technical use in modern sociology derives more specifically from the work of Max Weber, which will be discussed in greater detail in chapter 4.

It was perhaps natural that the disappearance of estates would have seemed to writers of the period to be bound to have its intended effect – the suppression of the causes of conflict in society – and, as we have seen, the early economists did not visualize classes replacing them as the sources of new conflict. In the work of David Ricardo, first published in 1818, we still find the assumption that classes are a natural and a balanced phenomenon of society. Only three years later, in his *Philosophy of Right*, the Prussian philosopher Hegel was to make an even more powerful claim for the fundamental harmony of classes within the state. His identification of social classes was idiosyncratic, but his acceptance of a concept of class was in itself sufficient to enable Marx to reconcile the views of philosopher and economist in a radically changed perspective, and the link lay through the concept of capital, which Hegel took up where Turgot had left off:

When men are thus dependent on one another and reciprocally related to one another in their work and the satisfaction of their needs, subjective self-seeking turns into a contribution to the satisfaction of the needs of everyone else. That is to say, by a dialectical advance, subjective self-seeking turns into the mediation of the particular through the universal, with the result that each man in earning, producing, and enjoying on his own account is *eo ipso* producing and earning for the enjoyment of everyone else. The compulsion which brings this about is rooted in the complex interdependence of each on all, and it now presents itself to each as the universal permanent capital . . . which gives each the opportunity, by the exercise of his education and skill, to draw a share from it and so be assured of his livelihood, while what he thus earns by means of his work maintains and increases the general capital. [Hegel 1962, pp. 129–30]

Opportunities for the individual depend partly on his share of the universal general capital and partly on skill, but they are also affected by the natural and accidental dissimilarities of natural, bodily and mental characteristics. Thus individuals are differentiated from one another. At the same time the universality inherent in the general movement of production and exchange distinguish individuals in general groups:

As a result, the entire complex is built up into particular systems of needs, means, and types of work relative to these needs, modes of satisfaction and of theoretical and practical education, i.e. into systems, into one or other of which individuals are assigned – in other words, into class-divisions.

These classes, three in number, Hegel terms the *substantial* or immediate class, the *reflecting* or formal class, and the *universal* class (ibid., p. 131).

The *substantial* class, that engaged in agriculture, Hegel so named because its ethical life depended directly on the family, the development of which Hegel, in common with most early anthropologists, erroneously linked with the emergence of private property as a result of the development of settled agriculture. The *reflecting* class, or business class, needed reflection and intelligence for its task of adapting raw materials and comprehended all those engaged in craftsmanship, manufacture or trade. Within these two classes Hegel does not distinguish in any way those who give instructions and those who receive them, and he makes it quite clear that for him individuals have the ability, at least up to a point, to influence their own class position. They are not allocated by a ruling class, as in Plato's *Republic*, nor do they suffer inevitably from the circumstance of birth, as in the Indian caste system. What is surprising about this is not his assumption of the power of individual will, since that, within limits, was the working assumption of any thoughtful Christian of the period, but the nature of the third class, the *universal* class, or class of civil servants, whose task, he stated, was to meet the universal needs of the community and for that reason required either private means or an allowance from the state to permit it to serve society. The idea of the state bureaucracy as constituting a distinct class of society shows clearly enough how far that concept had come since it was first identified in the middle of the eighteenth century, and how much importance was attached to the bureaucracy in Prussia; as a corps of officials who administered without ruling, civil servants constituted an administrative class and not a ruling class, for the state itself was the universal expression of all particular interests within it. But after the time of Hegel's immediate disciples the idea of the bureaucracy as a distinct class was to recede and to re-appear only when, in a twentieth-century context, its power had become evident and overwhelming in the East European socialist states after 1945.

It seems clear that for Hegel each individual must, whether he likes it or not, belong to one of the three classes. Yet as an educator, it is interesting to note, he recognizes that people may shrink from 'surrendering' their individuality to a class; he urges them not to hold back, since without such 'surrender' they cannot attain 'substantive being'. The implication of one of his later additions to his original text, that persons could persist as mere private individuals, seems reasonable, if contradictory; but for Hegel life outside civil society is not an acceptable alternative to life within that highest expression of its being which he terms the state.

For Hegel, then, the fundamental class division in society is that between industry and agriculture, between town and country, and between freedom and dependence, but freedom was only to be found in the acceptance of order, which, with its attendant freedom, was particularly to be found in the town. The universal class of the bureaucracy ensures that order and freedom are maintained and, by pursuing its own interests, achieves the good of all.

3   Class as struggle

The concept of the origin and maintenance of class structures as the product of struggle between social groups was not original to Marx. It too originated with the writers of the French Enlightenment. The initial spur to it was given by a writer who, though keenly interested in the origins of inequality between men, nevertheless explained them entirely in individual terms and without consideration of the privileged social groupings which might be involved. This was Jean-Jacques Rousseau, who achieved instant fame through his prize essay, *Sur l'origine de l'inégalité parmi les hommes*, published in 1755.

The theme was taken up by the Encyclopédistes and, as we have seen, considered by the Physiocrats, who (with the possible exception of Mirabeau) regarded the balance between classes as economically natural and necessary. Believers as they were in the value of agriculture and of scientific farming, none of them can wholly have ignored the responsibility of the governing classes for the way in which France was being run, and if they did not succeed in converting the government to a belief in their doctrines, nevertheless they spread that subtle sense of unease which later generations have seen as the prelude to the French Revolution.

In his *De l'esprit* (1758) Rousseau's contemporary Helvétius spoke of the greatest good of the greatest number as being the proper end of legislation. Although in so saying he specifically excluded legislation directed at the interests of particular groups, there is no doubt that his ideas were influential in helping to place on the agenda of reform the interests of the large number of dispossessed which France contained. For, as he pointed out, if the distribution of wealth were too unequal, the situation would be exacerbated as riches were gathered into a smaller number of hands, and the time would be reached when the nation would be divided into two classes (that is parts), of which 'one was abounding in excess and the other lacked necessities' (Helvétius 1909, p. 233). The consequences of persistent inequality would be disrespect for the law.

It is interesting to see the same theme being treated by Jonas Hanway in England in 1767:

laws are the instruments whereby the fabric of government is kept in repair, that under the shelter of it we may live in plenty, peace and freedom, defended against the rigorous blasts of times and seasons. But in proportion as we cease to feel a religious awe for this, we shall certainly become indifferent whether it stands or falls, not considering that we shall be buried in its ruins. If by long familiarity it grows cheap to the higher classes of the people, the transition in the esteem of the vulgar is too easy to imagine, as our history abundantly testifies. [Hanway 1767, pp. iv–v]

And he adds:

In proportion as injurious practices prevail, tho' within the letter of the law, and we impose the hardest, instead of the easiest terms of happiness to each other, our very liberty will become the instrument of mutual oppression. It is one great instance of our defection from virtue and even from humanity, that our fellow subjects, the infant poor of these cities, have perished in numbers sufficient to have made up a potent army and a formidable navy. [ibid.]

For Hanway, this was but a preface to a very detailed statistical analysis of the returns of the poorhouses of the regions round London, which indicated that his words were true, and that indeed the situation of the poor was unimaginably bad. His warning, that it was for the rich to act in extending compassion to their fellow subjects, was one which in due course, was to be taken up in England.

It is a measure of the difference between the situations in Britain and France that the attention of the French Enlightenment became focused firmly on the political structures of the nation as a whole. Thus we find Holbach in *La Politique Naturelle*, published in 1773, still certain that liberty was to be found not in the equality of all but in the equal protection of the laws. Where he felt that things had gone wrong was that the monarch and the monarchy of the past had been able to corrupt the political process by bribing the representatives of the Third Estate into perfidy and by fomenting conflict between the different orders and ranks of society. That his words were to be proved abundantly true some twenty years later, during the Reign of Terror, is an ironic comment on their usefulness.

Hanway, on the other hand, was under no illusion about the ultimate effect of an incorrect policy:

The equal object of a free government is to preserve both *rich* and *poor*; to prevent their oppressing each other; to support subordination and oppose any riotous tending to level men's conditions; this being as contrary to the possibility of government, as repugnant to the decrees of providence. That we have inadvertently erred in our politics, by pursuing such measures as have driven many subjects off the glebe, where they and their fathers earned their bread in husbandry, is generally allowed – this has destroyed the little property of members, and put them on a level with what we call the *poor*, which they were not before. [Hanway 1767, p. 119]

Here Hanway is clearly edging towards the concept of strife between classes. In 1771 John Millar of Glasgow (1735–1801) had published his *Observations Concerning the Distinction of Ranks in Society*, later editions of which were called simply *The Origin of the Distinctions of Ranks*. Since this was a fundamental work, one widely hailed in its time, it comes as something of a surprise to discover, first of all that the word 'class' does not appear in it at all and, second that the whole discussion of the origins of ranks is not couched in terms of classes as we understand them.

Millar cannot be criticized on the grounds of logicality or scientific zeal, for his book is comprehensive and detailed. He begins with the division between the two sexes and proceeds, through the acquisition of wealth, moveables, pasture and cultivation, towards the development of civilization and government and the emergence of the elegant arts as a prelude to opulence and luxury. Next he considers the division between parents and children, in which he finds the principle of government. Just as children need the protection of a father, so the tribe comes to require the protection of the senate or council of elders; the chief, who himself comes from an ancient family of hereditary succession, probably descended from a leader in war, habituates others to follow his opinion 'in planning as well as in conducting the several expeditions'. Ultimately, the militaristic tendencies of mankind lead them into longer and longer wars, developing more and more structures for the purpose. But at this interesting point, instead of continuing his argument, Millar breaks off with a curious plea for paying colliers more and for freeing slaves, in each case through the operation of a universal Act of Parliament. And there he stops.

Millar was exceedingly prominent both at the University of Glasgow and in the Whig politics of his native country. It will not be supposed that this small work constitutes the whole of his thought on the subject; nor does it. But to disentangle his thought from his writing with precision is rather more difficult. The most interesting evidence for his true views on the subject of ranks is to be discovered not in this earlier work but in his major study entitled *An Historical View of the English Government from the Settlement of the Saxons in Britain to the Accession of the House of Stewart* (1787). In chapter 5, entitled 'The state of property, and the different ranks and orders of man produced by the settlement of the Saxons in Britain', he begins with a very definite statement which appears to range him firmly on the side of those who believe that in matters of class all is for the best in the best of all possible worlds:

The distribution of property among any people is the principal circumstance that contributes to reduce them under Civil Government, and to determine the form of their political constitution. The poor are naturally dependent upon the rich, from whom they derive subsistence, and, according to the accidental differences of wealth possessed by individuals, a subordination of ranks is gradually introduced, and different degrees of power and authority are assumed without opposition, by particular persons, or bestowed upon them by the general voice of the society. [p. 84]

Millar's views seem clear enough. The distribution of property is the cause of people's subjection to political government. From it – and in itself it is largely accidental – there results, 'without opposition', a division of power and authority between the well-to-do and the rest. This follows from the fact that the poor are dependent on the rich. It is surprising, therefore, to discover that almost immediately Millar gives historical examples which demonstrate exactly the opposite. The Saxons, it appears, found the native British poor, invaded their territory and appropriated their land by means of their own valour and activity. Certainly, they were 'obstructed by the vigorous opposition of the natives, who seemed to have disputed every inch of the ground with their enemies', but it is from this process of disputation, and not from an assumption that the process developed 'without opposition', that historically the three 'ranks or orders' which Millar identifies in pre-Conquest society appear to have emerged. These three ranks derived from the division between the 'military people' and the peasants as a consequence of the fact that

these warriors, who in general were denominated *thanes*, came soon to be arranged in two classes; the one consisting of those heads of families who had acquired allodial property; the other of such retainers as held lands, by a military tenure either of the king or of any other allodial proprietor. [Millar 1787, p. 89]

Third, there was the clergy, giving rise to a later observation:

in every country where religion has had so much influence as to introduce a great body of ecclesiastics, the people, upon the first advances made in agriculture, and in manufactures are usually distributed into the same number of classes or orders. [ibid., pp. 212–13]

The fourth class which emerges at this latter stage is that of the artificers and tradesmen.

Here Millar is clearly at least halfway towards the conflict theory of the origin of class, insofar as his first three classes, which were, in fact, the historic estates, proceed from a struggle between the invaders and the native inhabitants. His judgement that the classes emerge 'without opposition' – if, indeed, it is not due to editorial accident or a last-minute change of plan in the work – can apply, on his historical evidence, only to the emergence of the clergy and the artificers.

But with Millar too the debate about the value or otherwise of class was soon to be swallowed up in a sequence of much greater historical events, namely, the onset and development of the French Revolution. In the course of the French Revolution, as we have already seen, the old division into estates was swept away. The king lost his powers permanently. The nobility were severely harassed but survived as a group through their numbers and the device of hereditary succession. The clergy was only briefly overthrown at the height of the Terror and was substituted by the worship of the goddess of Reason. And in the turmoil a corporal from a poor Corsican family rose rapidly through the social structure to emerge in 1804 as Emperor, at the apex of a new social structure which bore at times an uncanny resemblance to the old. It was the possibility of the 'career open to talents', with its inevitable connotation of rising in the social scale, that most impressed contemporaries as the product of the revolution.

The French Revolution was certainly a conflict between estates. Was it also an important example of class conflict, as later writers were to claim? Who were the protagonists? Those under attack were clearly enough defined: they were the king and the nobility, upon whom was heaped the whole of the blame for the earlier deficiencies of the French government and society. Nobility became in itself a cause for revenge. Thus Lavoisier, the chemist, and Condorcet, despite his moral and uplifting view of the inevitability of human progress (to which he gave brief expression in his days in prison), went to the guillotine along with many others who had been less enlightened in seeking to better the lot of mankind.

On the other hand, it is far from easy to identify exactly who was doing the attacking. Leading the fight, at one stage at least, was Marie Maximilien Isidore de Robespierre. Robespierre was a member of the provincial *noblesse de la robe*, who led the battle against his fellow aristocrats from the standpoint of a devout believer in the works of Rousseau and in the equality of man. Those who initiated the French Revolution, the men who stormed the Bastille on 14 July 1789, were, as Rudé has shown, mostly members of the artisan, urban class (Rudé 1964). They were, besides, men of mature years and not raging youth. Those who decisively changed the course of French history by storming Versailles and bringing the king back to Paris were the market women of the capital, who resented their inability to force the government to respond to their traditional rights and needs and who needed the food. Those who made up the great French revolutionary armies that carved their way through the political structures of Europe in a few brief years and altered its shape for ever were drawn from all social classes by the system of universal military conscription. The social origins of Napoleon's marshals were many and various, and in the new Napoleonic empire even aristocrats once again found useful employment.

In the draught of the French Revolutionary and Napoleonic wars, Britain (both England and Scotland) became one industrialized nation, the first on the face of the globe. As yet this was not the case in France, though the Revolutionary Wars stimulated the first growth of industrialization and necessitated the manufacture of arms and ammunition on a hitherto unknown scale. It was not until the time of Napoleon that the network of military canals linking Paris with the provinces was built which paralleled that constructed by private enterprise in England during the previous thirty years, and it was not until after 1815 that France really entered upon its phase of industrialization.

Marx's theory of class

It is important to bear these facts in mind when we turn to the interpretation of world history presented by Karl Marx (1818–83). Marx was born some three years after the conclusion of the wars, and he grew up, taking this industrialization for granted, in the early years of the railway era. It was a world which was marked in France, as it had been earlier in Britain, by increasingly sharp contrasts between the rich and poor. The process of industrialization brought hitherto unheard of numbers of people together to work in the new factories, while the modest improvements in public health initiated by the Age of Reason, were already beginning to bring about that rapid rise in population through natural reproduction which has continued to be a feature of the world in our own time.

It was, then, into this world that Karl Marx was born. His social background was unusual, and this in itself is essential to an understanding of the nature of his philosophy (McLellan 1972). To begin with, he came from a Jewish family and from a long line of rabbis, but the family had been forced, in conservative reaction following the Napoleonic Wars, to be baptized and to accept Christianity. This was because the territory in which the Marx family lived, the Rhineland, after a period in which it had been administered as a Département of the French Empire, had been reunited with Prussia by the Treaty of Vienna. Through this action the Allies had unified what had become under French administration one of the most industrially advanced areas of Germany and the large, and largely underdeveloped, conservative northern empire of Prussia.

It also re-emphasized the intellectual heritage of Hegel, who from his position at the University of Berlin had come to dominate German philosophy and to leave behind a small school of devoted disciples, the Young Hegelians, who had influence on German thought that was out of all proportion to their relatively small numbers and their failure to advance the doctrines which Hegel had left them. As with most other intellectual influences, the young Marx was eventually to revolt against Hegelianism, but not before he had absorbed from it most of its fundamental outlook, including the concept of the stages of history, which was to have a profound effect on German historiography in the nineteenth century. Having been unable either to obtain a university teaching position or to succeed as a radical journalist in opposition to the Prussian state, Marx eventually took the path into exile, and it was there that he began to study the works of the English economists, as well as absorbing the prevailing radical influence of the Utopian socialist writers. It was to these three intellectual influences that Marx was to give a distinctive twist in the preparation of a synthesis of world history which was at the same time to serve as a guide for political action.

In the view of Karl Marx, the concept of class is fundamental. For classes are the basic actors upon this historical stage, and the transfer of power from one class to the next forms the process by which, in his view, human society has evolved from one phase to the next. These phases form a sequence in man's development in relation to the development of his productive capacities, for Marx, like the Physiocrats, defined each class in terms of the relationship of its individual members to these processes.

From the period of *The Paris Manuscripts* to the day of his death Marx regarded class as being the most important single fact in political economy. He returned to the subject again and again, but never completed a detailed analysis of it; the final chapter of *Capital*, entitled 'Of the classes', breaks off after a few lines and has remained unfinished. Consequently, although it is obviously of great importance to try to understand what Marx meant by the term 'class', it is a task of supreme difficulty. What is worse is the fact that his admirers and disciples have worked so hard at trying to make good the deficiencies of Marx's own writings that they have by now made it extremely difficult to distinguish between what Marx himself thought and what they think he ought to have thought.

It is clear that Marx regarded classes as the fundamental organizational structures of society. Classes derived from the division of labour, but they had evolved away from the infinite number of small social groups which would be created merely by this form of differentation. Nor were they measures of people's wealth or resources; what united individuals within a single class were their relations to the factors of production. 'Modern class differences are by no means based on "trade"; rather the division of labour has created very different types of work within the same class' (Dahrendorf 1959, p. 11).

Marx borrowed from Ricardo the belief that labour formed the foundation of all value. Like Ricardo, he was not 'inattentive to the different qualities of labour, and the difficulty of comparing an hour's or a day's labour, in one employment, with the same duration of labour in another' (Ricardo 1895, p. 15), but he did not believe that this was because each form of work and its remuneration had 'long ago been adjusted, and placed in its proper position in the e of value' (ibid.); instead he thought that certain classes (those /arded by profits and rents) were unjustly expropriating the rewards of those who were paid wages.

Ricardo and others before him had said that the workman sold his labour to the capitalist; for Marx, however, what he sold was his *labour power*, that is to say, his agreement to work for the capitalist for a definite time or for a definite output. Once he had worked for the time necessary to pay for his wages and the cost of the materials, the product of his work went to the capitalist in the form of profit. It was through the expropriation or seizure of this surplus, by accumulating capital which was nothing but stored-up labour power, that the capitalist became a capitalist. The labourer therefore produces primarily for the capitalist and not for himself:

Hence, also, the product of his activity is not the object of his activity. What he produces for himself is not the silk that he weaves, not the gold that he draws from the mine, not the palace that he builds. What he produces for himself is *wages*, and silk, gold, palace resolve themselves for him into a definite quantity of the means of subsistence, perhaps into a cotton jacket, some copper coins and a lodging in a cellar. And the worker, who for twelve hours weaves, spins, drills, turns, builds, shovels, breaks stones, carries loads, etc. – does he consider this twelve hours' weaving, spinning, drilling, turning, building, shovelling, stone breaking as a manifestation of his life, as life? On the contrary, life begins for him where this activity ceases, at table, in the public house, in bed. [Marx and Engels 1962, vol. I, p. 82]

Competition between seller and seller, buyer and buyer, and buyer and seller would cause severe fluctuations in the price of commodities, but the inverse relationship between wages and capital would, for Marx, lead inevitably to the continuing impoverishment of the worker and to his increasing alienation from the object of his work. Earlier economists had believed, as many still do today, that increases in production would lead to greater return for the worker as well as for the capitalist. Marx denies this absolutely:

Even the most favourable situation for the working class, the most rapid possible growth of capital, however much it may improve the material existence of the worker, does not remove the antagonism between his interests and the interests of the bourgeoisie, the interests of the capitalists. Profit and wages remain as before in inverse proportion. [ibid., p. 98]

Hence as labour becomes more and more unsatisfying, competition intensifies and the worker's conditions deteriorate. The introduction of new machinery simply makes matters worse, since it leads the capitalists to discharge workers, and for Marx the laws of economics determine that they can never find employment as remunerative as that which they have lost (a view that empirical observation suggests has, for more than a century, been demonstrably false).

It was for this reason that contemporary society had, in Marx's eyes, come to be dominated by the two great classes, the bourgeoisie and the proletariat. But the actual structure of the society of his day Marx perceived in much more complex terms. We have already seen how in *Capital*, the key statement of his views, Marx wrote not of two classes but of three, 'wage-labourers, capitalists and landowners' (see p. 11); in the same passage he goes on to explain why on theoretical grounds he regards these entities as fundamental, despite the confusion presented to the observer by the social scene. At the same time, by finally accepting the Ricardian categorization of classes, we should note, he dismissed by implication the Hegelian view both of the unity of agricultural and industrial spheres and of the distinct role of the bureaucracy, a subject which Marx – despite its importance to his contemporaries – almost completely neglected (Lichtheim 1962, p. 384).

In England, modern society is indisputably most highly and classically developed in economic structure. Nevertheless, even there, the stratification of classes does not appear in its pure form. Middle and intermediate strata even here obliterate lines of demarcation everywhere (although incomparably less in rural districts than in the cities). However this is immaterial for our analysis. We have seen that the continual tendency and law of development of the capitalist mode of production is more and more to divorce the means of production from labour, and more and more to concentrate the scattered means of production into large groups, thereby transforming labour into wage-labour, and the means of production into capital. And to this tendency, on the other hand, corresponds the independent separation of landed property from capital and labour or the transformation of all landed property into the form of landed property corresponding to the capitalist mode of production.

The first question to be answered is this: what constitutes a class? – and the reply to this follows naturally from the reply to another question. What makes wage-labourers, capitalists, and landowners constitute the three great social classes? [Marx 1962, vol. III, p. 862]

What indeed? And, perhaps, first of all, why three social classes? Certainly, this tripartite division was not invented by Marx, nor did he claim that it was. It stands in the first paragraph of Ricardo's s it appeared originally in the work of the Physiocrats and

e of the earth – all that is derived from its surface by the united application of labour, machinery, and capital, is divided among three classes of the community; namely, the proprietor of the land, the owner of the stock or capital necessary for its cultivation, and the labourers by whose industry it is cultivated.

But in different stages of society, the proportions of the whole produce of the earth which will be allotted to each of these classes, under the names of rent, profit, and wages, will be essentially different; depending mainly on the actual fertility of the soil, on the accumulation of capital and population, and on the skill, ingenuity, and instruments employed in agriculture. [Ricardo 1895, p. 1]

Marx's answer to this question – essentially the question which had been asked and answered by Turgot – rejected fertility of soil, skill, ingenuity and instruments employed in agriculture and even population. The answer which Marx gave lay solely in the relations of domination and subjection which he saw as being created among men by the process of production. In his era, the era of capitalism, the fact of capital determined the differences in property relationships between the three classes.

First of all, the development of capitalist production had converted a large proportion of the population (for Marx, the majority) into workers, or, as he termed them, the proletariat. Their economic conditions made their interests wholly different from, and antagonistic to, those of the capitalists, those who owned capital within the society. Landowners, who for Marx were a remnant of the feudal period, had interests in common with the capitalists through their ever-present need to raise their rents or diversify investment, and hence are frequently in Marx's writing lumped together to form that amorphous class which he terms habitually the bourgeoisie. These two main classes, the bourgeoisie and the proletariat, therefore found themselves dependent on each other for their very existence but, for the same reason, hopelessly antagonistic to one another, for the existence of the capitalists as a class depended on the expropriation of the product of the workers, leaving them only the barest pittance necessary for survival.

So far Marx was only building on the concept of the relationship between the proprietors and the industrial classes envisaged by Turgot. He goes beyond it, however, in adding the prediction that the tendency of this process is constantly to diminish the resources of the proletarian to the point at which his destitution will ultimately drive him to social revolution.

The bourgeois, on the other hand, gains from his position not only wealth but also political power, for it is in the nature of the capitalist system of production that political power will pass into the hands of the bourgeois class: 'The executive of the modern State is but a committee for administering the common affairs of the whole bourgeoisie' (Marx and Engels 1962, vol. I, p. 36). The economic relationships between classes, therefore, formed the basis of the structure of society and underpinned the structure of government itself. Consequently for Marx class is not purely an economic relationship; it is also a political one. There is an equation in any given historical period between a class and the state, the nature of the state varying with the nature of its economic structures.

It will be interesting to pursue later the questions of the origins of the words 'bourgeoisie' and 'proletariat' and to consider the implications of the specific use of these words in Marx's context. At this point it will be sufficient simply to indicate that there are considerable uncertainties about both the indentification and the application of these terms. For Marx, class was so fundamental a fact of his system that he never consistently worked through his definition of it; although he alludes to it on many occasions, on each supplying some new identificatory tag which determines or designates a specific class, there is no grand, overarching definition either of a class or of the terms 'bourgeoisie' and 'proletariat'. This is true not only in the case of the landowning class mentioned above but also, in the even more important case of the agricultural workers. Marx recognized in *Capital* that 'all production of surplus value has for its natural basis the productiveness of agricultural labour' (Mészáros 1971, p. 139), yet, in common with many intellectuals of his period who lived in towns and far away from the processes of agricultural production, Marx had a considerable amount of inherited contempt for the rural workers. In the *Communist Manifesto* he had actually spoken favourably of capitalism in so far as it succeeded in rescuing the agricultural worker 'from the idiocy of rural life' (Marx and Engels 1962, vol, I, p. 38).

Marx himself does not give any clear explanation of why the economic interests of landowner and capitalist should coincide, any more than he does of why those of worker and farm labourer should be treated as identical. A farm is not simply a factory in the open air. The reason why he does not seems quite plain, on the other hand. In rejecting Hegelianism, Marx retained its most distinctive reasoning process, the dialectic, as the key to unlocking a materialist conception of history. At each historical stage thesis would call into existence antithesis, ultimately to be negated or transcended by it and so raised into synthesis. If the conflict between capitalist and worker were to give rise to a new kind of society, it could only be through the reduction of all class antagonisms to the primary conflict. It was, therefore, for philosophical and not economic reasons that Marx identified landowners with capitalists, even though his favoured term for the dominant class of the capitalist era was the 'bourgeoisie'.

Early in his journalistic career, before Marx had broken with the Young Hegelians or had begun to study political economy, he had observed that the members of the Prussian state parliament tended to speak in the name of classes rather than as individuals. Even at this early period, therefore, we can see the germ of the second central idea which he was to associate with his concept of class, namely, that of struggle. Grounded as he was in the tradition of the dialectic of Kant and Hegel, Marx saw the antinomy between bourgeois and proletariat as essential to the identification of both. 'Individuals form a class only insofar as they are engaged in the common struggle with another class,' he wrote in *The German Ideology* (Dahrendorf 1959, p. 14). This common struggle may not be self-conscious; indeed, in its initial stages it is not self-conscious and is not likely to become so for some time, for the dawning consciousness of a class as such is the thing that brings it into the political arena. Therefore, although for Marx the bourgeoisie was already organized as a class in his time, he predicted that in due course the same thing would happen to the proletariat, and that through the growth of class-consciousness the struggle between the two would be intensified. Until the fact of consciousness dawned on the proletariat it would not be 'a class for itself', a self-conscious organization capable of effective political and social action (Giddens 1973, p. 93).

Marx believed that this self-consciousness was, in fact, the dawning of the realization of a class's real situation, and that until this dawning came the members of the class existed in a state in which they did not understand how things really were. Class-consciousness, therefore, was the perception of reality, the understanding of the capitalist system as it 'really was'. In response to it, on the other hand, the interests of the bourgeoisie would be correspondingly strengthened and unified, swallowing up the independent interests of the landowning classes with those of the mercantile and entrepreneurial classes in one common bourgeois class interest. As the workers began to form coalitions, so the bourgeoisie would resist them more and more firmly. As the forces of production developed, so the workers would move from their period of dawning self-consciousness as a class seeking economic rewards into the realm of political action and into the struggle with the bourgeoisie. The proletariat would then become conscious of itself not only as an economic organization but also as a politically aware class, expressing itself through a political party.

The bourgeoisie would respond by using repressive measures, by co-opting the ablest members of the proletariat into its own class and generally by using every device possible to attain and maintain its dominance of that class. Ultimately, however, the collision of the two classes would lead to a social revolution, with consequences which Engels spoke of as being infinitely greater than those of the French Revolution (Marx and Engels 1975, vol. IV). The power of the bourgeoisie would be broken, the state structure smashed and the dictatorship of the proletariat established.

Does this mean that after the fall of the old society there will be a new class domination culminating in a new political power? No.

The condition for the emancipation of the working class is the abolition of all classes, just as the condition for the emancipation of the third estate, of the bourgeois order, was the abolition of all estates and all orders. The working class, in the course of development, will substitute for the old civil society an association which will exclude classes and their antagonism, and there will be no more political power properly so-called, since political power is precisely the official expression of antagonism in civil society. [Marx and Engels 1976, vol. VI, p. 212]

Marx himself was contemptuous of philosophers who stayed in their studies. In his *Theses on Feuerbach* he said: 'The philosophers have only interpreted the world, in various ways; the point, however, is to change it' (Marx and Engels 1962, vol. II, p. 405). Hence we can tell from his own actions how he sought to nurture an understanding of its position in the mind of the proletariat, to encourage it to develop the crucial attribute of class-consciousness. It was through the growth and education of working men's political parties and organizations. The role of the party of the proletariat which he envisaged was not peculiar to Marxism, but the hope for a very specific future, to be realized through revolutionary means, was. An important first step was to be the foundation of trade unions wherever they did not yet exist, since through such unions and similar working men's associations the necessary organizational experience could be acquired. Further, Marx envisaged his social revolution as a trans-national event. Hence the slogan of the *Communist Manifesto*, 'Proletarians of the world, unite!', was to be given expression through the creation of a working man's international, an organization designed to draw together the common interests of proletarians in all the countries of Europe in order to make the ultimate social revolution a worldwide revolution. This, the most original and distinctive feature of Marx's theory of class, was, ironically, to give more trouble to his followers than any other aspect of his theory.

There is no reason to doubt Engels when he says, on behalf of Marx, that he believed that after the period of the dictatorship of the proletariat, when the remnants of bourgeois society have been extirpated, the state will simply wither away, leaving a classless society.

The next question is: how is this transition from bourgeois society to the socialist society of the future to be achieved? By revolution, certainly, but why by revolution? And what form is this revolution to take? In one sense, of course, Marx based his prediction of a revolutionary future for proletarian organization on the historical fact of the French Revolution. 'Revolutions are the locomotives of history' – that is, some such powerful period of social transformation seemed logically to be required for the radical transformation of existing society, based on existing relations of production. Also revolutions had been responsible, in Marx's view, for the accession to political power of the bourgeoisie, in the course of which they had displaced the old feudal class and had enthroned themselves in European states.

Undoubtedly here Marx was thinking principally of the France of Louis-Philippe. After 1848 he spent a considerable amount of his time studying revolutions in various parts of the world, particularly in France but also in Spain and Germany, and his quest for information took him as far afield as Ireland in one direction and India in the other. Of the United States he knew surprisingly little, despite the period in his later life during which he was a correspondent for the *New York World*. Only twice in his entire, gigantic corpus of writings does he refer to Latin America, which at the time of his work made up the bulk of the independent states of the world.

Both references are unfavourable. To a Russian who wrote to him he took the trouble to explain that in certain instances, of which he thought Russia might be one, the existence and retention of structures of primitive communism (the *mir*), might enable a country the more easily to achieve a social revolution.

Of the timing of his expected social revolution Marx said nothing. He patiently watched the ups and downs of the trade cycle and, in the case of France, attempted to relate them to the political changes which brought about the accession of Louis Napoleon. He ceased to write in the early 1870s and died in 1883, leaving his colleague and disciple Frederick Engels to carry on his work. Accordingly, in so far as they are predictive, his theories assumed projections from data gathered not later than 1870, and the fundamental work of political economy from which the theory expounded first, in its semi-complete form, in the *Communist Manifesto* (1848) is based dates essentially from 1844. Modern writers, therefore, have been able to say that, on this basis alone, Marx's predictions may be regarded as outmoded, as Engels himself freely admitted.

Marx's empirical writings

'It is self-evident that this unavoidable neglect of contemporaneous changes in the economic situation, the very basis of the processes to be examined, must be a source of error,' Engels wrote. 'But all the conditions of a comprehensive presentation of current history unavoidably include sources of error – which, however, keeps nobody from writing current history' (Marx and Engels 1962, vol. I, p. 119).

In his approach to current history Marx was, as Engels is at pains to point out, concerned 'to trace political events back to effects of what were, in the final analysis, economic causes'. This assertion of the primacy of the economic has itself, as we shall see, been an embarrassment to later Marxists. Some have claimed that it is a dogma. Some have hotly denounced critics of Marx for treating it as a dogma. Others again, as we shall see later, have dismissed it and have asserted the primacy of the political. However, the evidence of Marx's empirical writings suggests that he sought the explanation for the political upheavals of his day in economic forces and watched the political scene closely for signs of the social revolution which, on theoretical grounds, he had predicted would come.

Elsewhere I have pointed out that Marx gives no explanation for why he expected the dénoument of the struggle between proletariat and bourgeoisie to take the form of a revolution. Rather, he seems to have assumed that some grand sequence of events, such as the one the French Revolution of 1789 represented for all nineteenth-century writers, must necessarily accompany the final transformation of society, and it was left to Engels to admit, towards the end of the century, that there were grounds for believing that the transformation could come about peacefully through the steady accretion of political power in the hands of the proletariat (Calvert 1970). Engels wrote:

All revolutions up to the present day have resulted in the displacement of one definite class rule by another, but all ruling classes up to now have been only small minorities in relation to the ruled mass of the people. One ruling minority was thus overthrown; another minority seized the helm of state in its stead and refashioned the state institutions to suit its own interests. This was on every occasion the minority group qualified and called to rule by the given degree of economic development; and just for that reason, and only for that reason, it happened that the ruled majority either participated in the revolution for the benefit of the former or else calmly acquiesced in it. [Marx and Engels 1962, vol. I, p. 123]

In *The Class Struggles in France, 1848 to 1850*, published in 1850, Marx argued that despite the apparent victory of the bourgeois forces in the establishment of the Second Republic, what had really happened through the ostensible setback to the cause of the proletariat which this involved was the intensification of the underlying class antagonism. Under Louis-Philippe, from 1830 to 1848, only a faction of the bourgeoisie had ruled, the finance aristocracy. The industrial bourgeoisie had been represented in the Chamber but excluded from power; the petty bourgeoisie and the peasantry were excluded from power altogether. These excluded classes, he believed, had been driven to revolt in 1848 by the combined effects of the potato blight and the general commercial and economic crisis after 1845. The Provisional Government brought the remainder of the bourgeoisie into the political arena; with them, however, came the proletariat also, whose representatives in the Hôtel de Ville had forced the proclamation of the Republic. Since they could not confront them directly, the Provisional Government, Marx argued, played one part of the proletariat off against the other by establishing the Mobile Guards, drawn, he alleged, from the 'lumpenproletariat, which in all big towns forms a mass sharply differentiated from the industrial proletariat, a recruiting ground for thieves and criminals of all kinds, living on the crumbs of society, people without a definite trade, vagabonds, *gens sans feu et sans aveu*' (ibid., p. 155). At the same time the government had to identify the Republic with social reforming ideas, in particular by the creation of the National Workshops to give employment to the unemployed. When the representatives of the workers forced their way into the Assembly and demanded war, they were, Marx argued, goaded into revolt so that they could be suppressed by force.

The sequel, he suggested, was an ironic one, for the adoption of universal suffrage by the bourgeoisie reduced it at once to a coterie in face of an alliance of larger classes. But on 10 December 1848 victory went not to the alliance or to the bourgeoisie but to 'the class that represents barbarism within civilization', namely, the peasantry. It was the peasants who, by their votes, put Louis Napoleon in power, but they were to be sorely disappointed, for his first action was to retain the salt tax, and the result of the legislative elections of June 1849 served simply to consolidate the hold of the representatives of the bourgeoisie on the Assembly. By the end of the same year the Finance Ministry was already back in the hands of the finance aristocracy, the faction that most effectively linked the returned landed aristocrats of the royalist factions with the bourgeois coalition. 'In general the combination of large landed property with high finance is a normal fact,' commented Marx. 'Proof: England; proof: even Austria' (ibid., p. 209). The return of 'the big wolves of the Bourse' was finally guaranteed by the reversal of the fundamental political gain of the Republic, the abolition once more of universal suffrage.

Marx expected this compromise to persist until a new economic crisis caused it to disintegrate. It was not long before he was proved wrong by the events described by him in *The Eighteenth Brumaire of Louis Bonaparte*, published in 1852. Engels later described this work as 'a concise, epigrammatic exposition that laid bare the whole course of French history since the February days in its inner interconnection and in so doing did not even need to treat the hero of the *coup d'état* otherwise than with the contempt he so well deserved' (ibid., p. 245). It is certainly epigrammatic, though far from concise, and it is crucial for an understanding of Marx's use of class analysis.

In it Marx sets out to explain 'how a nation of thirty-six millions can be surprised and delivered unresisting into captivity by three swindlers' (ibid., p. 252). The February Revolution is now seen as only a prologue to the June Days, in which the defeat of the leaders of the proletariat left that class leaderless and doomed to defeat in the search merely for limited aims.

It had proved that in countries with an old civilisation, with a developed formation of classes, with modern conditions of production and with an intellectual consciousness in which all traditional ideas have been dissolved by the work of centuries, the republic signifies in general only the political form of revolution of bourgeois society and not its conservative form of life, as, for example, in the United States of North America, where, though classes already exist, they have not yet become fixed, but continually change and interchange their elements in constant flux. . . . [ibid., pp. 252, 255]

Marx sees power during this period as being in the hands of a mere faction, which he terms the 'bourgeois republicans'. Between December 1848 and May 1849 they were squeezed out by the mass of the bourgeoisie.

This mass was, however, royalist. One section of it, the large landowners, had ruled during the restoration and was accordingly Legitimist. The other, the aristocrats of finance and big industrialists, had ruled during the July Monarchy and was consequently Orleanist. The high dignitaries of the army, the university, the church, the bar, the academy and of the press were to be found on either side, though in various proportions. Here, in the bourgeois republic, which bore neither the name Bourbon nor the name Orleans, but the name Capital, they had found the form of state in which they could rule conjointly. [ibid., p. 264]

It was a ministry of this coalition that Napoleon summoned on assuming power; the ascendancy of the coalition of the bourgeoisie was, Marx asserted, countered by the emergence of the Social Democrats, representing a coalition between the petty bourgeoisie and the workers. By the 'petty bourgeoisie' or, perhaps more accurately, the 'lesser bourgeoisie' Marx means people like shop-keepers who own their own businesses, and it is at this point that he makes an interesting and significant comment on the relationship between a class and those who represent it.

One must not form the narrow-minded notion that the petty bourgeoisie, on principle, wishes to enforce an egoistic class interest. Rather, it believes that the special conditions of its emancipation are the general conditions within the frame of which modern society can be saved and the class struggle avoided. Just as little must one imagine that the democratic representatives are indeed all shopkeepers or enthusiastic champions of shopkeepers. According to their education and their individual position they may be as far apart as heaven and earth. What makes them representatives of the petty bourgeoisie is the fact that in their minds they do not get beyond the limits which the latter do not get beyond in life, that they are consequently driven, theoretically, to the same problems and solutions to which material interest and social position drive the latter practically. This is, in general, the relationship between the political and literary representatives of a class and the class they represent. [ibid., p. 275]

For Marx, then, Social Democrats represent the interests of the petty bourgeoisie but are not necessarily petty bourgeois in their own origins, any more than Louis Napoleon, whom, as we have already seen, Marx regarded as representing the peasantry, was himself a peasant. A class can be *represented politically* by a group, even a very small group, and even by individuals who are not members of it. This cannot happen until conditions are right, but it need not happen even then, for class action depends not simply on the existence of classes, but also on the conscious awareness of their class interest by their members. Bonaparte represented 'a class, and the most numerous class of French society at that, the small-holding peasants' precisely because of their anomalous status in this respect.

The small-holding peasants form a vast mass, the members of which live in similar conditions but without entering into manifold relations with one another. Their mode of production isolates them from one another instead of bringing them into mutual intercourse. The isolation is increased by France's bad means of communication and by the poverty of the peasants. Their field of production, the small holding, admits of no division of labour in its cultivation, no application of science and, therefore, no diversity of development, no variety of talent, no wealth of social relationships. [ibid., p. 333]

Hence

In this way the great mass of the French nation is formed by simple addition of homologous magnitudes, much as potatoes in a sack form a sack of potatoes. In so far as millions of families live under economic conditions that separate their mode of life, their interests and their culture from those of the other classes, and put them in hostile opposition to the latter, they form a class. In so far as there is merely a local interconnection among these small-holding peasants, and the identity of their interests begets no community, no national bond and no political organisation among them, they do not form a class. They are consequently incapable of enforcing their class interests in their own name, whether through a parliament or through a convention. They cannot represent themselves, they must be represented. [ibid., pp. 333, 334]

Here is a practical application of Marx's distinction between a class *in itself* and a class *for itself* (i.e., self-consciously aware of its ordained role in the future evolution of society). It was this consciousness and this awareness which Marx was, of course, seeking to stimulate through his historical as through his philosophical writings. The democrats of his day, whom he had earlier identified with the petty bourgeoisie, saw, on the other hand, no distinction of classes but only the undifferentiated masses of the people. 'Accordingly, when a struggle is impending, they do not need to examine the interests and positions of the different classes,' he remarked. 'They have merely to give the signal and the people, with all its inexhaustible resources, will fall upon the oppressors.' This accounted both for what he saw as their failure and for their failure to understand the reasons for it.

Three other ideas contained in *The Eighteenth Brumaire* are of special importance. Two of them are directly relevant to the question of why Bonaparte emerged as Emperor. Both the 'party of Order' and the democrats had, Marx believed, failed to realize the paramount significance of controlling the 'lever of executive power'. Control of the 'parasitic' state apparatus was essential to the maintenance of the class position of the bourgeoisie in economic terms, while its political position required its strengthening for its own protection, and they were prepared to accept any measure to that end. Bonaparte, on the other hand, offered them not just a name or a symbol but, in his Society of 10 December, an organization of the lumpenproletariat which gave him the class base and organizational instrument he needed (ibid., p. 274, p. 285, p. 295) ultimately to convert the army of the state itself into his willing supporters.

His success in seizing control of the state might seem to have been a severe setback to the prospect of social revolution. Marx sought to deny this. It was, on the contrary, a necessary part of the intensification of class antagonisms which would have to precede the ultimate revolution, which he thus personifies:

First, it perfected the parliamentary power, in order to be able to overthrow it. Now it has attained this, it perfects the executive power, reduces it to its purest expression, isolates it, sets it up against itself as the sole target, in order to concentrate all its forces of destruction against it. And when it has done the second half of its preliminary work, Europe will leap from its seat and exultantly exclaim: Well grubbed, old mole! [ibid., p. 332]

Europe did indeed leap from its seat in 1870–1, but it was to witness the spectacle of the Paris Commune being suppressed by the forces of the Provisional Government of what was later to become the Third Republic with a degree of ruthlessness which left the capital a shambles. Marx saw in the Commune nothing less than the shape of the proletarian revolution to come. 'Its true secret was this,' he wrote in *The Civil War in France* (1871). 'It was essentially a working-class government, the produce [*sic*] of the struggle of the producing against the appropriating class, the political form at last discovered under which to work out the economic emancipation of labour' (ibid., p. 522).

Its suppression, moreover, was for Marx the most telling proof of the underlying ferocity of the class struggle. He claimed:

The civilisation and justice of bourgeois order comes out in its lurid light whenever the slaves and drudges of the order rise against their masters. Then this civilisation and justice stand forth as undisguised savagery and lawless revenge. Each new crisis in the class struggle between the appropriator and the producer brings this fact out more glaringly. [ibid., p. 535]

Indeed, in suppressing the Commune the Provisional Government had acted in conjunction with, and with the approval of, the Prussians, demonstrating a degree of identity of bourgeois interests which the proletariat, Marx claimed, could learn to counter through the International Working Men's Association.

In *The Civil War in France*, therefore, are joined the detailed (though very brief) analysis of historical events and the philosophy of history which that analysis was held to support. The detailed analysis of the competing interests is kept to a minimum in favour of the argument of a direct clash between the two great entities of bourgeoisie and proletariat. The Commune represents the proletariat; who or what comprises it is not discussed. Similarly, Thiers represents the bourgeoisie as a whole. The sophisticated divisions are omitted; the questions of the autonomy of the executive power and the class role of the army are minimized; and Marx asserts his belief that the haste in the suppression of the Commune was designed to forestall a general peasant uprising – without, once again, considering in detail how far a real identity of interest might exist between those peasants and the urban masses of Paris. What we are left with is the claim that the intensification of struggle has reached a new level, and this in turn suggests that the revolution to come will come soon.

One of the reasons why his immediate disciples expected the revolution to come soon was because of the inclusion of a small but extremely significant detail. Following through his consistent view that 'transitional' classes would be retained late into the struggle between the bourgeoisie and the proletariat, Marx foresaw two main periods of transfer between the two classes. One would occur fairly early on in the industrialization process, which was, of course, the period in which he was actually writing. During this period a circulation of individuals would occur between the proletariat and the bourgeoisie. In so far as this prediction was based on the actual observed fact that there was indeed such a circulation of individuals between classes in the countries in which he was living, this was a very safe prediction, and indeed it is certain that industrialization could not be possible without it. However, Marx also envisaged another point at which a significant transfer of individuals would occur. This would be at the culmination of the process of the intensification of hostility between the two classes, when a significant group of revolutionary intellectuals (now usually known by the Russian term 'the intelligentsia') would secede from the bourgeoisie to the proletariat to generate the social revolution.

In times in which the class struggle nears the decisive hour, the process of dissolution going on within the ruling class, in fact within the whole range of old society, assumes such a violent and glaring character that a small section of the ruling class cuts itself adrift, and joins the revolutionary class, the class that holds the future in its hands. Just as, therefore, at an earlier period, a section of the nobility went over to the bourgeoisie, so now a portion of the bourgeoisie goes over to the proletariat, and in particular a portion of the bourgeois ideologists, who have raised themselves to the level of comprehending theoretically the historical movement as a whole. [ibid., p. 43]

Despite the deceptive present tense used in the *Manifesto*, this is, as will be obvious, a statement about the as yet unknown future. Its conditional form, equally, may be reversed: 'If the intellectuals secede, then the revolution will come.' But what if when they come to understand the historical processes at work, they decide that they are better off where they are? Marx does not say, and indeed it appears that he never envisaged this possibility. In his later work Engels, with more experience of the accommodation of both the ruling and the working classes to the advancing industrialization of Europe, did come to realize that revolution might not be the only possible outcome, and indeed that the domination of the proletariat might be accomplished without it, just as its demands for better working conditions had already been met in part by the time the English edition of *The Condition of the Working Class in England* appeared in 1892.

Marx arrived at this position, in fact, despite such empirical evidence as that furnished, for example, by the United States, where in his day no classes, in the sense that he envisaged them in Europe, could be discerned. As Plamenatz (1954) notes, in one letter he ascribes this divergence from prediction to the importance of the ethnic question, despite the fact that this would call in doubt the primacy of the economic forces in society which he, in contradistinction to some later Marxists, never doubted. For the motive power in the class struggle was for Marx the progressive impoverishment of the proletariat which he professed to have discovered as a 'law' under capitalism, and the consequent need for capitalism to expand constantly in search of new markets. It was the belief in this law that led him and his followers, including Engels himself, to ignore the evidence that in the absence of new markets, capitalism, like any other economic system before it, would simply recede into a 'steady state', supplying the available market with renewable necessities.

The revolutionary intellectuals, therefore, would be aware of Marxian economics, and the role that they had to play, just as they would be aware of the Marxian philosophy of history and of the secession of parts of the nobility to the Third Estate in the French Revolution, which Marx rather inconsistently dismisses as 'irrelevant to the class struggle'. It is not irrelevant to Marx's own views on that struggle. For just as it was the self-assumed task of Marx himself to impart to the proletariat the news of its historic mission, so in turn it would be the duty of these revolutionary intellectuals, following in his footsteps, to hasten the emergence of class-consciousness among the proletariat as a whole and to make it an effective instrument for its task. The question of how far they might go in assuming that role of representatives of the proletariat, which Marx's observations on the role of representatives of other classes had left open to them, was consigned to the interpretation of a later generation.

It was, again, on the basis of hints embodied in the empirical writings, rather than on that of general, theoretical ones, that later

Marxists developed their attitudes towards others of the seven classes Marx had identified in the France of his day. They were particularly contemptuous of the role of the petty – more accurately, 'small' – bourgeoisie, which they came to see as fundamental to the survival of the 'reactionary' governments after 1871. 'Petty bourgeois', like 'lumpenproletariat', became a term of abuse rather than of analysis. At the other end of the scale, although belief in the internal contradictions of capitalism remained, the creation of the giant trusts made its analysis considerably more difficult, blurring the distinction between 'finance capital' and 'industrial capital', and the definition of these terms in concrete economic terms was not pursued with rigour. In Bismarck's Germany, with its military base, the introduction of social security schemes softened the sense of confrontation, and Kautsky, leader of the German Social Democrats, was able to argue on this basis that the capitalist class 'rules but does not govern'.

Marx himself would not have been surprised at the adaptability of the capitalist system. His panegyric on what the capitalist had achieved reads oddly now, but its inclusion in the *Communist Manifesto* (ibid., pp. 38–9) was a shrewd psychological thrust. Great enemies create great movements, and Marx saw the bourgeoisie as a redoubtable opponent indeed.

It is probably from this very emphasis on he strength of the bourgeoisie that he derived the distinctive feature of his revolutionary theory which has caused more controversy perhaps than any other. This is the rule of the dictatorship of the proletariat, a transition to the abolition of all classes and the classless society.

First, there is the question of why the rule of the proletariat must be a dictatorship. In an age in which constitutional government was coming into existence in Europe – and Marx himself had been among the radical writers most loudly demanding its introduction – it seems surprising that he should have regarded the ending of capitalism as being marked by the introduction of a dictatorship of any kind. Yet it is fundamental to all his philosophy to think dialectically, and the destruction or negation of the bourgeois society was something which would demand an iron hand. We are quite clear about what the political structure of the dictatorship would look like, for Marx expressed his admiration for the government of the Paris Commune of 1871 and hailed its structure as the form of the socialist state of the future (ibid., vol. II, p. 519 and pp. 521–3).

We are, unfortunately, much less certain about what he meant by the 'abolition' of all classes. It could mean simply that the government of the proletariat would enforce the equalization of property ownership, which would render the class struggle void, and in particular, as the Russians were subsequently to do in 1917, make it impossible for a capitalist to employ labour in a private capacity. But Marx the philosopher is here using a technical term drawn from the Hegelian sphere of the dialectic. The thesis, which is the bourgeoisie, has called into being the antithesis, which is the proletariat. The struggle between these two has reached the point at which the negation of the thesis by the antithesis gives rise to the synthesis, which is the dictatorship of the proletariat and the establishment of classless society. The society cannot be other than classless, since it is impossible for a society of only one class to exist: by definition, the existence of a class within society requires the coexistence of at least two classes. If there is only one class, the proletariat, there are no classes. Yet, dialectically, the argument ought not to end there. The classless society should in turn generate its own antithesis, raising the conflict of opposites to a higher level, in turn to be resolved by a new and possibly unimaginable synthesis. Such is the logic of the dialectic, and for a materialist such as Marx there could be no divine intervention or other agency which would bring the process of a dialectic to a halt. On Marx's own grounds, therefore, there is reason to doubt the soundness of his conclusions, and it would be a matter of considerable interest to explore some of the alternative resolutions which were in due course propounded by other writers who accepted Marx's methods without necessarily accepting his conclusions.

There is the possibility that in using an extremely imprecise term, *aufhebung*, Marx was deliberately evading the issue himself. Certainly, the word has various and even diametrically opposite meanings, though there is, I think, no serious doubt that what Marx meant by it was in fact, simply 'abolition'. But granted this, there remains the question of how the classes are to be abolished. By whom, is clear enough. The identity of the classes to be eradicated is self-evident, if one assumes that one can apply the uncertain definitions of the classes concerned in any given concrete instance. But the agency is not established, and it is this which future generations, beginning with the instigators of the Russian Revolution, were to have to decide for themselves.

As we have already seen, Marx was certainly not the first to distinguish classes in society, or to identify them in economic terms, or to establish conflict as a basis for their existence; nor did he claim to have done any of these things:

and now as to myself, no credit is due to me for discovering the existence of classes in modern society, nor yet the struggle between them. Long before me bourgeois historians had described the historical development of the struggle of the classes, and bourgeois economists the economic anatomy of the classes. What I did that was new was to prove:

(1)   That the *existence of classes* is only bound up with particular *historical phases in the development of production*;

(2)   That the class struggle necessarily leads to the *dictatorship of the proletariat*;

(3)   That this dictatorship itself only constitutes the transition to the *abolition of all classes* and to a *classless society* .... [ibid., p. 452]

In his speech at the graveside of Karl Marx, Engels attributed to him two 'discoveries':

the law of development of human history: the simple fact, hitherto concealed by an overgrown ideology, that mankind must first of all eat, drink, have shelter and clothing, before it can pursue politics, science, art, religion, etc. [and] the special law of motion governing the present-day capitalist mode of production and the bourgeois society that this mode of production has created [namely, surplus value]. [ibid., p. 167]

As he had earlier said in a brief biography of Marx published in 1878, it was the 'discovery' of surplus value that

removed the last justification for all the hypocritical phases of the possessing classes to the effect that in the present social order right and justice, equality and right of duties and a general harmony of interests prevailed, and *present-day* bourgeois society, no less than its predecessors, was exposed as a grandiose institution for the exploitation of the huge majority of the people by a small, ever-undiminishing minority. [*ibid.*, p. 166]

Engels was also right to recognize that these 'discoveries' – which, it should be noted, had been hotly contested by other thinkers, many of them possibly no less intellectually capable than Marx himself – would not have had the impact on European and subsequently world society that they have if it had not been for that other attribute of Marx's character, that of the revolutionist. However inspiring his conclusions might have been, his theory of classes would have had less dynamism if it had not been associated with two other things: a view of world history as stages culminating in the prediction of the realization of an ideal society, and Marx's tireless energy in working to realize this society at the earliest possible date.

The proletariat and the bourgeoisie

No examination of what the concept of class meant for Marx would be complete without some consideration of the meaning of the key terms he employs. We have already seen how the Physiocrats and Turgot both employed the word 'capital' freely, though in those days normally in the plural form, 'capitals'. It was in 1761 that the word *capitaliste* was first used by Jean-Jacques Rousseau to describe someone who possessed capital and could make use of it. The etymology of the word 'capital' in this context is interesting however, since it appears to stem directly from the original in Dutch. It took a very long time to be absorbed into English, where the word 'capitalism' did not appear until 1867, long after the period when its origin could be attributed to anything other than to the socialist writers, and even then in a context which strongly suggests some general knowledge of the writings of Marx himself.

The terms 'proletariat' and 'bourgeoisie' are much more interesting. As is well known, the term 'proletariat' derives from the Latin word *proletarii*, which was used in the Servian Constitution to designate the lowest class, those that had no resources except their offspring (*proles*). In this context it would have been familiar to any educated man of the eighteenth or nineteenth centuries. But how did it make the transition to describing a class of modern society? In his *Marx Before Marxism*, McLellan has a note on its emergence in German:

It was a romantic philosopher, Franz Baader, who, with reference to his native Bavaria in 1835, seems first to have used the word 'proletariat' and pointed out its significance for society. In an essay entitled *Über das dermalige Missverhältnis der Vermögslosen oder Proletairs zu den vermögen besitzenden Klassen* (1835), he described the law of the accumulation of capital in a few lines and claimed that neither charity nor police measures nor a constitutional state with citizenship limited to property holders could help the working classes, who should be given the right to defend their own interests, under the guidance of the Church, by forming associations. [McLellan 1972, p. 19]

The spelling of the word *Proletairs* here is extremely interesting, for the form is highly unusual in German. In French, however, the word *proletaire* had been in use since the time of Montesquieu, who had employed it in 1748 to describe Roman society, as indeed had many other writers on various occasions from at least as early as the fourteenth century. It was, surprisingly enough, the great individualist Jean-Jacques Rousseau who first used it to refer to modern society in 1751 in *La Nouvelle Héloïse*, but in French it appears to have remained in this adjectival form until the year in which Baader himself wrote, so his pre-eminence in coining the word 'proletariat' need not be disputed. It does not seem to have been used in English in its ancient sense until 1861, however, when for the first time it appears to have displaced the Latin word. Its use to refer to the lowest class of the community in modern society, often with hostile connotations, dates in English from 1853.

Although undoubtedly familiar today to all students of politics, the term has never found easy acceptance in English, in which in the nineteenth century the phrase 'labouring classes' and in the twentieth 'working classes' or 'working class' have held a scarcely disputed prominence. So far is this true that the very use of the word 'proletariat' acts as an indicator of whether or not a writer has Marxist sympathies, except when he happens to be discussing or quoting from Marx himself. Yet there does not seem to be any very substantial difference between the two terms which would encourage this distinction. Indeed, it is possible that for the majority the implications of the term were those that resisted its acceptance into English most strongly, since it would have been truly difficult, even in the late nineteenth century, for anyone other than a German philosopher to regard members of the British working classes as possessing nothing except their offspring. Their possessions might have been few and certainly inadequate, but they were not negligible, and as for their counterparts in France, where the term was adopted much more easily into the jargon of socialist discourse, it was precisely during this period that French society too was beginning its evolution away from the pattern foretold by Marx, a small but essential element of which was the acquisition of savings by the urban working classes.

If the term 'proletariat' has a fairly clear and defined meaning, the same cannot be said of 'bourgeoisie'. Not only do the two terms not come from the same language of origin, but they have virtually nothing else in common except their frequent use in a pejorative sense, though on this occasion the pejorative sense was well established before the adoption of the term 'bourgeoisie' as a term of political economy.

The origins of the term 'bourgeois' go back into the very foundations of the French language itself. Etymologically it is derived from the Germanic word for 'fortified place', which is found in Anglo-Saxon as *burh*. From the Germanic languages it became the Low Latin term *burgus*, retaining its meaning of 'fortified place'. Early in the year 1007 there appears for the first time the derivative form *burgensis*, meaning by this time the inhabitant of a town (which was no longer necessarily a fortified location). This was because by this period there had already begun that startling growth of towns which gave two senses to the emerging French word *bourg*: the one retaining the old sense of an inhabitant of a fortified place, the other meaning the inhabitant of an agglomeration of settlements immediately outside the ramparts, which in later years were to acquire the term 'false town', or *faubourg* (Pernoud 1960, p. 21). As Pernoud points out, the date 1007 itself is accidental, in that the word happens to be contained in a charter issued by Count Fulk Nerra by which he established a 'free town' near to the abbey of Beaulieu, close to Loches. The inhabitants of this town were to be given important rights of protection against the abbot, but there was in the charter a saving clause which provided that 'if the *Burgenses* attacked the monks or their servants and took their goods, they would pay a fine of 60 *livres*.' As Pernoud says, the terms of this contract pose, in the most direct way, the problem of the relationship between this emerging group of townsfolk and the established order of feudal society into which it was so rapidly thrusting itself.

To put the problem in historical perspective, we have to take account of the startling growth of trade that was taking place in Europe at the time, which was on a scale unheard of since the days of the Roman Empire. From the year 954, when the first pilgrim is reported to have made his way across Europe to pay homage at the shrine of Santiago de Compostela, the habit of pilgrimage had grown rapidly, necessitating a chain of hostels and facilities for sick pilgrims around which, if they did not exist already, there soon arose settlements. Along these routes pioneered by the pilgrims an increasing number of merchants also began to travel, and the inhabitants of key strongpoints sought to defend their right to take part in this fruitful and remunerative trade against the attacks of would-be feudal overlords and territorial masters. In the eleventh century the rush to found new towns was truly startling:

All the Villeneuf, all the Villenave, Villefranche, Villefranque and conversely Francheville or Franqueville, all the Chateauneuf, Neuf-chateau, Neufbourg, Bourgneuf, Beaumont, Claremont, Beaufour, the Neuville, Neuvic, Neuvy, Sauveté, Salvetat, Bastide, Ferté, etc. and their derivatives or combinations, bear witness that we are dealing with towns without an antique past, sprung from our soil in the feudal period. And one can add to them the names which evoke some sort of 'twinning' with other celebrated towns: Fleurance, which is an echo of Florence, Bruges in the Béarn, Granade on the Adour, Boulogne (from Bologna), Cordes (from Cordova), Pampellonne, Valence, Barcelonnette, etc. And even the memories of crusades and the evocation of the Holy Land, such as Neuvy-Saint-Sépulcre, Nazareth-Bon-Puisaye, etc. [Pernoud 1960, pp. 19–20]

About the year 1080 the word *burgensis* made its way into French, the language of the people who lived in the towns them-selves, and appears in the form *bourgeis*. From that moment onwards it became for the Middle Ages a term which distinguished a part of society which was neither noble nor of the serf or villein class. The dawning realization of common interests of those who lived in towns was finally attested in 1240 by the appearance of the word *bourgeoisie* itself. It became then the common term in French for the mercantile or trading members of society, considered collectively.

In 1302, as we have already seen, the States General, represent-ing the entire nation of France, including representatives of the towns, was convoked for the first time. The purpose of Philip IV in summoning this meeting, which brought under national control the system of provincial estates which had grown up within the previous century, was not only to raise taxation, an increasingly acute problem for the Crown, but also to demonstrate the support of his people in his struggle against the Pope. By this time the movement to found new towns, and the granting of new charters, had definitely come to an end; indeed, during the long reign of Louis IX (1226–70) only one new charter was granted, to the town and port of Aigues Mortes at the mouth of the Rhone, which had been deliberately founded by the king as a port of embarkation for the Holy Land and as such was a royal city and dockyard. But the bourgeoisie had come to stay.

As we have also seen, once established this position was not essentially disturbed down to the time of the French Revolution, the feudal system remaining intact despite the growth of new interests and the important role which the problem of finance was to play for the French monarchy throughout. Obviously, the members of the pre-revolutionary nobility tended to look down upon the bourgeoisie as uncultivated and interested primarily in money; they resented its wealth more, since they needed it themselves so badly. By the Revolution, therefore, the term was well established in casual use as a term with a pejorative meaning. It is highly significant, however, that the term remained uniquely French, so much so that when Werner Sombart came to write his monumental work on *Der Bourgeoisie*, he rejected the German equivalent for the term, *Bürgertum* (adj. *bürgerlich*), and used the French one. In English the French word can be found in the writing of both Clarendon in 1674 and Addison in 1702, in each case referring, naturally, to French society, so that the term would have been familiar to any member of the educated classes in England who had sufficient knowledge of French or who had made the Grand Tour.

Nevertheless, the picture is of a term that remained more or less static, with a well defined meaning, and therefore it is noteworthy that only in the period in which the growth of the middle classes in France really began to get under way did new derivatives appear, beginning in 1831 with the term *embourgeoiser*, the verbal form meaning 'to become a member of the bourgeoisie'. Although the term was certainly known to Marx before the period of his residence in Paris, it seems to have been during this period that it acquired the strong pejorative meaning which it has retained both in the works of Marx and in the minds of many of those who have already read Marx without necessarily sympathizing with his views down to our present time.

However, its prominence stems not only from its use as a term designating one of the two great classes of society but also from the fact that its German adjectival form, *bürgerlich*, meaning 'civil' or 'civic', designated for Hegelians the total structure of society or 'civil society'. For Marx, then, 'civil society' and 'bourgeois society' were synonyms, and what he was arguing for was no more and no less than the overturn of all the assumptions on which the legitimate social order of his day was based. In his view, 'civil society', as the term had been understood since the time of Locke, was a misnomer concealing the class domination of society by a selfish minority.

Earlier writers, of course, had regarded townsfolk as essentially parasitical upon the countryside, a view which in England was most energetically presented by Marx's contemporary, William Cobbett.

It would be hard, however, to regard the qualities of selfishness and greed so often ascribed to the bourgeoisie as unique to town dwellers; in the twentieth century, with as little reason, they have been ascribed to the peasantry or rural smallholding class *en bloc*. And, moreover, it seems only fair to point out that Marx himself was a town dweller, a man who, to judge by the evidence of the interiors of the rooms in which he lived (lovingly reconstructed by the Soviet State in the Karl Marx Museum in Moscow), enjoyed a Victorian middle-class style and standard of living and lived throughout his life on the surplus value of the labour of others. Small wonder, then, that he expressed his admiration, even if apparently reluctantly, for the achievements of the bourgeoisie.

It is unfortunate, though, that Marx should have chosen to designate one of the two classes of crucial importance to his theory by a term which so conspicuously lacks the economic objectivity which he sought in his theoretical writing. The pejorative implications of the term 'bourgeoisie' not only impeded an appreciation of the merits of Marx's theory but also built in a permanent confusion between the economic criteria of the relations to the factors of production on which he himself would have insisted and the dislike, purely emotional and not at all scientifically based, of the superficial evidence of a particular form of lifestyle at a particular period in European history. Time and again this confusion can be seen in the works of later writers, for the term 'bourgeoisie' has never ceased to be pejorative, and in the twentieth century it is profoundly difficult to employ the term without automatically using it as a term of criticism and disapproval.

In English this has meant that it has never gained popularity except among those who use it in a consciously Marxist sense. The preferred term in England was and remains 'the middle classes', in the plural. It was in this sense that Engels himself understood the equation of terms, although for Marx, it should be remembered, 'the middle classes' meant the classes or strata between bourgeoisie and proletariat, or what he and later Marxist writers have called the 'petty bourgeoisie'.

'I have used the word *Mittelklasse* all along in the sense of the English word middle class (or middle classes, as is said almost always),' Engels wrote in 1845, in the preface to the German edition of *The Condition of the Working Class in England*.

Like the French word *bourgeoisie* it means the possessing class, specifically the possessing class which is differentiated from the so-called aristocracy –

the class which in France and England is directly ... in possession of political power. Similarly, I have continually used the expressions working men (*arbeiter*) and proletarians, working class, propertyless class and proletariat as equivalents. |Marx and Engels 1975, vol. IV, p. 304|

About the habit of using a number of different words as equivalents in social science discourse, the less said the better, perhaps. But the equation of 'middle class' with 'bourgeoisie' is a significant matter, not merely a problem for translators. For 'middle class' in English does not have the disparaging overtones that the French word has on the Continent. These are well demonstrated in the work of Werner Sombart (1967), an impressionistic work, like an essay in style, which, despite considerable analytical skill, is thin on evidence. The references which he so sparingly gives can hardly be regarded today as a valid overall basis for the facts presented.

For Sombart is not concerned with the bourgeoisie as a class doomed to act out a role on the historical stage which, with all its shortcomings, has a certain undeniable grandeur; he is concerned with what he sees as the worship of wealth by the bourgeois himself, who, as an individual, comes to rate money above what it will purchase and to see the pursuit of money as the sole end of existence. It is a theme to which Marx himself gave expression in the *Paris Manuscripts* and which Sombart elaborates into a denunciation of the destruction of ethics to which he considers 'the spirit of capitalism' gives rise. It is one extremely popular in all ages with those who feel they are not as well done by as they might be and, on a higher ethical plane, can be seen as a modern injunction to the rich, for their own good, to follow the biblical injunction to sell all they have and give it to the poor.

Business is his sole preoccupation; is it any wonder that all else within him dries up? Everything about him becomes a wilderness, all life dies, all values disappear; in short, his environment is like that which Nature produces for the colonist. The home of the capitalist undertaker becomes for him, to all intents and purposes, something foreign. Nature, Art, Literature, Politics, friends – all vanish into nothingness. He has no time for them. |Sombart 1967, pp. 351–2|

No doubt this picture ought logically to be true. But is it? Most people engaged in business or industry seem to find time for recreation, family life and even politics. In fact – and perhaps this is the problem – they seem to have the resources to enjoy each and every one of these things quite a lot, irritating as this may be to those who do not!

With Sombart, then, we move away from the hard facts of economic life, disputable as these may be, and into the realms of quasi-sociological speculation, where the development of the bourgeoisie is attributed to a mysterious spiritual entity called 'the spirit of capitalism', which appears at different times, in different places, in varying degrees, offering different capacities for development and needing varying lengths of time in which 'to come to full bloom'. Before leaving Marx's own writings and following the subsequent development of Marxist theory up to and into the era of 'advanced capitalism', therefore we should consider the important and so far unresolved question of the duration attributed by Marx to the elements of class society.

The question is raised by a statement in *Communist Manifesto* itself: 'The history of all hitherto existing society is the history of class struggles.' How far, if at all, is this true? The great social divisions of the Middle Ages had been legal divisions of estate, not economic divisions of class. The bourgeoisie, which Marx claims to be the ruling class of the capitalist era, orginated literally centuries ago, in the High Middle Ages. Only when the productive forces within it were fully developed did it burst its bonds and assume political control over the new order. Yet in that order it had necessarily called into existence the industrial proletariat which was in turn to destroy it.

Marx himself did not seek to resolve the identification of class and estate, which Max Weber was subsequently to be at pains to reassert. It was Ferdinand Toennies who addressed the issue of conflict between the two opposing concepts of *social collectives*.

Estates and classes are based essentially on the facts of economic life. But their significance reaches over into political affairs and into the intellectual and moral sphere. Estates are related to one another like the organs or limbs of a body; classes are engaged in a contractual relationship. Classes look upon, and deal with, one another basically as opponents, who depend on one another nevertheless as a result of their mutual interests. The relation between classes turns immediately into emnity, when one class is dissatisfied with the actions of another, when one accuses the other that the contract is inadequate or that its conditions have not been observed. Hence, estates change over into classes, when they engage in hostile actions or engage one another in war. These struggles are class struggles, even if they are called struggles between estates. [Toennies 1931, p. 12]

To take this literally would be to introduce a new criterion for the identification of a class – that it should be engaged in war – which would take the concept well away from its Marxian resting-point. It would also blur what seems to be the crucial contradiction between the *Manifesto* and Marx's later writings, namely, that whereas the bourgeoisie may (or may not) have existed as a class before its assumption of power, it cannot (if Marx is to be consistent) have done so for long in a state of self-awareness, unless we are to take account of other factors in explaining its ultimate realization of power. We can certainly accept the contention that Marx did not see the stages of history as arriving like circus elephants, each holding on to the tail of the one before it. But in default of a concept of class in earlier times, the assertion that the struggles of those times should be seen as class struggles is certainly suspect within the terms of his more developed theory of history. It may be argued that the *Communist Manifesto* is not to be taken as a fully developed statement of Marx's views anyway, but, given the fact that millions since have seen it as the epitome of Marxism, it is more important rather than less to subject it to critical attention. If there is to be no class struggle in the future, and if it cannot be shown that there was class struggle in the past, why should we believe that there is class struggle in the present?

4   Class, status and power

As we have already seen, for the English-speaking world the term 'class' never had the sharp precision which it was given in the eighteenth century in France. Consequently, though popular, it did not easily accommodate itself to the new Marxist usage, which in any case did not achieve any very great acceptance in Britain, still less in the United States, in the nineteenth century. A further difficulty was the technical problems impeding the definition of 'class' in terms of identifiable, objective criteria which could be labelled and applied consistently, and to this topic we will have to return at greater length. The concept slowly emerged, therefore, of class as a self-assigned, constant picture of one's place in the world, defined not only, and possibly not even dominantly, in terms of one's economic position but also in terms of other variables, now commonly labelled status and power.

It would be misleading to label all such treatments of class as non-Marxist, for two reasons. The first is that there is no necessary consistency between them, and that the relationship between them is such that the differences are sometimes greater than they are between any one of them and Marxist approaches broadly construed. The second is that although such views of class have been conceived in the post-Marxist period, it would be misleading in many respects to see them, as many writers still assert, wholly as a reaction to Marx. Indeed, many of them directly incorporate Marx's own ideas, without necessarily accepting the accretions of subsequent generations of thinkers. Nor is there any compelling logical reason why these accretions should be accepted; in this sense all such approaches must be considered, at least *ab initio*, equally valid unless demonstrated otherwise. Marxism is an important strand in modern thought everywhere, but it is not by any means the only one, and in many cases it does not even dominate the day-to-day thinking of those who profess to be Marxists. In this way we are all Marxists, and we are

Up to this point I have been
specifically to refer to an economic
earlier meanings, defined by the Pl
centre of his world view by Marx. The
reason for regarding this set of usages
others as 'wrong', and it would be misle
to restrain the use of the term in this
alternative approaches. What they have
view of class as a distinct 'social' pher
collective' based on varying economi

retire entirely f
scholar, he v
imperial
becam
the
r

.... often
indentifiable in terms of attributes of status used in the social sphere
to identify, delimit and even restrict membership. Naturally, this is
confusing, and though I have tried to use the phrase 'social class' in
these contexts to limit the possibilities of confusion, I am aware that
in doing so I may inadvertently be giving the impression that to use
the simple word 'class' to describe social status groups, as many
millions of people do, is to be regarded as incorrect. In this respect,
as in others, as we shall see, there has been a remarkable degree of
convergence in recent years, though not, unfortunately, with much
resulting gain in clarity.

Finding an alternative term to designate these approaches, on
the other hand, is very difficult indeed. It would be anachronistic to
term them pluralist approaches, and although they relate to an
essentially operational use of the term 'class', it would be misleading
in the extreme to term them positivist approaches, since they bear
no relation whatsoever to the historical quasi-religion of positivism
as outlined by Auguste Comte. In many ways, the best term that
seems to fit them is 'Weberian approaches', but in using this term it
is necessary to state at the beginning that though Max Weber gave
the first definitive statement of some of the concepts of the class
upon which they are based, Weberian thought differs substantially
from the way in which it has been interpreted subsequently, and the
degree of diversity has now become very great indeed.

Max Weber

Max Weber (1864–1920), was Professor of Economics successively
at the universities of Freiburg, Heidelberg and Munich, where he
died suddenly of pneumonia, leaving much of his work unfinished.
Despite consistently bad health, which forced him eventually to

⎧m university teaching and to work as a private ⎦ prominent in opposition politics in the last years of ⎦rmany, wrote regularly for the Press, and ultimately ⎦ member of the Commission which wrote the first draft of ⎦eimar Constitution. This experience, coupled with his legal ⎦ning, gives his work a highly analytical quality, which, however, ⎦s somewhat obscured because much of it has had to be reconstructed from the notes of his students. His views on class, although they are unquestionably of immense importance, are particularly difficult to distinguish, since his writing on this subject is seriously incomplete.

Weber uses the term 'class' (*Klasse*) in a very individual way. For Weber, class is above all a concept to be seen in apposition to 'estate' (*Stand*), a term which appears to have caused enormous difficulties to the translators of Weber, since the English term 'estate' is in some respects misleading and, in addition, lacks the adjectival form (*ständlich*) which is so useful in the German. In *The Theory of Social and Economic Organization* Weber defines a class as 'any group of persons occupying the same class status'. This latter term is already defined:

The term 'class status' will be applied to the typical probability that a given state of (a) provision with goods, (b) external conditions of life, and (c) subjective satisfaction or frustration, will be possessed by an individual or a group. These probabilities define class status in so far as they are dependent on the kind and extent of control or lack of it which the individual has over goods or services and existing possibilities of their exploitation for the attainment of income or receipts within a given economic order. [Weber 1965, p. 424]

The definition of class for Weber, therefore, has two important inherent characteristics: it is multiple, and it is both subjective and objective. From this he deduces that there may be more than one type of class. A 'property' class is determined by the differentiation of the property it owns. An 'acquisition' class is determined primarily by the opportunity its members have to exploit their services in the market. And a 'social' class is composed of multiple class statuses, between which the observer can detect regular and consistent movements of individuals or generations (ibid.).

The relationship of property classes is such that it lies along a continuum; some classes are positively and others negatively privileged, while yet others, each of which forms a sort of middle class, lie somewhere on the scale in between. Along this continuum a number of smaller groups stand out, distinguished from those that lie on either side of them by a special combination of characteristics. These are the social classes, of which the 'working class' forms a particularly large, regular and distinguishable group. Other groups thus specially identified are the petty bourgeoisie (*Kleinbürgertum*) and the intelligentsia, or intellectual class. Neither social classes nor property classes, however, can be identified with the traditional estates (*Stände*) which are distinguished by a defined mode of living, a formal system of education for their position or the prestige either of birth or of education.

Thus for Weber the difference between classes lies not in their relationship to the means of production but in their relationship to the means of consumption, the market place, independently of any formal legal status or ascribed status that they may receive on other accounts. (cf. Cotgrove 1967, p. 213).

This emphasis on the market situation is consistent with Weber's other interests in the development of modern society, as symbolized by his most famous work, *The Protestant Ethic and The Spirit of Capitalism*. For Weber's concept of class fits into a view of society as a growing entity which expands and develops new potentialities; consequently, he believes, far from becoming simpler and more constrained, class, in common with other forms of stratification, is becoming more diffuse and complex. The development of new potentialities within the process of industrialization gives rise to new subgroups, which in turn form the nuclei of rising classes which displace existing class groups – insofar as those class groups can be said to have a permanent basis, for classes for Weber are not fixed; the combination of awareness and self-consciousness which distinguishes them is something which in due course may be superseded by changes in society.

It is impossible, however, to consider the notion of class in Weber without dealing with other equally important concepts. First among these is the notion of status. The translation 'class status' used above is particularly confusing in this respect and should probably be rendered rather as 'class situation'. For 'status' in Weber is the nearest equivalent to the German word *Stand* when it is modified from its traditional German meaning of 'estate' to mean what in English is signified by the word 'status'.

In English the term 'status' has a very precise legal meaning. It means 'the legal standing or position of a person as determined by his membership of some class of persons legally enjoying certain rights or subject to certain limitations; condition in respect, e.g. of liberty or servitude, marriage or celibacy, infancy or majority' (*OED*). As a legal concept it has long since been adopted into the English language, and thus we find it in Boswell's *Life of Johnson* in 1791 and subsequently in many other references. Put more simply, status is the right to certain privileges, and consequently it can be measured in a fairly simple, linear way. High status means the possession of more rights and privileges; low status means the possession of fewer rights and privileges. These rights, if they are to be effective, must be sanctioned by law. It is for this reason that the word 'status' in English bears such a close resemblance to the implications of the Continental term 'estate', to the extent that the two terms may be indistinguishable, as they are in German. Weber defines social status in the following terms:

The term of 'social status' will be applied to a typically effective claim to positive or negative privilege with respect to social prestige so far as it rests on one or more of the following bases: (a) mode of living, (b) a form or process of education which may consist in empirical or rational training and the acquisition of the corresponding modes of life or (c) on the prestige of both, or of an occupation. [Weber 1965, p. 428]

Status is, then, a description of the honour or respect in which a person is held. Honour brings with it privileges, but also responsibilities. It may give one relatively privileged access to valuable economic resources, but such access is not necessary to the acquisition of status or to its maintenance; 'poverty is not as such a disqualification for high social status but there again it may influence it' (ibid., p. 428). It is for this reason that Weber sees status position, or *Standische Lage*, translated in the above extract as 'social status', as a form of social stratification cutting across the boundaries, where defined, of class position. The distinction, however, is in itself a complex one. Anthony Giddens puts it like this:

The contrast between class and status group, however, is not, as often seems to be assumed, merely, or perhaps primarily, a distinction between subjective and objective aspects of differentiation. While class is founded upon differentials of economic interests in market relationships, Weber nowhere denies that, under certain given circumstances, a class may be a subjectively aware 'community'. The importance of status groups – which are normally 'communities' in this sense – derives from the fact that they are built upon criteria of grouping other than those stemming from market situations. The contrast between classes and status groups is sometimes portrayed by Weber as one between the objective and subjective; but it is also one between production and consumption. Whereas class expresses relationships involved in production, status groups express those involved in consumption, in the form of specific 'styles of life'. [Giddens 1973, pp. 43–4]

In his essay 'Class, Status and Party' in *Economy and Society*, Weber not only extends his concept of class in systematic fashion but also supplies the link between class and status group which explains their interrelationship. What classes have in common with status groups, and for that matter with political parties, is that they are all 'phenomena of the distribution of power' within the society. However, though political power is clearly dependent on each of the three phenomena, the phenomena themselves are not independent of one another. The distribution of property, the distribution of honour and the distribution of political activity are dependent, each in its own way, on the other two. As Weber himself writes:

With some over-simplification, one might say that 'classes' are stratified according to their relations to the production and acquisition of goods; whereas 'status groups' are stratified according to the principles of their *consumption* of goods as represented by special 'styles of life'. [Gerth and Mills 1948, p. 193]

Put like this, it is evident that the consumption of goods will be very closely dependent on their production and acquisition, and that the acquisition of goods for Weber is not inseparable, as it is for Marx, from the process of production. For Weber there exists a much greatter range of economic possibilities in any given economic situation, corresponding to the visibly increased potentialities of late as opposed to early nineteenth-century society.

However, the flexibility which Weber introduces into the concept of class extends very much further in the case oof the concept of status. If this is a subjective characteristic, it is subjective in the mind of the observer as well as that of the observed. The extent to which a claim to honour is made, or is acknowledged by others to be valid, is not explored by Weber, who observes (and was, indeed, possibly the first to observe) a clear distinction between the economic order within which is the place of classes and the social order within which he finds the place of status groups. What he does, of course, is to explore at considerable length the way in which honour, originating in the 'charisma' of outstanding personal qualities, perceived by others in an individual, can be translated

into political power and ascendancy. The way in which this ascendancy is established, and the ways in which it is subsequently translated into the continuing basis of political power in society, was what occupied a great deal of Weber's published work. Clearly, it is not inseparable from his concept either of class or of status, even though the discussion is not closely related to it.

There is a tendency, in most studies of Weber, to emphasize those respects in which his theory differs from that of Marx. In one respect, however, it is very definitely the product of the same intellectual tradition. This is in the assumption that the phenomena of industrial society in the social world are to be seen as uniquely characteristic of any one society and fundamentally different from those of societies that have existed before.

This assumption is as pronounced in Weber as it is in Marx, if not more so. Classes are seen as essentially the phenomena of modern industrial society: the difference between the two writers lies in their expectations and projections of what will become of the classes in future. Nor are the two thinkers so very strikingly different in their treatment of the theme of the survival of pre-capitalist relationships in capitalist society. It is true that Weber is explicit, where Marx is silent, about the importance of the concept of honour, as exemplified in social estates. Marx, who was married to the daughter of an aristocrat but was always short of money, could hardly have failed to be aware, even if he did not choose to discuss, the distinction between honour and property relationships. The extent to which Marx recognizes the survival of non-class relationships in industrial society is, of course, somewhat obscured by that famous rhetorical flourish of the *Communist Manifesto*: 'The history of all hitherto existing society is the history of class struggles' (Marx and Engels 1962, vol. I, p. 34). In the English edition of 1888 Engels himself qualified this statement by suggesting that it was meant to refer only to 'written history', and that the emergence of classes was by that time much better understood than it had been when the *Manifesto* was written. But with our far greater knowledge not merely of pre-history but also of medieval history we are in a position today to make judgements that are very much more authoritative than those of Marx, Engels or even Weber.

It was, as we have already seen, as estate and not as class that social differentiation was perceived in pre-modern times. The struggle between these entities was the struggle, therefore, between estates and not between classes. The distinction between estates and classes made by Ferdinand Toennies has already been cited above. In the same article Toennies went further in distinguishing between the two types of social organization, finding the key to their distinctiveness in the concept of individualism. Following Sombart, Toennies stresses the extent to which the 'stranger' (in particular, the Jew) had played in the development of mercantile (and hence of capitalist) society. This collective had little in common with either estates or classes. And Toennies, as a Continental observer, was struck by the distinctive features of British society, which had developed in a way that was totally different from that predicted by Marx. There the distinction between propertied and propertyless classes, he thought, was distinctive and unique.

The persistence of medieval ways of life in England, is a remarkable exception in this respect. Both ruling estates are still vigorously alive and they are still strongly represented politically. The middle class is made up of capitalists and of the entire stratum which is known as the bourgeoisie in France and Germany. But in Great Britain a middle stratum between the bourgeoisie and the working class is hardly worth mentioning. This is explained simply by the diminished significance of centuries past of the artisan and even more of the peasantry. English-language literature does not recognise the organisation of the people in 'estates' whether these are ruling estates or bourgeois estates, estates of birth or of occupation. Only three classes are recognised: upper, middle, and lower. The differentiation of estates is neither established linguistically nor theoretically, even though the social position or rank to which someone belongs is often discussed. Such discussion points at least to the existence of estates, partly of birth and partly of occupation. [Toennies 1967, p. 18]

This point has given rise to some interesting complications. For example, one recent writer, following the line originally laid down by Marx, emphasizes the curious uncertainty that hovers round the term 'bourgeoisie'. He writes:

Strictly speaking, the bourgeoisie never constituted a social estate of the feudal system; consequently they were never a middle class of the estate system. The social-status system – the estates system – based upon the landed economy of feudal society was never able to assimilate the townsman. The bourgeois social order was not only different from the feudal order but also antagonistic to it. [Cox 1970, pp. 145–6]

As we have already seen, this is not historically accurate. The townsmen were, in fact, assimilated – indeed, the nature of medieval society, and the peculiar emphasis placed on the importance of semi-divine kingship, would have been inconceivable without the existence of a category of townsfolk. Certainly, there is no evidence that the feudal system, as historically understood nowadays, predates the emergence of towns to any significant extent, nor that the system of relationships characteristic of the feudal era ever existed without towns; William the Conqueror, who established in England the feudal system in the most complete and coherent form known in Europe, lost no time after his successful conquest in proceeding to London to be hailed as king and crowned as Westminster. And the first significant building work he undertook in his new kingdom was the erection of the White Tower, on the edge of the City of London, to overawe the citizens and to inform them that he was now master.

The development of stratification

Independently of Max Weber, Thorstein Veblen in the United States was working on his celebrated and irritating book *The Theory of the Leisure Class*, first published in 1918. This, the first native American study of class structures, and in literary skill far ahead of most, profoundly influenced intellectual trends in the most advanced capitalist society of its day and helped to influence that diversification of interpretations which has continued to be such a marked feature of the American literature.

The focus of Veblen's work is squarely on the emergence of a privileged class in society, symbolized by leisure. Leisure, meaning the absence of need to work, has important consequences for the stratification of society which go beyond the emergence of a privileged or parasitical group of individuals. For Veblen, the leisure class is not simply an elite but something much larger, and it emerges not in industrial society but in pre-modern times, when

The leisure class as a whole comprises the noble and priestly classes, together with much of their retinue. The occupations of the class are correspondingly diversified, but they have the common economic characteristic of being non-industrial. These non-industrial upper class occupations may be roughly comprised under government, warfare, religious observances, and sports. [Veblen 1918, p. 2]

The emergence of this leisure class coincides with the appropriation of property within the community, but once well established is followed by the emergence of a second class, 'whose office is the performance of a vicarious leisure for the behoof of the reputability of the primary or legitimate leisure class'. This class is the servant class. For Veblen the most significant thing about this class is its focus upon the person of its master: 'The master's person, being the embodiment of worth and honour, is of the most serious consequence.' The care of this person and the performance of services for him is, however, but the focus of a sphere of conspicuous consumption, symbolized by the wearing of liveries and other signs of the ability to maintain a substantial retinue, such as the provision of spacious servants' quarters. This retinue shares in the benefits produced by the existence of the leisure class but cannot be counted as part of that class, though it cannot be separated from it either. Veblen points out that the actual number of the personal services performed by each servant must necessarily decrease as the number of servants increases, and that therefore the employment of these servants may be regarded as essential mainly for prestige purposes. Secondly, he observes, a scale of values obtains such that the service of men, though possibly inferior to that of women, is preferred, since it gratifies the desire of the master to illustrate his capacity for dominance over them, men being preferred for this purpose because of their greater strength.

It is a serious grievance if a gentleman's butler or footman performs his duties about his master's table or carriage in such unformed style as to suggest that his habitual occupation may be ploughing or sheep herding. Such bungling work would imply inability upon the master's part to procure the service of specially trained servants; that is to say, it would imply inability to pay for the consumption of time, effort and instruction required to fit a trained servant for special service under an exacting code of forms. [Veblen 1918, p. 61]

To the extent, therefore, that the servant is part of the master's household, he shares both the attitudes and expectations of that household and its economic status. He has, therefore, an interest in the maintenance of the system as it stands.

Now that the keeping of personal servants is extremely rare, and many domestic duties are performed by machines, Veblen's thesis may seem of only marginal importance. It lies, however, at the commencement of a series of studies which had sought to explain the phenomenon of 'deference'. Veblen wrote:

In modern civilised communities the lines of demarcation between social classes have grown vague and transient, and wherever this happens the norm of reputability imposed by the upper class extends its coercive influence with but slight hindrance down through the social structure down to the lowest strata. [ibid., p. 84]

Through this process, then, one can see members of the 'lower' classes following the example of the 'upper' classes in voting as in the patterns of their behaviour and their standards of good conduct. And, even more significantly, these standards are set in practice by the leisure class, to whose status, therefore, all other members of society will wish to aspire.

Veblen is also of considerable interest for his emphasis on the emerging role of engineers in society. These technical specialists, with no exact correspondence in the pre-industrial world, were conspicuously important in American society, in which their social influence was not restrained to the extent it was in Europe by preconceptions about their position in society.

Veblen's analysis of the leisure class is of particular concern to us, since it emphasizes a feature that in retrospect appears to be a distinct weakness in Weber's theory of class. Weber, in defining estate, or status, as based on consumption, gives it a degree of internal logic and economic coherence which the traditional term 'estate' did not have. The division of medieval society by estates was not, as we may already have deduced, purely a matter of consumption. Certainly, the lord consumed a great deal more than the peasant, and furthermore his status, like that of the leisure class for Veblen, was marked out by his ability to support a large number of retainers in the process of vicarious consumption. But the status ascribed to him cannot be defined in terms of consumption alone, otherwise we would have to hold that abbots, whose consumption was severely circumscribed by the nature of their rule, had a lower social status than had lords, which was clearly not the case.

Mousnier emphasizes the extent to which historical stratification has rested on non-economic criteria of

social esteem, position, rank, honour and prestige among individuals and social groups (such as families, organizations, colleges, communities) and mutual recognition of these differences in a given society.... [Mousnier 1973, p. 16]

by according them second place in his list of scales of stratification. He is extremely careful to stress the precise applications of this to the concept of *Stande* in German:

Social stratification by 'order', subdivided into 'estates' (in German *Stande*, in French *Etats*), is extremely common. It consists of a hierarchy of degrees ('estates or conditions') each one distinct from the other and organised not according to the wealth of their members nor their consumption capacity, nor yet by their role in the production of material goods, but according to the esteem, honour and rank that society attributes to social functions that can have no connection at all with the production of material goods.

In feudal France up to the middle of the fifteenth century as well as in the France of fealties that followed this period, social prestige, honour and rank were ascribed to the military profession and fitness for leadership and perfection that derived from it. [ibid., p. 25]

The element of military skill in stratification, however, was not as quickly recognized in the Europe of the inter-war period. There the most important thinker was the German Theodor Geiger, whose work was subsequently to be strongly influential on the concept of class expressed by Dahrendorf. In his *Zur Theorie des Klassenbegriffs und der proletarischen Klasse* (1930), Geiger accepted the basic Marxist contention that class was based on the ownership of the means of production, but with qualifications. Other criteria also operated to ascribe people to specific classes, and he saw no wholesale confrontation between the two major classes, between which he saw a disparate body of unrelated occupations in a middle class that belonged to neither one nor the other of them. This issue of the varied nature of society he took up again in his *Die soziale Schichtung des deutschen Volkes* (1932), in which he undertook an analysis of the economically active population in Germany, and divided them into no fewer than five groups. Their social position was, he thought, determined not only by their relationship to the factors of production but also by such criteria as the size of the enterprises in which they worked, the degree of independence they had in their jobs and the extent to which specialized qualifications were necessary to undertake them. The tendency of this work to revise a fundamentally Marxist view of society in an accommodation to an evidently different pattern of economic development from that predicted by Marx himself was extended in his major publication *Die Klassengesellschaft im Schmelztiegel* (1949). 'Certainly Marxist theory has been falsified by political postulants,' he agreed. 'The similarities, however, are worth not less than the easy objections of their bourgeois opponents' (Geiger 1949, p. 36).

Although the concept of power makes a fleeting appearance in Geiger's earlier work, albeit purely in relation to industrial power or capacity, in his later work he appears to have regressed from this towards a more strictly Marxian concept of class as based essentially on economic criteria. It is particularly interesting to contrast

Geiger's view of class with the almost contemporary view of R.H. Tawney in England.

In his *Equality*, published in 1931, Tawney launched an attack on the British class 'system', complaining not that the advance of production had failed to disturb a basically satisfactory and predictable trend towards division in the two major classes but, on the contrary, that the preservation of traditional class structures was stifling individualism and ensuring that merit and rewards continued to be separated. It was the sickness of class that prevented Britain from becoming a common society, joined together by a common culture. Yet many of the attributes by which Tawney defined class membership were marks of status instead.

Tawney's conception of class was wide and flexible, distinguishing class from simple occupation and asserting its cultural rather than its material aspect on the one hand, but denying on the other that an absence of class consciousness indicated an absence of class. This enabled him to conduct an examination of social justice in terms not simply of wealth or income, but of all the other opportunities, accesses and advantages which whilst they might be sustained by or lead to monetary privilege, were not themselves simply financial; education, health, recruitment to positions of power and benefit. [Barker 1978, p. 144]

It was logical that it should have been in the United States that the attempt was made to bring together these competing approaches and that it was done under the auspices of a broadly Weberian concept of society. The social experience of the United States, as an immigrant culture in which traditional European social distinctions had failed to survive (and were, indeed, consciously eliminated by the egalitarianism of the official ideology), was such that any treatment of social stratification had to take into account more than one attribute. At the same time there emerged important differences of emphasis which we must not overlook. American writers generally were impatient of the distinction between money gained in one sense and money gained in another. The United States did not have, in their opinion, a proletariat: the opportunity to rise in terms of income, and hence in terms of opportunity and consumption, was available to every American who was prepared to work hard, and in the extreme fluidity of American society of the period it is indeed hard to find empirical evidence with which to refute this claim. Inevitably, this meant the development of a concept of class which was much wider than that propounded either by the Marxists or by Max Weber himself.

At the same time, the economic basis of class in relationship to production failed to survive in its original sophistication. Rather, it was assimilated to a simple rank order based on income, the statistically easiest method of determining a person's position in the economic hierarchy. For an American, after all, one dollar was much like another. Veblen's study of the leisure class, moreover, did not encourage people to emulate the individuals whom he had delineated. Members of the leisure class were regarded as being idle layabouts, good for nothings who contributed nothing to the good of society and whose parasitical and useless existence was tolerable only insofar as it did no significant harm to the society as a whole, of which they were such a small and insignificant part. This attitude was the easier to sustain in view of the fact that by the beginning of the twentieth century members of this class played no significant role in American politics. The great wealth of the giant trusts, moreover, was in the hands of self-made men such as Andrew Carnegie and John D. Rockefeller. The one member of the privileged classes who had political power at this period, Theodore Roosevelt, made it quite clear, through his almost frenetic activity, that he was no idler and that in his activity lay his claim to political power.

In the United States the nature of political power was essentially separable from that of the economic organization of society in a way that it was not in the older unitary states of Europe. The size of the country, the nature of the federal system and the fact that political activity was associated within urban areas principally with the hard work and energy of relatively poorly paid immigrants or their descendants combined to separate in the minds of American writers the concept of power from the concept of class or status; in relation to the notion of 'party', class and status were not, in fact, 'alternative phenomena of the distribution of power' in American society. Party was the fundamental instrument for the organization of power, and class and status alike had no political effect except by way of party. Hence in their thought the notion of party as a structure came to be assimilated directly to the concept of power, as a dimension of stratification. In the hands of Lipset and Bendix this emerged as a new and fundamental restructuring of the Weberian tradition, and one which was to have the most fundamental impact on American views of social stratification thereafter.

For Lipset and Bendix it was class, status and power that were the three fundamental axes of stratification within their society, and not class, status and party that were three phenomena of the distribution of power. Power was not for them directly related to class and status. It was in fact, within American society, apparently quite distinct from them. The belief in the possibility of rising from the log cabin to the White House went with the belief that political power was open to any member of American society, regardless of his wealth or past occupation. Power was, in fact, an attribute of professional politicians, whose occupational strata, therefore, were distinct from the societies whom they served. Status, on the other hand, was more likely to be acquired through power rather than power through status. Furthermore, rightly or wrongly, by the inter-war period the patrician element that had surrounded Theodore Roosevelt had become something of an aberration. Certainly, to be a Henry Cabot Lodge or a Charles Bonaparte was to have good family connections and hence status, but by the 1920s it was not necessarily to be as powerful within the American political system as were people of much more humble origins, such as Warren Harding or Calvin Coolidge.

A decisive influence on the new formulation was that of Talcott Parsons, who wrote in 1954:

Of the two major types of what above were called diffuse function associations, the political may be treated as a relatively minor factor except for the groups actively participating in political function. The high level of horizontal mobility means that membership in the local political unit is of secondary significance and easily changed. Similarly party affiliation is for most of the 'public' loose and easily changed except with the numerically small extremes involved in political activism of the proto-fascist or communist variety. The question of where those actively engaged in political careers belong presents another order of problem. Perhaps the most important point to note is that in sharp contrast to many societies, a 'political elite' or 'ruling class' does not have a paramount position in American society, but at best those making a political career are even at the top *among* the elite elements. Moreover, there is little continuity from generation to generation in this type of affiliation. [Parsons 1954, p. 119]

Politics, then, could be treated at least partially as an 'occupational role' and did not invalidate, while it did complement, the 'broad generalization' that the American system of stratification revolved mainly about the integration between kinship and the occupation system. The crucial link between the two systems was to be seen in the person of the husband and father, who, being the same person, became the 'instrumental leader' of the family and whose occupational earnings constituted the main source of family income.

Hence there *has to be* a broad correlation between the direct evaluation of occupational roles, income derived from those roles, and status of the families of the incumbents as collectivities in the scale of stratification. It is essentially this broad correlation to which we would like to apply the term 'class status', so far as it describes American conditions. Somewhat more broadly we may repeat the definition of class status given in the earlier paper as that component of status shared by the members of the most effective kinship unit ... As thus defined, class status is, it should be clear, not a rigid entity, but a fairly loosely correlated complex. Family status relative to specific occupation and income may be enhanced (or depressed) by canons of taste in the fields of expressive symbolism, by connections with other families of certain orders of prestige, through kinship or for example memberships in voluntary associations or purely informal mutual entertainment relations. It may also be enhanced or depressed through choice of residential location, through prestige of educational institutions which members have attended or children are currently attending, and through various other channels. To a considerable degree it is arbitrary where the 'constitutive' elements of class status are held to end, and their 'symbolic' penumbra to begin. All that is here contended is that the family–occupation–income complex is by and large the core of the wider complex. [ibid., p. 120]

Only in the most general sense, therefore, could the American class complex be made to yield a 'single unequivocal scale of classes'. A number of factors made identification of this extremely difficult. On the one hand, consumption was mass and general, so that it was difficult to distinguish between the consumption of different groups. Secondly, the opportunities for income were relatively compressed, so that it was difficult to distinguish people who were very much richer than others. The 'business managerial elite' could not be described as unequivocally 'top' in an occupational sense, since they were keenly contested by many professionals. The emphasis on the nuclear family meant that families tended not to transmit careers in the way that they did in Europe. Contrary to Marxian predictions, the industrial labour force had not grown in proportion to the growth of the productivity of the economy, while at the same time a large number of white-collar and service occupations had appeared, many of them semi-independent. The drudgery of work had enormously diminished. And the farm population, itself also much diminished in proportion to the whole (in 1940 it was about 15 per cent), ranged in income right across the scale and was not internally stratified. Above all, the degree of horizontal and vertical mobility remained very considerable, particularly by contrast with that possible in Europe.

Although all the points that Parsons made were undoubtedly correct, it did not follow that American sociologists and other writers were entirely happy to accept a loose and virtually indefinable concept of class. To follow this path would have meant the virtual disappearance of the concept of class, and although this may have certain advantages, it was not in fact the route that was taken. Rather, theorists tended to concentrate on a relatively limited number of axes of stratification and increasingly found themselves driven back towards a quasi-Weberian framework for the analysis even of American society. In this movement the pressure to clarify and simplify for the purposes of the mass instruction of large numbers of students must also have played its part. Few students would be entirely happy to accept the Parsonian approach as an effective solution to the practical problems of society, and American society has traditionally been based above all on the practical.

It was with their attention fixed firmly on the practical application of their definition of class that Lipset and Bendix established in 1951 three criteria of social stratification which together they regarded as constituting the concept of class. Since the behavioural revolution of the late 1920s, they observed, the literature in the field had become more and more methodological, and consequently discussions of class and status in the literature of American sociology had become 'increasingly ahistorical'. However, it was their belief that the analysis of social class ought to be

concerned with an assessment of the chances that common economic conditions and the common experiences of a group would lead to organised action.

It followed that

the analysis of class must combine the study of present facts (of social stratification) with an assessment of possibilities for future development, and this cannot be accomplished without a study of changes in the social structure during the historical past. We would propose three interrelated variables to facilitate such an enquiry: economic position, status, and power. [Lipset and Bendix 1951, p. 248]

Though for Lipset and Bendix these three variables were but different aspects of the stratification of class, their position was almost immediately modified by others, who retained as a synonym for 'economic position' the more common and traditional formulation of 'class' itself. Class, status and power thus came to be recognized as the three principal axes of stratification within society, class being defined principally in terms of economic position, but in a Weberian rather than a Marxist sense, in that it was the relationship to the market and not the relationship to the forces of production that tended to determine economic position. As Lipset and Bendix themselves stressed, the separation of ownership from control in modern industrial society, coupled with its growing complexity, made a purely economic concept of class meaningless in the eyes of most Americans and, indeed, in the eyes of many others as well.

Ironically, in their discussion of class Lipset and Bendix had occasion to refer to the work of J.A. Schumpeter. For Schumpeter, who was an economist, had taken a view of class which was almost diametrically opposed to theirs. In 1943, in his important book *Capitalism, Socialism and Democracy*, he had written:

Social classes ... are not the creatures of the classifying observer but live entities that exist as such. And their existence entails consequences that are entirely missed by a schema which looks upon society as if it were an amorphous assemblage of individuals and families. It is fairly open to question precisely how important the phenomenon of social classes is for research in the field of purely economic theory. That it is very important for many practical applications and for all the broader aspects of the social process in general is beyond doubt. [Schumpeter 1943, p. 14]

Where Lipset and Bendix on the one hand and Schumpeter on the other did agree was on the importance of power. Schumpeter was dismissive of Marx's own views about class on the valid and reasonable ground that he had never worked them out properly. 'The theory of his chief associate, Engels, was of the division-of-labour type and essentially unMarxian in its implication,' he had written. Neither economics nor bare force, as Lassalle had asserted, could alone explain the phenomenon of governmental authority, and without governmental authority there could be no true political power.

It was similarly in the conflict with authority rather than in the ownership of the means of production that Dahrendorf (1957) found the basis of class promotion; it was in differential access to positions of authority, and hence to power and prestige, that he saw the basis of class conflict in the twentieth century. To this extent, therefore, Dahrendorf built on the work not only of Geiger but also of Marx himself, whom he sought to reformulate rather than to disprove.

Though Schumpeter has no time for the predictive aspects of Marxism – the statement that socialism is the only possible kind of classless society he regards as no more than 'ingenuous tautology' (Schumpeter 1943, p. 19) – he was strongly influenced by Werner Sombart and the German sociologists of the early twentieth century, and he accepted the concept of bourgeois society. He regarded it as a society motivated by economic considerations: 'going up and going down means making and losing money' (ibid., p. 73). The prizes offered by it are for ability, energy and exceptional capacity for work, but they are not proportional to the amount of energy displayed, and spectacular prizes are offered to very few. In his work on 'Social classes in an ethnically homogenous environment', first published in 1926, he had made very clear the importance to the individual which he attached to class:

We have said that allegiance to a certain class is a foreordained fact for the individual – that he is *born* into a given class situation. This is an objective situation, quite independent of what the individual does or wants to do, indeed limiting the scope of his behaviour to a characteristic pattern. The individual belongs to a given class neither by choice, nor by any other action, nor by inate politics – in some, his class membership is not individual at all. It stems from his membership in a given clan or image. The family, not the physical person, is the true unit of class and class theory. [Schumpeter 1951, p. 148]

By contrast with American writers who regard class as objectively real, such as the Lynds (1937), Hollingshead (1967) and those of the Functionalist school, in addition to those already mentioned, the European Schumpeter considers mobility within classes and between classes to be extremely rare.

Whatever historical period, whatever set of social circumstances we may select, we shall always be able to make two assertions that are not likely to be successfully contradicted. In the first place, only in very exceptional cases – so exceptional that they are of no particular significance to the explanation of social processes – is it possible for an individual to enter a 'higher' class at a single bound. An example might be a position of sovereignty, achieved by virtue of a *coup d'état*, affording the usurper immediate entry into the top levels of the aristocratic class. A sudden downfall from the class to which one once belonged constitutes, so far as I can see, no more than a mischance devoid of basic interest. In the second place, it is *as a rule* practically impossible for the physical individual to effectuate the transition to a higher class *for himself*; and in the over-whelming majority of cases it is impossible for him during his own lifetime to modify decisively the class situation of the true class individual, the family. The occasional cases, however, in which one or the other of these eventualities may occur can no longer be put aside as 'basic uninteresting exceptions'. [Schumpeter 1951, p. 164]

It is only the individual who is born into the social class for Schumpeter, however, thus enabling families gradually to rise or fall in the social scale, in which process they may be assisted by chance. The rise and fall of whole classes also engaged his attention. In examining this phenomenon he carried his definition of class well back into the period of feudal knights, thus implicitly contradicting the assumption of Marx that classes are themselves the products of capitalist society. The ability of classes, as defined, to remain in control, however, depended not only on their emergence to power but also on their development of the techniques needed to attain that power. All around him Schumpeter saw evidence of the fact that the decaying aristocracies of Europe were in this respect almost a bad joke, though it was always possible for exceptional individuals to rise even out of the aristocratic clubs to positions of political power. In Britain, on the other hand, the rise of the middle class to political power in the nineteenth century had given the country a uniquely talented and able ruling group – a group, moreover, conscious of its destiny to rule and prepared to seize hold of the opportunities thus presented to it. He pointed out:

The warlord was automatically the leader of his people in virtually every respect. The modern industrialist is anything but such a leader. And this explains a great deal about the stability of the former's position and the instability of the latter's. [ibid., p. 220]

Many writers, of course, were not prepared to accept class as real at all, and some who appeared to accept it, such as T. A. Marshall, diffused it in an indefinite spectrum of gradings so that it lost all sense of coherence (Marshall 1938, 1950 and 1964). Periodically reviews of the work of sociologists – a characteristic feature of that somewhat interestingly collective discipline – such as those of Pitrim Sorokin (1928), C. H. Page (1940) and H. W. Pfautz (1952) attempted to forge some sort of consensus among the widely differing works of their colleagues, but they produced mainly bewilderment. Thus Page found that class was: an economic and educational community (Ward 1906), capital indicating talent

(Sumner 1959), an economic, political and ideological concept based on interests (Small 1905), a social fact based on physical, moral and mental inequalities (Giddings 1898), stratification by income qualified by inheritance and competition (Cooley 1956), and a kind of status produced by wealth or power (Ross 1920). At least these six writers were agreed on one thing: that class was in some way a real, objective concept.

The social psychologist Richard Centers, who devoted a series of research projects to examining class structure within American society and who gave rise to the simple, sixfold classification of American society into upper-upper, lower-upper, upper-middle, lower-middle, upper-lower and lower-lower classes, argued that at least they were subjectively real. They were real, that is, in the perception of individuals who designated them. And, in an attempt to bridge the gap between these and all other existing theories, the British writer Walter G. Runciman, in his *Relative Deprivation and Social Justice*, returned to the threefold distinction between class, status and power in society and coupled it with the use of the new psychological concept of 'relative deprivation' to explain why individuals felt themselves moved to act in particular ways, given the facts of their social situation. 'All societies are egalitarian,' he wrote. 'But what is the relation between the inequalities in a society and the feelings of acquiescence or resentment to which they give rise?' (Runciman 1966, p. 3).

The threefold division of class, status and power, therefore, has now spread outside American society into the English-speaking world generally, and it may be expected to continue to dominate the field of social studies in a non-Marxist context. But the problems presented by the task of operationalizing concepts remain as severe as ever; these will be discussed at greater length in Chapter 7.

5   Class in advanced capitalism

Leninism

After the death of Marx in 1883 his colleague and collaborator
Frederick Engels continued his work, becoming until his own death
in 1895 the undisputed authority on the meaning and application of
Marx's work. Many critics have accused Engels of distorting and
even vulgarizing Marx in the process of defending him (McLellan
1977; Kolakowski 1978) by emphasizing the mechanical, determin-
ist elements in Marx's philosophy and creating the pseudo-
historical 'science' of 'historical materialism' in a well-meant
attempt to save Marx from oversimplification at the hands of other
scholars. Such concepts as the alienation of the worker from his
product or the consciousness of social classes – concepts which in
other hands could have been used to stress the role of the individual
and the voluntary nature of social action – were, on the contrary,
subordinated to the action of economic forces. Engels is thus the
true founder of the 'dialectical materialism' which, as 'diamat',
forms today the indigestible staple intellectual food of Soviet
political education.

Lenin, who was only 13 when Marx died, therefore absorbed a
version of Marxism already modified in the direction of determin-
ism and dogma, being particularly strongly influenced by
Plekhanov's *An Outline of the Monistic Conception of History*.
Significantly, it is from Engels rather than from Marx himself that
Lenin chose in later years to quote, as in his encyclopedia article
(1913) on Karl Marx (Lenin 1967, vol. I, p. 4ff.). And it was his
political skill as much as his command of Marxism that led him at a
very early age, while still a law student, into the leading position in
Social Democratic agitation in the capital, St Petersburg. He was
banished to Siberia in 1895, returning only to go into exile in 1900.
It was in exile that he wrote *What is to be Done?* (1902), in which he
made his first extended statement about the application of Marxism

to Russian conditions, and with it effected a decisive alteration of emphasis in the Marxist concept of class.

What is to be Done? is a demand for revolution, not gradualism, which Lenin labelled 'opportunism'.

History has now confronted us with an immediate task which is the most revolutionary of all the immediate tasks confronting the proletariat of any country [he claimed]. The fulfilment of this task, the destruction of the most powerful bulwark not only of European, but (it may now be said) of Asiatic, reaction would make the Russian proletariat the vanguard of the international revolutionary proletariat. [ibid., p. 120]

But crucial to this task was, he believed, the elucidation of the relationship between consciousness and spontaneity in the awakening of the masses. There had been waves of strikes in Russia in the 1890s, certainly, but this did not mean that the Russian proletariat was on the point of attaining spontaneously a Social Democratic class-consciousness.

We have said that there could not have been Social Democratic consciousness among the workers. It would have to be brought to them from without. The history of all countries shows that the working class, exclusively by its own effort, is able to develop only trade union consciousness, i.e., the conviction that it is necessary to combine in unions, fight the employers, and strive to compel the government to pass necessary labour legislation, etc. [ibid., p. 122]

But from where was this class consciousness to come?

The theory of socialism, however, grew out of the philosophical, historical, and economic theories elaborated by educated representatives of the propertied classes, by intellectuals. By their social status the founders of modern scientific socialism, Marx and Engels, themselves belonged to the bourgeois intelligentsia. In the very same way, in Russia, the theoretical doctrine of Social Democracy arose *altogether independently* [my italics] of the spontaneous growth of the working-class movement; it arose as a natural and inevitable outcome of the development of thought among the revolutionary socialist intelligentsia. [ibid.]

In support of the view that it is for the intelligentsia to awaken the proletariat he cites Kautsky: 'The vehicle of science is not the proletariat, but the *bourgeois intelligentsia....* Thus, socialist consciousness is something introduced into the proletarian class struggle from without ... and not something that arose within it spontaneously' (ibid., p. 129). Though socialist theory is correct, he asserts, bourgeois ideology is older, more developed and more effectively disseminated. What is needed, therefore, is developed and systematic agitation to expose the tyranny of the government and to arouse the consciousness of the workers, and for this the Social Democrats must go among the workers, but not among the workers alone – they must agitate among all classes of the population. The key to such successful agitation, he argues, is an All-Russian newspaper, the only way in which a broad movement can be held together without the dangerous exposure of local groups to police scrutiny and the infiltration of the organization by spies.

History records that it was Lenin's faction of the Social Democrats – the so-called 'majority' faction, the Bolsheviks – organized on such principles, who ultimately seized power in October 1917, and hence they must be deemed to have been successful. But the Marxist theory of class had been altered in the process. The proletariat was now deemed incapable of attaining true class-consciousness without the aid of bourgeois intellectuals, such as, in his own terms, Lenin was himself. No less important was the fact that the organization, the party, created to unify the proletariat in the struggle was a clandestine organization, composed of members of various classes and, as events were to prove, capable of developing a consciousness of its own which could turn it into an elite, a chosen group, representing but not of the class that it purported, in Marxian terms, to represent. Interesting too is the reference to social status rather than relation to the means of production which defines Marx and Engels as members of the bourgeoisie. The confusion between class and status which, as we have already seen, Weber was later to elucidate is implicit in Marx (as in, for example, his distinction between the various grades of bourgeoisie) but is explicit here and is the more significant because in the feudal Russia of Lenin's day the bourgeoisie neither reigned nor ruled, unless by 'bourgeoisie' one means the Tsar, the nobility and the Civil Service.

In 1905 Lenin argued forcibly, and his views were consistent with Marx's own works, that the Social Democrats should support the democratic revolution, despite the fact that it would lead to the immediate strengthening of the bourgeoisie, arguing that they would for ever be blamed if instead of channelling and harnessing the revolutionary zeal of the proletariat, they frustrated it. When the rising failed he argued for the revision of military tactics for the 'armed uprising' which would be the revolution to come and in which 'the party of the class-conscious proletariat' would have to 'discharge its duty' (*Lessons of the Moscow Uprising*, ibid., p. 583). But the creation of the Duma and the determined efforts of Stolypin to establish a secure landowning peasantry eroded political support for revolutionary parties in Russia, and in the event it was only the disasters of the Great War that revived them.

The success of the October Revolution in Russia established the Leninist interpretation of Marx as a new norm. Following their seizure of power, the Bolsheviks instituted a new form of government based loosely, as Marx had wished, on the structure of the Paris Commune. Ministers and their Ministries were abolished and replaced by People's Commissars responsible to the Party for the conduct of their office. Each member of the government received the pay of an ordinary worker. By enthusiastic exhortation, every effort was made to ensure that people would work in future for the good of the community as a whole and not for a mere material reward. In the first few heady weeks and even months after the revolution, it was widely believed, not only in Russia but also outside and not only by supporters of the Bolsheviks but also by their bitter opponents, that their success was but the herald of a worldwide revolution. With the ending of the Great War in November 1918, this view was revived spectacularly when the defeated states of Germany and Hungary in particular underwent severe internal turmoils, culminating in the latter case in the short-lived socialist government headed by Bela Kun (Lane 1971, pp. 20–1).

The Bolsheviks, therefore, lost no time in trying to create an organization to make their worldwide role as the vanguard of the proletariat in all countries effective. There was no point, in their opinion, in trying to make use of the existing structures of international working class co-operation, and beyond all certainly not that of the Second International, whose inefficacy had been so adequately demonstrated by the failure of the socialist movements to foresee, still less prevent, the onset of the Great War itself. A new, Third International (Comintern) was therefore formed on 2 March 1919, from which agents went out to convince the proletarians of other countries of their mission to carry out a unified worldwide revolution under Russian leadership. Its foundation came too late to take full advantage of the post-war collapse of order in Europe, and most of its efforts came therefore, with Lenin's backing, to be directed towards Asia, where, however, the series of revolts of the 1920s were ultimately to culminate in their largest single disaster down to that time, the suppression of the Shanghai Insurrection of 1925.

Through this chain of events a two-stage modification of Marxian thought took place. In the course of the October Revolution and its immediate aftermath Lenin came essentially to equate the proletariat with the party he headed, which had assumed the new and distinctive name of the Russian Communist Party (Bolshevik) (RCP (B)). No longer did the Party simply represent the proletariat; increasingly he spoke as if it were the proletariat. Subsequently, with the formation of the International, the Russian proletariat in turn assumed an identification with the worldwide proletariat.

From the moment he heard of the February Revolution in Russia Lenin had insisted on its class character. 'State power in Russia has passed into the hands of a new *class*, namely, the bourgeoisie and landowners who had become landowners,' he wrote in *The Tasks of the Proletariat in our Revolution* (September 1917). 'To this extent the bourgeois-democratic revolution in Russia is completed' (Lenin 1967, vol. II, p. 23). The necessary condition for a socialist revolution in Russia had thus been fulfilled; by virtue of the increase in participation in politics in Russia which it had engendered and the emergence of 'dual power' of state and Soviets, Lenin now claimed in effect that it was a sufficient condition. The war had brought Europe generally to the point of proletarian revolution. The Soviets, already in existence, constituted 'a new form or rather a new *type of state*' (ibid., p. 32), similar to that of the Paris Commune. 'Marxism', he wrote, claiming orthodoxy for his own interpretation alone, 'differs from the petty-bourgeois, opportunist "Social Democratism" of Plekhanov, Kautsky and Co. in that it recognises that what is required during these two periods is *not* a state of the usual parliamentary bourgeois republican type, but a state of the Paris Commune type' (ibid., p. 33). The embryonic form of this state, the state of the period of the dictatorship of the proletariat, already existed, and the change of name of the Bolshevik Party which he proposed would show their determination to assume power within it. Earlier, in *The State and Revolution* (August 1917), he had argued that this rule of the proletariat should be a dictatorship and had outlined the principles of organization that in its early stages the Bolsheviks were in fact to follow:

The theory of the class struggle, applied by Marx to the question of the state and the socialist revolution, leads as a matter of course to the recognition of the *political rule* of the proletariat, of its dictatorship, i.e., of undivided power directly backed by the armed force of the people. The overthrow of the bourgeoisie can be achieved only by the proletariat becoming the *ruling class*, capable of crushing the inevitable and desperate resistance of the bourgeoisie, and of organising *all* the working and exploited people for the new economic system.

The proletariat needs state power, a centralised organisation of force, an organisation of violence, both to crush the resistance of the exploiters and to *lead* the enormous mass of the population – the peasants, the petty bourgeoisie and semi-proletarians – in the work of organising a socialist economy. [ibid., p. 285]

The proletariat, then, is to lead the peasants, the petty bourgeoisie and semi-proletarians, but who is to lead the proletariat? In *Can the Bolsheviks Retain State Power?*, written just before but published just after the October Revolution, Lenin supplies the answer indirectly:

We are told that the 240,000 members of the Bolshevik Party will not be able to govern Russia, govern her in the interests of the poor and against the rich. These 240,000 are already backed by no less than a million votes of the adult population .... We therefore already have a 'state apparatus' of *one million people* devoted to the socialist state for the sake of high ideals and not for the sake of a fat sum received on the 20th of every month. [ibid., p. 402]

On the evening of the October Revolution, Lenin wrote to the members of the Party's Central Committee:

If we seize power today, we seize it not in opposition to the Soviets but on their behalf.

The seizure of power is the business of the uprising; its political purpose will become clear after the seizure. [ibid., p. 450]

The 'we' who were to seize power, however, were not the Party members as a whole, whose Central Committee was not even told of the impending coup until this brief letter of justification reached them. This became abundantly clear in Lenin's proclamation *To the Citizens of Russia!* the following morning.

State power has passed into the hands of the organ of the Petrograd Soviet of Workers' and Soldiers' Deputies – the Revolutionary Military Committee, which heads the Petrograd proletariat and the garrison. [ibid., p. 451]

Speaking to the Seventh Congress of the RCP(B) in March

1918, Lenin reaffirmed that, as he had outlined in *State and Revolution*, he and his colleagues, in seizing power, had sought to create

a new type of state without a bureaucracy, without police, without a regular army, a state in which bourgeois democracy has been replaced by a new democracy.

What they had actually created, however, was rather different, and in apologizing for the fact, Lenin laid the blame on the haste with which the new government had had to move.

In Russia this has scarcely begun and has begun badly. If we are conscious of what is bad in what we have begun we shall overcome it, provided history gives anything like a decent time to work on that Soviet power. I am therefore of the opinion that a definition of the new type of state should occupy an outstanding place in our Programme. [ibid., p. 609]

In Lenin's lifetime it was still permissible to criticize him freely, and among the most trenchant critics of his seizure of power was Rosa Luxemburg, who until her early death argued that any revolution that did not originate in the spontaneous action of the proletariat could not become a proletarian revolution and would not lead to the proletariat's becoming the ruling class. In so doing she was continuing in what had before 1917 been the dominant strain in the interpretation of Marx's own writings, as we have already seen, but October 1917, by establishing Bolshevik rule, had also established what was to become Leninist orthodoxy. The Spartacists in Frankfurt, who had denounced the German Party as '*a party of leaders*, which is out to organize the revolutionary struggle and to direct it from above, accepting compromises', were denounced by Lenin, who called their 'Left' views 'an infantile disorder' (ibid., vol. III, p. 354). In one of his last works, *Our Revolution* (January 1923), he rejected the argument that Russia had not yet been ripe for proletarian revolution on two grounds: that the war had created abnormal conditions, and that Russia, lying as it did on the boundary between West and East, was bound to introduce variations on the European pattern (ibid., p. 766).

A year later Lenin was dead. Once Stalin had succeeded in consolidating his power as the ruler of what was now known as the Soviet Union, orthodoxy was revised to establish the principle of 'socialism in one country'; through the enforced collectivization of agriculture and the expropriation of the *kulaks*, or medium and small landowners, the Soviet Union set a drastic example to other countries of what the working out of the class struggle might actually mean in the phase of the dictatorship of the proletariat. Collectivization was regarded with great hostility and resisted with great bitterness, the peasants destroying their crops and killing their animals rather than hand them over to the state. Ultimately, the need to survive and the establishment of the Machine Tractor Stations to supervise the peasants on behalf of the Party brought an end to the resistance (Mitrany 1951). The Soviet Union was considered ripe for its new constitutional order, established in the Soviet Constitution of 1936, in which the role of the Party as the vanguard of the working class was spelt out, and the duty to monopolize power on behalf of workers' organizations (although these organizations are still spoken of in the plural) was clearly set out. Since 1936 the official orthodoxy in the Soviet Union has been that there the class struggle has come to an end. There are still two classes in the Soviet Union, the workers and the peasants, but they are not antagonistic, being incapable of forming contradictions within the proletarian state and hence of giving rise to a new stage in the development of the dialectic. In addition to them, Soviet sociologists officially recognize the existence of one separate 'stratum', the intelligentsia, which consists of members of neither of the other two classes but whose interests, as determined and expounded by the Communist Party of the Soviet Union, are identical with theirs (Lane 1971, pp. 34–6).

Maoism

By the mid-1920s it was already all too painfully obvious that the Marxian analysis of European society was seriously inadequate as a guide to action in the rest of the world. In still overwhelmingly rural China, the failure of the infant Chinese Communist Party to seize power in the towns, as evidenced by the fiascos in Canton and Shanghai, led the young Mao Tse-tung to make his own assessment of the real structure of Chinese rural society.

This major analysis of a class structure of a non-European society was based on the official Soviet view of Marxism set out in Bukharin's *Historical Materialism* (1921), but all the same it was indeed revolutionary in its indications. Mao first published in 1926 his article 'Analysis of All The Classes in Chinese Society'. It was issued in translation again only in 1953, and then in a heavily revised version. But the original was of very great importance in explaining the difference between the Chinese revolutionary experience and that of the Russians. What is particularly interesting about it is that although Mao in fact diverged substantially from the trend of analysis foreshadowed by Marx, and his originality lay not in his methods but in his subject of analysis, in true polemic fashion he made generalizations, alleged to be of universal applicability, on the basis of the unique experience of his own country:

In any country, wherever it be under the heavens, there are three categories of people: upper, middle and lower. If we analyse things in more detail, there are five categories: big bourgeoisie ... middle bourgeoisie ... petit bourgeoisie, semiproletariat and proletariat. As regards matters in the countryside ... the big landowners are the big bourgeoisie; the small landowners are the middle bourgeoisie; the peasant landowners are the petit bourgeoisie; the peasants who own part of their land and rent the rest are semi-proletariat; and the agricultural laborers are the proletariat. In the cities, the big bankers, the big merchants and the big industrialists are the big bourgeoisie; the money lenders, the merchants of middling importance, the owners of small factories are the middle bourgeoisie; the shopkeepers and master craftsmen are the petit bourgeoisie; the shop assistants, the street vendors and the handicraft workers are the semiproletariat; and the factory workers and the coolies are the proletariat. These five categories of people all have a different economic position and a different class nature. Consequently, they adopt different attitudes towards the revolution, i.e., complete opposition to the revolution, partial opposition to the revolution, neutrality to the revolution, participation in the revolution or being the principal force in the revolution. [Schram 1963, p. 144]

Naively, Mao, who knew no foreign languages and had no knowledge of the outside world, wrote:

The attitude of the various classes in China toward the national revolution is more or less identical to the attitude of the various classes of Western Europe toward the social revolution. [ibid., p. 144]

This article appeared a month after another entitled 'An analysis of the various classes of the Chinese peasantry and their attitudes toward revolution' (January 1926) and reproduces long passages from it. It is somewhat surprising, therefore, to find that this earlier article, so clearly related to the other one, is distinctly different in its approach and includes a very detailed observation of the different groups of peasantry which was clearly based on Mao's own personal experience. It avoids, moreover, the identification of interests of elements of town and countryside, which Mao was later to abandon almost completely – though, following the success of the Chinese

Revolution in 1949, he continued to pay the lip service to the 'leading role' of China's tiny proletariat (only about 2 million out of a population of 395 million at the time) which Marxist theory enjoined.

No matter where you go in the villages, if you are a careful observer, you will see the following eight different types of people: big landlords; small landlords; peasant landholders; semi-landholders; share croppers; poor peasants; farm labourers and rural artisans; *éléments déclassés*. These eight types of people form eight separate classes. Their economic status and standard of living differs, this in turn influences their psychology, so that their attitudes towards revolution also differ. [ibid., p. 172]

The middle landlords have disappeared. The semi-landholders, share croppers and poor peasants, numbering in all between 150 and 170 million, are regarded as part of the semi-proletariat. The share croppers and the poor peasants are distinguished from the farm labourers who form the agricultural proletariat.

These farm laborers possess neither land nor tools, nor do they have any circulating capital. Hence they can subsist only by their labor. With their long hours of work, their low salaries, the treatment they receive, and insecurity of their employment, they are worse off than the other workers. This group of people is the most distressed in the rural areas and should be given the greatest attention by those who are organizing peasant movements. [ibid., p. 175]

The importance of Mao's analysis lies in his recognition that virtually all elements of Chinese society were capable of being turned to revolutionary account, but the degree to which they could be made to do so would vary according to both the approach made to them and their specific sense of their own situation. Nevertheless, apart from the landlords, there was none that he did not consider would be of some value among the 100 million to 120 million peasant landholders who were becoming marginal in economic terms as a result of the civil wars and the exactions of the war lords and had to 'work longer hours, rise earlier, work longer and devote more attention to [their] job, simply in order to maintain [their] standard of living'. The majority, if not keen on the revolution, would not oppose it.

The sophistication of Mao's observations of human kind is best seen in his treatment of the *éléments déclassés*, a French phrase, earlier used by Bukharin, for which no equivalent exists in English.

The *éléments déclassés* consist of peasants who have lost their land, handicraftsmen who have lost all opportunity of employment as a result of oppression and exploitation by the imperialists, militarists, and the landlords, or as a result of flood and drought. They can be divided into soldiers, bandits, robbers, beggars and prostitutes. These five categories of people have different names, and they enjoy a somewhat different status in society. But they are all human beings, and they all have five senses and four limbs, and are therefore one. They each have a different way of making a living: the soldier fights, the bandit robs, the thief steals, the beggar begs and the prostitute seduces. But to the extent that they must all earn their livelihood and cook rice to eat, they are one. They lead the most precarious existence of any human being. [ibid., p. 176]

Mao adds:

The number of *éléments déclassés* in China is fearfully large; it is roughly more than 20 million. These people are capable of fighting very bravely, and, if properly led, can become a revolutionary force. [ibid., p. 176]

When these articles appeared Mao himself was already in the province of Hunan, observing the organization of the peasant movements in the central and southern sections of the province. The organization took about nine months, and from October 1926 onwards the organized peasants set to work to smash 'the local police, the evil gentry and the lawless landlords'. Mao reported enthusiastically in 1927 on the effects and described their methods:

In force and momentum, the attack is just like a tempest or hurricane; those who submit to it survive, those who resist perish. As a result, the privileges the feudal landlords have enjoyed for thousands of years, are shattered to pieces. The dignity and prestige of the landlords are dashed to the ground. With the fall of the authority of the landlords, the peasant association becomes the sole organ of authority, and the slogan 'All Power to the Peasant Association' has become a reality. Even trifling matters, such as quarrels between man and wife, have to be settled by the Peasant Association. Nothing can be settled in the absence of Association representatives. *Whatever nonsense the people from the Association talk in the meeting is considered sacred.* The Associations actually dictate in all matters in the countryside, and it is literally true that 'whatever they say, goes'.

The peasants had been fantastically successful.

What Mr Sun Yat-sen wanted to but failed to accomplish in the forty years he devoted to the national revolution, the peasants accomplished in a few months.

Mao added, regardless of Marxist orthodoxy:

To give credit where due, if we allot ten points to the accomplishments of the democratic revolution, then the achievements of the urban dwellers and the military rate only three points, while the remaining seven points should go to the peasants in their rural revolution.

He was sarcastic at the expense of those who considered that the Peasant Associations were going too far:

A revolution is not the same as inviting people to dinner or writing an essay or painting a picture or embroidering a flower; it cannot be anything so refined, so calm and gentle. . . . a revolution is an uprising, an act of violence whereby one class overthrows the authority of another. [ibid., pp. 181–2]

In his detailed description of the methods by which the peasants broke the authority of the landlord class, Mao first gives an account of how a Marxist social revolution could actually achieve the task of eliminating the bourgeois classes. He distinguished a graduated series of political blows, beginning with the auditing of accounts, the levying of contributions for the relief of the poor and major demonstrations in which the landowner's house was mobbed and his goods and animals taken or destroyed. Then came

Parades through the villages in tall paper hats. Such things have been staged many times in various places. The local bullies and evil gentry are crowned with tall paper hats bearing slogans such as 'local bully so-and-so' or 'so-and-so, one of the evil gentry'. They are walked on a lead and escorted by big crowds both in front of them and behind them. Sometimes gongs are beaten and flags waved to attract attention. This form of punishment, more than any other, makes the local bullies and evil gentry shudder with fear. He who has once been crowned with the tall paper hat loses face for ever and can never hold up his head again. . . . [ibid. p. 185]

For exceptionally evil cases, for whom the tall paper hat was considered inadequate, the punishment was either imprisonment or shooting. Mao adds cynically that formerly it was the landlords who had been able to shoot the peasants as they pleased without reprisal, and it seemed unreasonable to say that the peasants 'should not now rise and shoot one or two of them'.

As a result of these means, substantial areas of China came to be subjected to revolutionary government for varying periods, culminating in the movement of the 'Long March'. It was during this period, when the revolutionaries had already begun to rule, that Mao made one of his most significant contributions to modern

Marxist theory, the doctrine of non-antagonistic contradictions. From a strict reading of Marx it was possible to believe – and to judge from Soviet propaganda, it appeared that the Russian leaders did believe – that there would be no more contradictions within socialist society. Such, however, was visibly not the case, and when Mao published his celebrated pamphlet *On Contradiction* in 1937, his thesis was basically: 'Contradiction is universal, absolute, existing in all processes of the development of things and running through all processes from beginning to end.' Contradiction, therefore, would continue to exist in the socialist state and did exist even under the social conditions of the Soviet Union where, in his words, 'A difference exists between the workers and the peasants; this difference is a contradiction, though, unlike that between labor and capital, it will not become intensified into antagonism or assume the form of class struggle' (ibid., p. 234). There had been, and were still, contradictions within the Chinese Communist Party itself, and therefore the party had to struggle against them. He could even envisage the possibility that if 'those people who have committed mistakes persist in them and increase the gravity of their mistakes, then it is possible that such contradictions will develop into antagonism' (ibid., p. 235). But clearly he expected his warning, his oblique hint about the possible fate that might befall those embracing 'erroneous ideologies', to be heeded and considered that this would be sufficient.

In dialectical terms, the doctrine of non-antagonistic contradictions is a much more satisfactory resolution to the problem of post-socialist society than is the notion of complete and absolute harmony. It is significant too that despite the destruction of millions of Soviet peasants in the forced collectivization Mao should still regard as 'non-antagonistic' the conflict between the peasants and the workers which he discerned – but then he needed the support of Stalin in the war against the Japanese on the one hand and the Kuomintang on the other. Nevertheless, the works of Mao were not widely known outside China until the success of the Chinese revolutionaries in 1949, and until the death of Stalin in 1953 his own pre-eminence as the interpreter of Marxist wisdom and the inheritor of Leninism was not seriously questioned. It was, indeed, during just this period that in the course of reissuing many of his earlier essays and articles Mao took the opportunity to amend them to conform with a more orthodox, Leninist view of Marxism.

Since the Chinese revolutionaries had come to power in alliance with a very substantial proportion of what they regarded as the bourgeoisie, they had naturally to recognize that a multiplicity of classes had survived the process of revolution. In seeking to eliminate class differences, however, their methods were very different from those of the Russians, and this difference reflects a very different concept of class itself. In showing what it was not, Robinson shows how far removed it had become from the economic factor identified by Marx. She writes:

Class is not defined by birth. An old mandarin or an ex-landlord may be an honorary proletarian; some of the most vicious of the organization men were once-poor ppeasants corrupted by power. *Class is defined by a state of mind, and the state of mind is revealed in conduct.* [my italics] When the record of a cadre is being examined, former status as a poor peasant will count in his favour, and a former bourgeois style of life is *prima facie* suspicious, but in neither case decisive. He must prove a *proletarian* attitude today, not proletarian origin in the past, to be liberated from mistakes and rejoined to the movement. [Robinson 1969, p. 15]

This concern at the survival of class contradictions within Chinese society was later the principal force impelling Mao towards the attempt ultimately to resolve contradictions by the launching in the 1960s of the Great Proletarian Cultural Revolution. In China great care was taken to prevent the intelligentsia from remaining a separate stratum by insisting that students, civil servants and soldiers should take part, for a fixed period every year, in the agricultural tasks of the peasantry. Through the close and continuous association between intelligentsia and the peasants in the countryside, Mao hoped to avoid the re-emergence of contradictions within socialist society and their development into antagonisms. Ironically, however, in the end it was to the soldiers that he had to turn to reinstate order in the cities when the workers, during the Great Proletarian Cultural Revolution, rose in revolt against the power given to students and others by the call to unify forces against the persons taking the capitalist road!

The survival of capitalism

In Western Europe Marxists continued the development of Marx's ideas through and past the Leninist stage, though from 1917 until 1956 the 'revisionist' strands in their thought were submerged in the consistent tendency to accept uncritically the claims of the Soviet Union at face value. Following Khrushchev's speech to the

Twentieth Party Congress, however, it was no longer possible to be uncritical. The legitimacy of the Soviet claim to hegemony had been destroyed. Though Mao had not yet proceeded to make his own claim to hegemony, and indeed at this stage was still defending Stalinism against what he saw as 'revisionism' in Soviet government, in Western Europe Marxist thinkers, coming now from a new generation and inheriting the unbroken German tradition of Marx himself, were in a position to make contributions of their own.

Among these thinkers class was still recognized as the prime fact in bourgeois society with which a Marxist had to reckon. But the realization of the early post-Marxists that class was a more complex thing than some of Marx's writings seemed to suggest was now intensified. Fortified by the new knowledge of Marx's earlier writings mentioned above, by 1973 Nicos Poulantzas was stating boldly that Marx's analyses of social classes never referred simply to one economic structure. 'Everything happens as if social classes were the *result of an ensemble of structures and their relations*, firstly at the economic level, secondly at the political level, and thirdly at the ideological level' (Poulantzas 1973, p. 63).

At one level, Poulantzas's work seeks, in what he terms the age of 'monopoly capitalism', to redirect the attention of fellow Marxists towards the task of identifying and defining classes in capitalist society to which insufficient attention had been given by his predecessors, such as the petty bourgeoisie. But unlike almost all Marxists before him, he did not hesitate to state bluntly that he considered Marx himself was wrong on certain issues, and as a result the Marxist concept of class emerges from his writing, which is in any case far from easy to read, virtually unrecognizable.

For Poulantzas, to begin with, classes cannot be defined empirically. 'Social classes are not empirical groups of individuals, social groups, that are "composed" by simple addition; the relations of these agents among themselves are thus not interpersonal relations.' Classes can be defined only by their position. 'Classes exist only in the class struggle.' But that position is separable from their real, objective economic situation, since a class can 'take up a class position that does not correspond to its interests' (Poulantzas 1974, pp. 14, 15, 17). Not satisfied with this, Poulantzas identifies also 'fractions' and 'strata' of classes, such as the state bureaucracy and the intellectuals; 'these fractions, strata and categories may often, in suitable concrete conjunctures, assume the role of relatively autonomous social forces' (ibid., p. 23).

What, then, are classes?

They are groupings of social agents, defined principally but not exclusively by their place in the production process, i.e. in the economic sphere. The economic place of the social agents has a principal role in determining social classes. But from that we cannot conclude that this economic place is sufficient to define social classes. Marxism states that the economic does indeed have the determinant role in a mode of production or a social formation; but the political and the ideological (the superstructure) also have a very important role. [ibid., p. 25]

As Parkin remarks eloquently: 'Given what now passes for Marxist theory, almost any imaginable bourgeois alternative seems preferable' [Parkin 1979, p. x].

How then did Marxist writers come to get themselves into such a fix? To begin with, following Marx himself, Marxist writers after the Russian Revolution had not ceased to note that there were still a multiplicity of classes, as they understood that term, in contemporary capitalist society, and they were at the same time fully aware that Marxian theory called for the intensification of class struggle and the consolidation of the warring classes into two competing entities. Thus in his *Historical Materialism* (1921), Bukharin, as we have already seen, had offered an analysis of capitalist society (which clearly influenced that of Mao) that included distinct intermediate and transitional classes, mixed-class types such as the 'railroad worker who owns a farm of his own' and *déclassé* groups of persons 'outside the outlines of social labour: the Lumpenproletariat, beggars, vagrants, etc.' (Bukharin 1925, p. 92). It was probably from Bukharin too that Mao absorbed the new interest, even among Marxists, in psychology, seen as a bridge between the material conditions of life and the formation of the ideological response to it.

In the 1920s, however, with a Social Democratic Government in power in Germany, it was possible to remain a Marxist while believing that Marx's ultimate scenario of a violent social revolution leading to the dictatorship of the proletariat was outmoded. After all, had not Engels himself suggested at one stage that it might be possible for the proletariat to come to power peacefully in Britain by means of the vote? And in England in 1924 a Labour Government did come to power, though briefly, and marked its accession to power by extending formal diplomatic recognition to the Government of the Soviet Union.

One could, therefore, accept Marx's ideas about the class

struggle without accepting the ultimate resolution which
foreseen for it, and the Social Democratic parties of W
Europe have inherited the tradition of talking in a fashion
much more radical than their actions actually seem to ju ...y.
Politically, this has a practical purpose, in that it enables them to
maintain a claim to be the spokesmen of the Left in their respective
countries – a claim which, though challenged repeatedly between
the wars by the organized left-wing revolutionary parties (and in
particular by the Moscow-aligned Communist Parties), was in fact
effectively challenged in that period only in Spain during the course
of the Spanish Civil War.

Alternatively, while retaining the belief in an ultimate revolution, it was possible to extend the time scale for the fulfilment of
Marx's predictions to a greater or lesser extent.

It was through this chain of reasoning that Kautsky, the German
Social Democratic leader, had moved, identifying the growth and
diversification of different types of capital and a long series of
qualifications to the unity of the classes.

Thus in his book *The Capitalist Class* (1908) Kautsky noted that
although the majority of peasants, small producers and shopkeepers evidently belonged to the proletariat, they still did not understand this because they were prevented from seeing it by the fact of
their ownership, however fragile that might be. In *The Class
Struggle* he noted that a large element of the propertyless, the
servants, were of little value to the revolutionary struggle, insofar as
they associated themselves with the employers and were depen-
dents on their master's good will for their own advancement,
benefiting at the same time from any increase in the capitalist
surplus. He was cynical about the value of the *déclassé* elements,
also regarding beggars as liable to exploit society rather than as the
exploited (Kautsky 1900a; see also Kautsky 1900b, 1903, 1964).

The second possible accommodation of post-Marxist thought to
the changing nature of capitalist society was to reassess the nature of
capital itself. There were two possibilities: either Marx misinter-
preted one or another key aspect of the nature of capitalism itself, or
capitalism itself had changed and hence his ideas needed to be
adapted to the changed circumstances. I propose to deal separately
with the major accretion to Marxist theory represented by Lenin's
development of the concept of imperialism and the subsequent
additions to that theory insofar as they have affected post-Marxist
concepts of class. When interpreting the internal response of

capital, to the threat posed by Marxism, as seen by Marxists, however, it is necessary to bear in mind the increase in resources which they considered that the development of overseas empires and the extension of European influence overseas brought to the strengthening of the bourgeoisie in its resistance to the proletariat's claims.

The weapons of the proletariat in its struggle against the bourgeoisie were, first, trade unions; second, the strong labour organization; and, third, a political party based on the working class. In *Late Capitalism* (Mandel 1975) Ernest Mandel gives a radical Marxist view of how capital responded to the challenge that the development of such organizations posed.

First of all, he says, the principal weapon of the bourgeoisie against the proletariat is the pressure of unemployment. The development of strong trade unions makes the maintenance of a high level of unemployment difficult, and the bourgeoisie is therefore unable to use the threat of unemployment directly. However, through the atomization of the proletariat, its division in the face of the bourgeoisie, it is possible for its will for collective defence to be weakened by allowing the level of unemployment to rise, thus reducing real wages, or by failing to return wages to their previous level after a downturn in the economy, or by forcing the price of labour down through financial manipulations, or by an increase in the intensity of labour, where possible by lengthening the working day, or by a combination of these factors.

At first sight, this does not appear to fit the facts in the Western European democracies, for in the post-war period the threat of unemployment has been very small, the length of the working day has long since been reduced to eight hours or less and a sophisticated trade union leadership knows very well when conditions are improving, or when it is being offered a bargain which seems to be unsatisfactory. However, closer examination suggests that there is at least some truth in the critique: though the formal length of the working day has been very much reduced, in practice the acceptance by trade union organizers of a relatively low basic wage in return for the expectation of high returns on a considerable amount of overtime means that workers have been working very long hours indeed on a voluntary basis in order to bring in substantial returns. This process has been very much facilitated in Britain and the United States by the existence of a large number of trade union organizations, often in competition with each other; the classic instance in which such competition does not occur, West German industry, owes much to the occupation by the Allies after the Second World War and the consequent imposition of a relatively logical and unified system of trade unions.

Mandel, moreover, sees the existence of social welfare schemes as merely a sharing of the surplus extracted from the workers. The same applies, of course, to increases in wages in times of relative prosperity. But there is a limit to the degree to which the bourgeoisie can respond, he argues. Although more surplus value can be extracted from the proletariat through productivity's increasing more than wages, or an increased intensity of labour, or the lengthening of the working day, or by any two of these, he believes that all three measures cannot in practice be applied together, since the resultant pressure would weaken the worker psychologically and physically to the point at which he is no longer economically sufficiently productive. Mandel subsequently notes that even among the bourgeoisie there are now substantial groups, such as health service doctors and social workers, who identify more with the proletariat whom they serve than with the bourgeoisie of which they are members. And he foresees that the capacity of the bourgeoisie to respond to the challenge posed by the proletariat must ultimately come to an end with the total mechanization of labour. At this point the transfer of labour into the sectors immediately preceding mechanization, such as supervision and semi-technical occupations, will become so great that the majority of the population will identify with the proletariat rather than with the bourgeoisie; consequently, the bourgeoisie will be unable to maintain its control over the system in its present form.

Moreover, Mandel agrees with Kautsky that 'the capitalist class rules but does not govern.' The representatives of capital within the state mechanism, therefore, are free to pursue their own personal interests as well as collective ones. With communist and social democratic representatives in Parliament, the capitalists are no longer free to use the state mechanism absolutely as they wish, and a combination of the two factors limits their capacity to respond to challenge even before it reaches the point at which automation becomes universal.

The contrary view may be represented by the work of Ferdynand Zweig, not a Marxist writer. In his *The Worker in an Affluent Society* (1961), Zweig argues from a conflict basis. 'No amount of sermons on the theme of social solidarity will do away with the basic conflict between capital and labour,' he asserts. 'But the conflict is also not the whole truth. There is an area of conflict and an area of solidarity, and the point is only that the problems of conflict should be treated within the sphere of solidarity' (Zweig 1961, p. 204).

Zweig argues that in the fully developed welfare state a process takes place which has been described as the 'embourgeoisement' of the proletarian. He no longer retains his previous fear of un-employment; he has entered the period of 'the revolution of rising expectations' and becomes much more acquisitive. 'If he has no ambition for himself, he has plenty for his children,' Zweig argues. So the members of the working class become more family-centred, more concerned to acquire material welfare and correspondingly much less interested in the class struggle. With the confidence born of the highest level of prosperity known in Western Europe down to that time, Zweig wrote:

It took the employer a long time to imbue the worker with his own values and to turn him into a full and willing partner in the acquisitive society, but he has finally succeeded, and the results seem to reinforce the working and the fabric of the society to make it more secure from inside. The acquisitive society has succeeded in expanding its frontiers and converting its natural antagonists to its own creed. It seems as if the acquisitive society has only now come into maturity, reaching a uniformity and regularity which could hardly have been foreseen a generation ago. [ibid., p. 212]

The consequence of the embourgeoisement of the working class would be either that they would lose consciousness of their role in the future socialist revolution, if that degree of consciousness had already developed, or that they would fail to develop it beyond the stage of trade union consciousness. The awareness of these possibilities, coupled with the dramas associated with the past role of social democracy in Germany, led other writers, in particular Gyorgy Lukács, to lay an increasing amount of stress on the role of the revolutionary intellectuals in generating revolutionary con-sciousness among the proletariat. (Lukács 1971). In so doing they built upon the thesis advanced by Marx in *The Poverty of Philosophy* (1847), in which he first outlined his theory of consciousness. The proletariat, considered as a group of individuals sharing a common situation in relation to the processes of produc-tion, was a 'class in itself'; for the realization of its historic role it had first to become, through the development of self-consciousness, a 'class for itself'.

What few Marxists were willing to accept until recently was the possibility that they were looking in entirely the wrong direction. The Italian anti-Marxist writer Mosca, writing at the end of the nineteenth century, had suggested that there might exist a 'political class', quite separate from the three classes defined by tradition – the upper, middle and lower classes, which monopolized political power and acted, if necessary, without reference to the wishes of the capitalists (Mosca 1939). In so doing, Mosca became one of the founders of the theory of elites, which for Marxism became somewhat more than a theoretical possibility when Kautsky made his remark about the distinction between governing and ruling. It was at any rate clear that the entire capitalist class could not rule. The question was: how far were the governments of capitalist countries actually reflections of their ruling class, if ruling class there was?

It was certainly tactically convenient for Marxists to assume that there was indeed some divergence between the two, for it permitted the Soviet press, for example, to portray the governments of capitalist countries as being in fear of the massive power of their own populations and to act on the assumption that sufficient pressure upon the systems of capitalist countries, administered in the right way, might actually bring about a change in policy favourable to the proletariat, and hence, by definition, unfavourable to the capitalist classes. Indeed, it was not long before the Soviet Union came to watch the shifts and turns in Western political life most intensely, evaluating, sometimes publicly, sometimes privately, whether specific changes in policy were desirable or undesirable. Though these might be seen in the long run as leading to the takeover of the government by the proletariat, this event was not necessarily to be expected overnight, and to this extent, it is interesting to note, they were following a tradition established by Marx himself in his acute study of the day-to-day events in other countries that took his particular interest. Though Marx attached overall importance to the shifts and changes in the world trade cycle and to the effect of economic development on the countries that interested him, he spent a great deal of his time discussing the actual turns and political changes among the members of the ruling bodies of those countries, the political parties and other people of power or influence.

To sum up, therefore, there were four principal ways in which most Marxist writers could accommodate Marx's predictions to the fact of the survival of capitalism.

The first was to embrace the principles of social democracy, and, like the German Social Democrats, to make their way to power by political organization and the use of the electoral system while remaining officially Marxist. The more viable this expedient was seen to be, the more people were seen to accept it; consequently, in those countries where it has been easiest to adopt this approach, the organized revolutionary Marxist parties have remained relatively weak, while in the post-Second World War period a surprising number of officially pro-Moscow Communist Parties have shown a startling gradualism in their approach to the problem of making revolution.

The second was to attribute every delay in the onset of the revolution to the wiles and ingenuity of the capitalists; to identify new and subtle ruses by means of which capital was resisting the inevitability of history; and to elaborate the Marxist concept of class to accommodate such factors as the embourgeoisement of the working classes and the emergence of rival groups within the proletariat as well as within the bourgeoisie, where Marx himself had predicted such contradictions would not only remain but also increase.

The third was to lay more stress on that congenial aspect of Marxist theory which came most naturally to writers, namely, the role of the revolutionary intellectuals. By emphasizing the extent to which the proletariat had to be guided in their revolution by those skilful in the analysis of social problems, these writers not only explained the delay in the onset of the revolution but also devised for themselves a colossal agenda which it would take them many years to complete.

Last, a few avowed Marxists were prepared to challenge the traditional views attributed to Marx concerning the identification of the capitalist class with the rulers of capitalist countries, and this separation of power from its economic basis proved tactically useful to communist governments in dealing with non-communist states. All these attitudes, however, had after 1916 to coexist with Lenin's assertion that he had discovered a new principle of capitalist development which had brought Marx up to date: Leninism was, he claimed, the Marxism of the age of imperialism.

From imperialism to international stratification

Lenin's theory of imperialism is now familiar to many, as is the fact

that in constructing it he drew upon the works of the Englishman
J. A. Hobson, and the German economist Rudolph Hilferding,
among others. Nevertheless, the synthesis which he expounded in
his 1916 pamphlet *Imperialism, the Highest Stage of Capitalism* is
distinctive in its overt Marxist base and is written with the
pamphleteering vigour which made him such a formidable political
leader. Its basic thesis was a simple one: that capitalism had
survived, because it had undergone transformation. It had spread
outwards from Europe to obtain control over collective territories,
and by making use of the resources drawn from those territories it
had been able to transcend the limitations of its own internal
economic structure.

Capitalism has grown into a world system of colonial oppression and of the
financial strangulation of the overwhelming majority of the population of
the world by a handful of 'advanced' countries. And this 'booty' is shared
between two or three powerful world plunderers armed to the teeth....
[Lenin 1967, vol. I, p. 681]

It was this system that had given rise to the Great War, in the middle
of which Lenin was writing, and here we must remember that Lenin,
in common with some of his followers, had been wholly taken aback
by the failure of the international proletariat to follow Marx's
predictions and to combine together to resist the onset of the war.
Their particular target of hatred was the leader of the German
Social Democratic Party, Kautsky, who had led his faction into the
lobbies in the Reichstag in support of the declaration of war against
France. Lenin devoted a prominent place in this pamphlet, therefore, to denouncing Kautsky and all those who thought like him.

  The development of the theory of imperialism, based as it was on
the visible signs of the division of the world between the territories
of the great powers, the expansion of great businesses, cartels and
trusts and the knitting together of the world system of trade and
exchange by the growth of the railways, had resulted in the effective
partition of the world between the 'imperialist' powers, of whom
Russia, the territory of special interest to Lenin, was most backward
economically and enmeshed in a semi-dependent relationship with
the other powers. Lenin wrote:

If it were necessary to give the briefest possible definition of imperialism,
we should have to say that imperialism is the monopoly stage of capitalism.
Such a definition would include what is most important, for, on the one
hand, finance capital is the bank capital of a few very big monopolist

banks, merged with the capital of the monopolist associations of industrialists; and, on the other hand, the division of the world is the transition from a
colonial policy which has extended without hindrance to territories
unseized by any capitalist power, to a colonial policy of monopolist
possession of the territory of the world, which has been completely divided
up. [Lenin 1967, vol. I, p. 745]

However, Lenin did not wish to confine his attention to a brief
definition, but to explain what, in his opinion, were the necessary
consequences of it. And from the point of view of Lenin's analysis of
the capitalist state, the feature he most wished to stress was the
'immense accumulation of money capital in a few countries', and
'the extraordinary growth of a class, or rather of the stratum of
rentiers, i.e., people who live by "clipping coupons", who take no
part in any enterprise whatever, whose profession is idleness' (ibid.,
p. 754). For Lenin, therefore, not only did the bourgeoisie of
developed countries undergo a transition of crucial significance to
the prospects of its further survival in a division into new and
distinct strata, but at the same time the imperialist states assumed a
dominant relationship towards the internal populations of other
countries. But the division within the bourgeoisie, more significantly, was also paralleled by a division of the proletariat into an
upper and a lower stratum. In the upper stratum were those workers
which the system of imperialism enabled the state to reward, while
the lower-paid jobs were reserved for distinct groups of workers,
often (and in particular in the United States) immigrants from other
countries. And he quoted approvingly Engels's comment to Marx:
'The English proletariat is actually becoming more and more
bourgeois, so that this most bourgeois of all nations is apparently
aiming ultimately at the possession of a bourgeois aristocracy and a
bourgeois proletariat *alongside* the bourgeoisie' (ibid., p. 760). In
effect, he said, a section of the proletariat had allowed itself to be led
by men bought by, or at least paid by, the bourgeoisie, hence
postponing the (to him) inevitable day of the social revolution.

In his critique Lenin was primarily concerned with the immediate
situation of the warring states in Europe and of the financial class
which dominated imperialist society. However, later writers were to
cast their eye upon the consequences of the relationship between
ascendant and dependent territories for the class structure not
simply of the dominant state but also of the subordinate one. The
works of André Gunder Frank and other dependency theorists
have stressed the emergence in formerly colonized states of a

national bourgeoisie and hence of an essential link in the process of maintaining the structure of dependency without the overt means of oppression (such as the use of armed force) which earlier writers might have predicted (Frank 1971, 1977). This theme has been taken up by a long list of writers in relation to the conditions of individual countries, particularly in Africa and Latin America.

Last, some theorists of international relations, and notably Johan Galtung (1974; cf. Horowitz 1972), have proceeded from this step to identify a sort of international class complex between states, acting as if they were individuals in a class structure. Thus there are, they suggest, Third World 'proletarian' states which stand in the same relation to the First World 'bourgeois' states as, in Marxist theory, do the members of the proletariat to the bourgeoisie. This development is particularly confusing insofar as the question of whether a state is 'proletarian' or not bears no relation to its internal class structure, though writers of this school follow the dependency theorists in ascribing to class relations in dependent territories the particular characteristics which tend to maintain, and indeed to extend, the pattern of dependency.

Advanced capitalism?

It is possible to argue that the term 'capitalism' may be applied correctly only to the economic conditions of the time of Marx, and that in this sense capitalism ended a long time ago. Certainly, it is generally agreed, even by Marxists, that modern capitalism is very different in kind from the capitalism of Marx's day. But the nature and degree of the differences between the two forms of capitalism, as well as their significance, is another matter. Capitalism has not succumbed to recurrent economic crises, nor to two world wars, nor to decolonization, which ought, according to Lenin's interpretation of imperialism, to have resulted in the downfall of the Western economic system.

In the 1920s the members of the Frankfurt school took up the theme of alienation and decadence within capitalist society, with particular reference to individual psychology and its manifestations in literature (Horkheimer 1978). In the post-1945 period, with the emergence of the United States as the world's leading capitalist state (and, indeed, probably the only one in which the term 'capitalism' is actually used confidently and with pride), that country has become the prime target for such criticism. From his vantage point in southern California, the refugee philosopher Herbert Marcuse coined the phrase 'repressive tolerance' to 'explain' the fact that despite the immense internal stresses to which it was subjected, the United States remained a liberal and tolerant society – tolerant even of his angry denunciations of what he saw as its materialistic lifestyle and philistine values (Marcuse 1972).

The United States has not moved as far as some other countries in extending political control over its economic system, but it has done so to an extent undreamed of before 1932. It is this fact that Jürgen Habermas has used to explain capitalism's success in surmounting crisis in his development of Marxism into what has generally become known as Critical Theory, a theory of social science which remains Marxist while embracing the belief in methodological rigour which in recent years has been more closely associated with the work of American empirical writers.

The term 'Critical Theory' refers to Habermas's belief in knowledge as critical self-awareness. Its unifying factor is seen to be communication, the ideal form of which will be full and undistorted, while in practice social forces bring about the systematic distortion of meaning in all forms of communication. The thinking individual has, therefore, through self-awareness, to liberate his understanding from these systematic effects, the most important of which is domination, before he can enter into collective understanding of collective phenomena such as class-consciousness and class interest (McCarthy 1978, p. 131).

For Habermas, the historical origins of class lie in the emergence of the state, when the ruler assures himself of the loyalty of his followers by allowing them privileged access to the means of production. Class, therefore, is not a phenomenon of capitalism alone, but it is a system of relations of domination that enables the 'material process of production' to be 'uncoupled' from the kinship system. The result is that economic organization can be extended to permit large-scale agriculture and the expansion of crafts to meet the needs of a larger society (ibid., p. 258).

This process, however, is not an automatic one. Habermas specifically rejects as inadequate explanations of the emergence of the state (and consequently of social classes) all five of the theories which he sees as previously having been advanced: the superimposition of a ruling class by conquest, the division of labour, the inequality of distribution, the need for irrigation, and the effects of a critical level of population density. These are for him merely system problems that overload the capacity of the kinship system to respond; they do not adequately explain why society responds in the way that it does, or why it responds in some cases and not in others. To these questions only 'an evolutionary learning process' provides an adequate answer.

Only with the help of learning mechanisms can we explain why a few societies could find solutions to the steering problems that triggered their evolution, and why they could find precisely the solution of state organization. [Habermas 1979, p. 160]

There are, however, permanent consequences for the state which, manifest as they have been since the earliest times, are no less significant in the era of advanced capitalism.

If we equate legitimate power with political domination, we have to maintain, among other things, that no political system can succeed in permanently securing mass loyalty – that is, its members' willingness to follow – without recourse to legitimations. [ibid., p. 180]

Since the need for legitimation stems from the relations of domination enforced by the state, they are inseparable from the nature of class society, though in earlier periods the class character of the conflicts generated may, for Habermas, have been disguised as conflicts between estates, groups or the like. Indeed, it is precisely because attention has been focused in the past on such crises that the class character of the state has been so easily overlooked.

The extent of what has to be legitimated can be surmised only if one contemplates the vestiges of the centuries-long repressions, the great wars, the small insurrections and defeats, that lined the path to the modern state. . . . These local insurrections against the offshoots of the modern state trickled away in the nineteenth century. They were replaced by social confrontations of artisans, industrial workers, the rural proletariat. This dynamic produced new legitimation problems. The bourgeois state could not rely on the integrative power of national consciousness alone; it had to try to head off the conflicts inherent in the economic system and channel them into the political system as an institutionalised struggle over distribution. Where this succeeded, the modern state took on one of the forms of social welfare state – mass democracy. [ibid., p. 193]

The modern social welfare state faces a much more complex steering problem than did its predecessors, but Habermas sees no reason why, with its correspondingly greater resources, it should not continue to discharge its task for a long time to come. This task is to deal with any and all of the four possible sorts of crisis that Habermas sees as possibly afflicting the modern state. Two sorts, which he terms 'system crises', affect the subsystems within the state; the economic system faces periodic economic crises, the political system crises of rationality. But since both depend for their resolution on the maintenance of legitimate power within the state, failure to deal with them can lead to a questioning of the identity of the political system itself, which he terms a 'legitimation crisis'. A parallel form of crisis in the socio-cultural system, the 'motivational crisis', he asserts, can also arise when certain aspects of the beliefs of citizens become dysfunctional – that is to say, when they threaten the maintenance of the economic order – but it is the possibility of a legitimation crisis that threatens the maintenance of the system as such.

At the moment I can see no possibility of cogently deciding the question about the chances for a self-transformation of advanced capitalism. But I do not exclude the possibility that economic crisis can be permanently averted, although only in such a way that contradictory steering imperatives that assert themselves in the pressure for capital realisation would produce a series of other crisis tendencies. [Habermas 1976, p. 40]

He adds:

Because in advanced capitalism politics takes place on the basis of a processed and repressed system crisis, there are constant disputes (among shifting coalitions and with fragmented class consciousness) that can alter the terms of class compromise. Thus whether, and to what extent, the class structure is softened and the contradiction grounded in the capitalist principle of organisation itself is affected depends on the actual constellations of power. [ibid.]

What Habermas is saying, in fact, is that although advanced capitalist systems remain class systems, their failure to act out the scenario predicted for them by Marx is due to the fact that the political sphere now guides, on the whole successfully, the economic, a conclusion previously reached independently, it might legitimately be pointed out, by the Keynesian school of economists in the West. For Habermas, however, this is not purely because economic crisis management has relieved strains on the political system, but because successful management attenuates the sense of class conflict at the same time as it acts to re-legitimize the political order. Class conflict can no longer simply be 'unmasked', since it no longer exists in the straightforward sense known to the capitalist society of the time of Marx. And since the state has to offer a satisfactory rationalization of its actions, it can no longer be identified purely with the interests of the bourgeoisie; in fact, the opposition between proletariat and bourgeoisie is not, it seems, intensifying but rather becoming vaguer and more diffuse.

Because the economic system has forfeited its functional autonomy vis-à-vis the state, crisis manifestations in advanced capitalism have also lost their nature-like character. In the sense in which I introduced the term, a system crisis is not to be expected in advanced capitalism. Of course, crisis tendencies that appear in its place can be traced back to structures that have resulted from the suppression – successful at first – of the system crisis. By means of this development we can explain the moderation of cyclical economic crises to a permanent crisis that appears, on the one hand, as a matter already processed administratively and, on the other hand, as a movement *not yet* adequately controlled administratively. This does not exclude constellations in which crisis management fails, with far-reaching consequences. But the appearance of such constellations can no longer be systematically predicted. [Habermas 1976, pp. 92–3]

What is of particular significance, however, is that at the same time Habermas rejects the belief that the state can be empirically proved to serve the interests of a specified limited class group, a Marxist fallacy which he regards as equivalent to non-Marxist elite theories. The state thus appears, as it has done increasingly in various Marxist authors, as something separate from class structures and class dominance (a theme to which we shall return below).

If few Marxists are prepared to go as far as to follow Lukács in holding that one can still be a Marxist while having disproved every one of Marx's basic premises (Mészáros 1971, pp. 54–5), collectively an accommodation has been reached with the idea that 'late' capitalism may, as 'advanced' capitalism, be a more durable construct than had previously been imagined.

6 Class in socialist states

The effect of the Bolshevik Revolution

Marx predicted that the socialist society would be a classless society. To this extent, his projected society is one of a recognizable genre of idealized Utopias. Other writers who have postulated such Utopias, from Plato to H. G. Wells and beyond, have differed from Marx in regarding stratification as an essential component of political structure. Plato's Guardians, or H. G. Wells's Samurai, were both attempts to recognize the distinctive role played by government in social structure and to relate it to a structure of society that would bring to the top those men particularly fitted to undertake the task. Marx was not, of course, the first person to reject such a notion or to call for the reversal of the division of labour (Durkheim 1964). There are strongly egalitarian trends in both philosophical writing and political action from the time of the ancients onwards, and, as we have already seen, the Christian (and indeed also the Islamic) message, emphasized the equality of believers before God.

The Paris Commune of 1871 – not a communist state, but one which Marx took as a herald of the communist state to come – was characterized by a high degree of egalitarianism. Lenin, in the early days of the Russian Revolution, imitated it by establishing that the Commissars of the new regime should be paid only as much as an ordinary worker. Civil servants in the period of 'war communism' received only ordinary rations, and differentials in pay were reduced to about 4:3, without, however, being wholly eliminated (Lane 1971, pp. 20–1, 30–2). It was characteristic of Stalinism that not only was any tendency towards egalitarianism in reward reversed but also the differences between rewards were accentuated to a far greater degree than they were even in Western capitalist societies of the period (Inkeles 1950). It was at the height of the Stakhanovite enthusiasm of the 1930s that the Soviet

Constitution of 1936, as we have seen, formally established the view that there remained only two, non-antagonistic classes in the Soviet Union (workers and peasants), and one stratum, the intelligentsia.

The lack of antagonism between workers and peasants which Stalin professed to find in 1936 had not been achieved without deliberate political action. The wholesale destruction of the distinctive class position of the peasantry and the 'proletarianization' of workers on state farms was, indeed, hailed by apologists of Stalin's regime as one of the most notable achievements of the Soviet Government. This policy was extended to the East European communist states in the immediate post-1945 period. It was Stalin too who introduced the concept of the 'class enemy': the individual who, by virtue of his membership, former membership or continued belief in the values of a class antagonistic to the proletariat (namely, the bourgeoisie), could be suppressed or even liquidated. Fearful of the bourgeois world, especially as a result of the experiences of the Second World War between 1941 and 1945, Stalin organized the wholesale liquidation of individuals by classes in the Ukraine and Poland and, in a rather less exhaustive fashion, that of selected individuals in the other states. That this concept of the class enemy is by no means dead has recently found its most chilling proof in Indo-China in the killing of all individuals suspected of bourgeois sympathies by the Pol Pot regime in Cambodia, the forced evacuation of Phnom Penh and the attempt to eliminate all remnants of class structure in that country by driving its citizens back into a state of primitive peasant cultivation reinforced by a repressive apparatus.

For a decade in Eastern Europe there was no effective opposition to the dominant Stalinist view. As one commentator has rightly pointed out, this was due not to the force of its intellectual argument but to other factors. Those who lived in the Soviet Union at this time, however, observed, as did Inkeles, that the effect of a series of new institutions for differential economic reward, including the labour-day and piecework system of payment on collective farms and the introduction of gradings, differentiation and separate pay scales for managers and technicians, had created as early as 1940 'an elaborately and precisely stratified status system within which at least ten major social-class groups could be distinguished for purposes of sociological analysis' (Inkeles 1950; 1968, p. 151).

The stratum of the intelligentsia could be divided into no less than four subunits: the ruling elite 'a small group consisting of high Party, government, economic, and military officials, prominent scientists, and selected artists and writers'; the superior intelligentsia; the general intelligentsia, incorporating most of the professional groups; and the white-collar group, extending through accountants and book-keepers down to ordinary clerks and office workers. The working class was equally differentiated between, at the one end, the highly paid, skilled and productive workers and, at the other end, those who, through their lack of skill or initiative, remained close to the minimum wage level. The peasantry, though less differentiated, incorporated a distinct group of well-to-do peasants, those particularly advantaged by the position or nature of their collective farms and even those who were more prosperous on the less prosperous farms. In addition to all these there was a residual group in the forced labour groups capable of being regarded as a class on its own, though drawn from all the other classes. These ten groups collectively made up Soviet society.

Membership in any one of these major social-class groups was predominantly determined on the basis of a complex of conditions, of which occupation, income, and the possession of power and authority were the main elements. Thus, the system was essentially based on differences in the functions performed by individuals in the productive process, the administrative apparatus, and the power structure, rather than on either hereditary and semi-hereditary factors, which were primary in defining social position in Tsarist Russia, or on ideological considerations, which predominantly determined the stratification patterns during the earlier years of the Soviet regime.

Yet while these divisions were essentially economic and functional, the valuation of the different occupations was markedly affected by cultural factors, such as the traditional tendency to rate brain work above physical labour. [Inkeles 1968, p. 153]

Inkeles noted, on the other hand, that there was a significant overlap between the major groups, so that an appreciable number of workers and peasants had average incomes higher than those of many white-collar workers, but he also observed that the major groupings based on income and power had distinctive styles of life characteristic of their position, and to this extent, if no further, the social class system contradicted the basic assumptions of the simple structure praised by Stalin. Those observers who approved of the system could take comfort from the fact that it was a very open system, in which there was a considerable degree of mobility, and people of relatively humble pre-revolutionary origins had been able to attain very high positions.

This mobility was created predominantly by the tremendous expansion of the national economy, but was given additional impetus by the high rate of national attrition accompanying the revolutionary process, by the de-classing – and in part physical elimination – of major portions of the former upper and middle classes, and by a political system which periodically removed large numbers of people from responsible positions by means of *chistka* or purge. [ibid., p. 156]

On the other hand, once a person achieved one of these higher positions his status in it was attested in two respects, which appeared to make further social mobility very much more difficult. First, the principle had been formally adopted by the Soviet Government that 'recognition and reward are to be determined not only by the *extent* of a man's contribution beyond the call of duty, but also by the *status* he held when he made this contribution' (ibid., p. 158). In 1935 formal military ranks were restored to the Soviet armed forces, and subsequently a series of laws required civil servants and other workers in state enterprises to wear formal uniforms, thus providing them with the most obvious and visible sign of their relative status and position. High status was at the same time rewarded in the most evident way by levying very low rates of taxation from those with high earnings, and the inheritance taxes originally introduced in 1926 were abolished.

While these structural trends seemed to run contrary to the dominant value of egalitarianism professed by communist ideology, they did not necessarily conflict with the belief that class, in the Marxian sense, had ceased to be an internal problem for Soviet society. Even Trotsky in the late 1930s went no further than to claim that Soviet society had, in fact, been captured by a new elite. It was not until the 1950s, and even then in Yugoslavia, which had already escaped from the Soviet orbit, that Milovan Djilas was to suggest that the new 'elite' was something more than that.

In his book *The New Class*, in which the Marxist standpoint was taken as given, Djilas renewed the attack on the practice of the socialist state. His target were the *apparatchiki*, the members of the Party and state bureaucracy. These men and women had, he claimed, created for themselves a privileged position within the structure of the formally socialist state. They enjoyed better economic returns, had disproportionate access to political power and were to some degree able to perpetuate their position in their families and their descendants through their control of the state and Party machinery.

The greatest illusion was that industrialisation and collectivisation in the USSR, and the destruction of capitalist ownership, would result in a classless society. In 1936, when the new Constitution was promulgated, Stalin announced that the 'exploiting class' had ceased to exist. The capitalists and other classes of ancient origin had in fact been destroyed, but a new class, previously unknown to history, had been formed.

It is understandable that this class, like those before it, should believe that the establishment of its power would result in happiness for all men. The only difference between this and other classes was that it treated the delay in the realisation of its illusions more crudely. It thus affirmed that its power was more complete than the power of any other class before in history, and its class illusions and prejudices were proportionately greater.
[Djilas 1957, p. 38]

The new class which Djilas described was 'the bureaucracy, or more accurately the political bureaucracy, of the new communist state'. It differed from earlier classes in coming to power not to complete a new economic order but to establish one and, in so doing, to establish its power over society. It developed out of the stratum of professional revolutionaries who had founded the Bolshevik Party and who, as professional revolutionaries, had made the revolution of 1917. It was the Bolshevik Party that was the core of the new class, which might be said 'to be made up of those who have special privileges and economic preference because of the administrative monopoly they hold'.

So far it might appear that he was merely describing an elite. But Djilas was well aware of the theoretical implications of claiming that it was also a class, and his argument is grounded in Marx's own views about the stages of historical development and the relations of classes to the forms of production.

It seems unusual that a political party could be the beginning of a new class. Parties are generally the product of classes and strata which have become intellectually and economically strong. However, if one grasps the actual conditions in pre-revolutionary Russia and in other countries in which communism prevailed over national forces, it will be clear that a party of this type is the product of specific opportunities and that there is nothing unusual or accidental in this being so.

Although the roots of Bolshevism reach far back into Russian history, the party is partly the product of the unique pattern of international relationships in which Russia found itself at the end of the nineteenth and the beginning of the twentieth century. Russia was no longer able to live in the modern world as an absolute monarchy, and Russia's capitalism was too weak and too dependent on the interests of foreign powers to make it possible to have an industrial revolution. This revolution could only be implemented by a new class, or by a change in the social order. As yet, there was no such class. [ibid., pp. 40–1]

Djilas saw the new class as being formed from the proletariat as the result of the monopoly which it established in the name of the working class over the whole of society. Like all other classes so designated in Marxist theory, it took its position from its distinctive relation to the factors of production.

As in other owning classes, the proof that it is a special class lies in its ownership and its special relations to other classes. In the same way, the class to which a member belongs is indicated by the material and other privileges which ownership brings to them.

As defined by Roman law, property constitutes the use, enjoyment, and disposition of material goods. The Communist political bureaucracy uses, enjoys, and disposes of nationalised property. [ibid., p. 44]

It was this special form of ownership, namely, collective owner-ship, which the class 'administers and distributes' in the name of society, that gives the new class its power and its privileges. The abolition of the special privileges of a new administration, documentation for which Djilas was in those days unable to find, was, in his opinion, the first and necessary step towards the democratization of communism, which otherwise would continue to be an essentially authoritarian doctrine. Nor, he suggested, was it in any way unusual to see in collective ownership the foundations of effective class domination. He suggested that this had been the case in many earlier historical communities, even, for example, that of Ancient Egypt, where the state bureaucracy administered collective property on their behalf.

Subsequently, other writers were to take up this theme and to expand it. But before we leave Djilas it would be worth noting the significance of his comments on class discrimination, as these too started a line of development which was potentially of great significance for the analysis of communist societies.

It is generally thought that Communist dictatorship practises brutal class discrimination. This is not completely accurate. Historically, class dis-crimination declines as the revolution slackens off, but ideological discrimination increases. The illusion that the proletariat is in power is inaccurate; so, too, is the proposition that Communists persecute someone because he is a bourgeois. Their measures do aim most harshly at the members of the ruling classes, especially the bourgeoisie. But those bourgeois who capitulate, or re-orient themselves, are able to assure for themselves lucrative posts and favor. What is more, the secret police often find able agents in their ranks, while the new power-wielders find them able servants. Only those who do not ideologically approve the Communist measures and views are punished without consideration as to their class or their attitude towards nationalisation of capitalist property.

Djilas adds:

It would be wrong to think that other forms of discrimination – race, caste, national – are worse than ideological discrimination. They may seem more brutal to all outward appearances, but they are not as refined or complete. [ibid., pp. 144–5]

Though for Djilas this tyranny over the mind is the most important feature, as far as the implications of his work for the Marxist concept of class is concerned, the dominant aspect is the nature of property that he distinguishes. In identifying the control and manipulation of state property as the distinctive feature of his 'new class', it has to be emphasized, he is working within the original Marxist postulates to create a very different concept of society and doing so, moreover, a century after Marx and in a stage of society about which Marx had relatively little to say.

Djilas himself was imprisoned by Tito, and his contentions found more favour initially among Western critics of communism than they did among the East Europeans themselves. Strict Party control of the means of the expression and dissemination of opinion severely constrained the ability of East European Marxists to form new, alternative views of Marxism. Besides, in the non-Soviet socialist countries a more urgent debate was being conducted about the desirable degree of independence of their respective states from the centralized control of the Soviet Union, as first Hungary, then Czechoslovakia and subsequently Romania attempted to sever some of its links with the Soviet Union. Only one of them actually succeeded in doing so, and that one, the state of Albania under the government of Enver Hoxha, remained a Marxist state but following the Chinese interpretation of Marxism rather than the strictly Leninist one (De George 1968).

Even without the Soviet dislike of independent thought in

Eastern Europe, it was scarcely likely that thinkers in this region, fronting as they did upon the still capitalist West, should be eager to rock the boat by discovering faults in their own society. Ironically, it seems to have been the very piety of the East Germans, who attempted to retrieve all the available works of Marx, that led to the publication in 1953 of Marx's *Grundrisse*, that collection of notes for possible future writings which served subsequently as such a useful quarry for Marxists eager to revise the works of the master by using his own writings.

Though these writers, therefore, still find it either necessary or desirable to ground their arguments on quotations from Marx, Engels and other approved writers of the past, in practice they have been able to examine in some detail the complex way in which the maintenance, and indeed strengthening, of status differentiations in socialist societies operate to frustrate the aim of classlessness. There is, and is likely to be, no confusion here between class and status, still less any crude belief (such as has frequently been denounced by Marxist apologists in the West) that by demonstrating the survival of status differentiations in socialist societies one is 'disproving' Marx's prediction of a classless society. Such a prediction, being intangible and not fixed in time, cannot be refuted; nor, for that matter, can it be verified. What can be shown is that in Eastern as in Western Europe status differentiation continues, is associated closely with the use and maintenance of political power and generally operates in all the ways in which class, in the sense that that term is popularly understood in Western Europe, is held to operate, and does operate, as a system of labelling designed to regulate society and to fix interests in the way desired by its rulers.

It was the events of October 1956 in Poland which made it possible for Stanislaw Ossowski to publish the book *Class Structure in the Social Consciousness*, on which he had been working for several years. Ossowski had studied under Stefan Czarnowski (1879–1937), a Durkheimian nationalist at Warsaw, where the Marxist Ludwig Krzywicki (1859–1941) had been head of the Institute of Social Economics from 1921 onwards. The Warsaw school had a strong tradition of empirical research into the social problems of the working class. Though Ossowski remains strongly in this positivist tradition of the pre-war period, he wrote within a Marxist framework, while at the same time denouncing the oversimplifications of the Stalinist period known in Poland as the period of the 'cult of personality'.

152   *Class in socialist states*

The conflicts between organisations, propagating class ideology on behalf of the same class, particularly after 1917, or the processes which in mono-party systems came to be called 'the estrangement of the party from the masses' showed that it is just as much possible to use class interests as a mask for party interests as it is to disguise class interests by means of universal or national slogans in organisations whose ideology is allegedly not class-bound.

These experiences and others like them have taught us that the relationship between social classes and large social organisations is more complicated than was assumed in the Marxian view of the dynamics of history; and that the antagonisms in which we may seek the driving force of history are at work on more than one level. [Ossowski 1963, p. 415]

Ossowski begins by explaining that his purpose is to clarify the meaning of terms. The literature of class and social stratification he points out, consists of metaphors of spatial relationships. The language of Marxist writing contains fewer spatial metaphors than the writing of non-Marxists, but because of the peculiar importance attached to the principal Marxist writers in socialist societies, the terms which they use have become unusually vague, he argues, and the fact that they *are* metaphors has ceased to be recognized. Ossowski therefore uses the past history of thinking about class, in particular that used in Christian religious writing, to illuminate the different formulations of class structure.

Amongst these differing formulations we find three basic aspects of that dichotomy, corresponding to the three categories of privileges enjoyed by the upper stratum: (1) the rulers and the ruled (or, to put it in a way closer to the sentiments of the ruled, those who give orders and those who must obey); (2) the rich and the poor; (3) those for whom others work and those who work.

The first relation is expressed in the term 'the ruling classes', while an alternative formulation for the second relation is 'the propertied classes' and 'the propertyless classes'. In opposing the 'exploiters' to the 'exploited' we are referring to the third relation only, but a moral evaluation is discernible in this last formulation. A moral evaluation is even more evident in such expressions as 'oppressors' and 'oppressed'. Here we have the moral aspects of the basic dichotomy, as they are seen from the viewpoint of those at the bottom. But when we disregard moral evaluations and ask in terms of which 'objective' categories a given relation between upper and lower stratum is conceived, it will, I think, become clear that this relation is confined to the three basic ones mentioned above. (ibid., pp. 23–4).

From this basis Ossowski goes on to point out that although in each age class divisions tend to be perceived in terms of dichotomies, in practice intermediate classes always exist. The different dichotomies may reinforce one another, but they may equally well conflict with one another. The grading of social classes may, it is true, depend on the assessment of a single, objective characteristic. It may, on the other hand, be a synthetic classification, one imposed by the observer upon the mass of material which he finds empirically before him.

Ossowski then proceeds to point out that Marx and Engels inherited a dichotomic perception of class along with a militant ideology of popular revolution:

Marx the revolutionary and Marx the dramatist of history developed a dichotomic conception of a class society. Marx the sociologist was compelled in his analysis of contemporary societies to infringe the sharpness of the dichotomic division by introducing intermediate classes. [ibid., p. 75]

With that rich knowledge of the corpus of Marx's writings which living in a socialist society in the late 1940s forced on writers, Ossowski is able to demonstrate how Marx at times speaks of a trichotomy of classes, introducing the concept of the petty bourgeoisie, regardless of whether he is talking about dwellers in town or in countryside. This intermediate class both possessed its own means of production and made use of them and is therefore distinguished by its work and its property from both the bourgeois capitalist class and the class of the propertyless workers. Also in his introduction to *The Peasant Wars in Germany* Engels introduces the concept of the lumpenproletariat, a stratum distinct from the rest of the proletariat and one also destined to play a different role. Furthermore, the boundary lines between the different classes are not fixed in the Marxist canon; they differ according to the different aspects of political or economic analysis which happen to be of interest at the time. The fact is, as Ossowski makes clear, if class analysis is successfully to explain the differences, as well as the similarities, between different forms of political or religious struggles, then two classes are not enough (ibid., p. 88). Last, the classic Marxist–Leninist conception of class is inadequate just where it would be most useful: in the analysis of the social structure of countries in which the means of production have been nationalized, the so-called socialist countries.

In addition to employing a detailed knowledge of Marx's and

Engels's writings to show up the internal differences and incon-
sistencies in their concept of class, Ossowski also makes considerable use of empirical material drawn from other ages and from
non-socialist countries. As he himself subsequently pointed out,
had his work been published a few years previously, it would on that
account have been subject to severe criticism and might, indeed,
have been banned entirely. Under the Stalinist interpretation of
Marxism, a comparison between the pre-socialist capitalist societies
and socialist states was regarded as quite improper. For this reason
it is interesting to see that when he makes such comparisons,
Ossowski is careful to do so in a way which suggests that he is not, in
fact, comparing the two, yet in a context in which the similarity of
events necessarily suggests itself to the reader. The reader is thus
left to draw his own conclusions from the material presented to him:
that classes have, in fact, survived into the era of socialist
construction, and that, furthermore, there is considerable doubt
about whether their relationship is non-antagonistic, as the canons
of dialectical materialism in its Stalinist interpretation suggest.

Thus he uses the growth of the new middle class of civil servants,
trade union officials, local government officers and the like in the
United States both to indicate that Marx's analysis of the sub-
mergence of classes in two dichotomies in the capitalist states has
not been borne out by events and to comment on how the new
middle class in the United States corresponds to the stratum of
non-manual white-collar workers in state and local government and
party officers in the Soviet Union, without in any way suggesting
that this latter group forms a class in the sense that the former does.
The inference is left to the reader.

The free use of material drawn from the study of capitalist
societies has continued to be a feature of Polish writing on the
subject of class, with inevitable effects on the interpretation in
Marxist writing of socialist societies. With the survival of capitalist
societies, this continued to be a necessary subject for Marxists, and
Julian Hochfeld (1911–66), in his work on class, stayed firmly
within the Marxist–Leninist tradition, while at the same time
establishing the differences between three categories of class
formulation: the mode of production, the economic order of the
socio-economic formation, and economic arrangement, the real
intertwining of dominant and coexisting modes of production. In his
emphasis on the distinction between a dominant mode of production and the actual economic order, regardless of whether each

directly related to the actual structure of classes in the society, Hochfeld and, subsequently, Wlodzimierz Wesolowski were able to draw on the critical work of other Marxist writers, and notably on the writings of the Italian Antonio Gramsci, whose *Prison Notebooks*, written during his long period of imprisonment under Mussolini, had in the meantime become freely available (Joll 1977).

Gramsci contributed to Marxist thought the key notion of *egemonia*, or hegemony. By this he meant that in each age a particular form of economic order was dominant, influencing all thought and ideas and art as well as the nature of economic, political and social processes. The hegemony of this economic order was not felt directly in terms of its actual translation into action; it was possible for it to pervade all thinking long before its translation into action had become a practical fact. Thus he believed that in his time the 'socialist mode of production' was already 'dominant' and on its way to achieving hegemony, which was not yet translated into action in the form of the construction of an actual socialist economic order. It followed from this belief that those classes which were most closely related to the dominant order would assume a greater importance in the social structure than those associated with the disappearing modes. Thus on this view a class may be dominant without actually holding political power; the aspect of dominance and efficacy are philosophically separated from one another, and a new flexibility is given to Marxist interpreters in the century-long debate over the relationship of the political superstructure to the economic base. Though the East European Marxists have not gone as far as the Western European followers of Louis Althusser in inverting the base and superstructure and in asserting the primacy of the political, nevertheless in adopting Gramsci's concept of *egemonia* they have instead practically ensured the separation of the two for analytical purposes.

Wesolowski, therefore, is able, at one and the same time, to talk in Marxist terms of the dominant class in socialist societies and to seek to understand the political activities of socialist as well as of capitalist societies in the borrowed non-Marxist terms of the power elite, at the same time bringing about, to some extent at least, a reconciliation between the traditional Marxist concept of a class and the control of politics by an elite. For Wesolowski class domination can be ensured by control over the means of production, the process and product of labour, the guarantee of this control through the fundamental laws of the state, and the legitimation of this control by the dominant ideological system (Wesolowski 1979, p. 58).

Elite power is a phenomenon of a different and distinctive type, though linked with class domination through a form of 'general dependance of the political process upon the phenomenon of class domination' and the consolidation or limitation of class domination by the acts of the power elite as appropriate.

For Wesolowski, therefore, class ceases to be the sole determinant of authority within a socialist society. Strata, not excluding something very much resembling the 'new class' of Djilas (who is, however, not quoted as one of Wesolowski's sources), continue to form the basic system of stratification in socialist societies. Nor do the contradictions of interests between these strata disappear: certain levels fall away but others remain. The existence of a nationalized economy creates a fundamental coincidence of interests, but both structural factors and the unequal distribution of goods continue to create objective contradictions of interests, basically revolving around departures from the principle 'to each according to his work'. Wesolowski does not note, though we should, that this modification of the Marxian principle 'to each according to his need' was introduced by Stalin in 1936, and its effective maintenance, even in terms of a fundamental principle of organization, in the writings of the new Eastern European Marxists is an interesting commentary on the extent to which the fundamental principles of Stalinism in dialectical materialism continue to be assumed in discussion. Wesolowski concludes by pointing out that sociology has an important role to play within socialist societies in furthering the understanding of the nature and extent of these contradictions and in attempting to provide the understanding necessary for the creation of better formulations and solutions to the longstanding problems of those societies.

An interesting by-product of Wesolowski's work is the extent to which he indicates that historical functional analysis, such as is used by writers in the United States to describe their own society, continues to have value within socialist societies, though of course in a Marxist context; such views would certainly not have been welcome a decade or so before.

The peculiar position of Poland and its distinctive sociological tradition has enabled Polish writers to take a distinctive and independent stand in their reformulation of Marxism. In other East European states the contradiction between the professions of

Marxism and the accomplishment of the state has been felt more keenly, nowhere more so than in the German Democratic Republic (GDR). There too Marxism was not simply an alien import but a living philosophical tradition. Yet the regime of Walther Ulbricht was the most rigidly Stalinist in Europe; hence it is instructive to study the writing of Rudolf Bahro, as represented by his most famous work *The Alternative in Eastern Europe* (*Die Alternative*). This is a bitter polemic on the differences between the ideal socialist society and the actually existing societies of Eastern Europe. For it appears to him that only in the capitalist countries today is it possible for communists to consider their task afresh; in the socialist countries this thinking virtually is stifled. Hence the world socialist system and the world communist movement are torn apart, he believes, by fundamental internal contradictions which have their main roots in the Soviet Union itself.

A superstructure has emerged from our revolution which seems only good for this purpose and for pursuing it in the most systematic and bureaucratic way possible. As all those involved are well aware, the rule of man by man has lost only its topmost layer. The alienation and subalternity of the working masses persists in a new phase. [Bahro 1978, p. 191]

Bahro's critique of Soviet socialism has implications as significant for the nature of class in socialist society as those of the critique of Djilas but goes well beyond it. It is the whole society he sees as standing 'propertyless against its state machine'. Bureaucracy rules all.

What is even more striking is that early in his analysis he mentions an authority shunned by all writers within the Soviet orbit since the time of Stalin, namely, Leon Trotsky. For he cites Trotsky as the first communist thinker to be confronted by his own supporters with the suggestion that the Russian Revolution might not objectively lead to the achievement of socialism. More important, he suggests that he is willing, if that proposition were to prove correct, to take up arms once again on the side of the oppressed. And in his search for the cause of the divergence between theory and practice Bahro is prepared to reach back even beyond Lenin, as far as Marx himself. For him Marx still stands at the beginning of a period of world historical development which he believes, with Gramsci, will last in all probability for centuries.

He is also painfully aware that to demonstrate that practice departs from the ideas of Marx is of no value, since it leads one into a battle of quotations in which accuracy is always assailable and the authority given to the quotation depends on the power behind the person saying it. However, it is useful to point out at this stage that this is a problem only for Marxists. For non-Marxists the demonstration that Marx's views of history are invalid is in itself an adequate justification for rejecting or modifying them, in precisely the same way as we would reject or modify the views of Darwin, Newton or Clerk-Maxwell as a result of further information about the phenomena of biology, gravitation or electromagnetism.

What Bahro is concerned to show is that Marx did not foresee the growth of bureaucratization, which he regards as the principal obstacle to the realization of Marx's (admittedly Utopian) belief in the realization of socialism.

An important aspect of Bahro's work is his examination of the nature of social stratification under socialism as it actually exists in Eastern Europe. He finds that in what he calls the state of 'proto-socialism' there is, in fact, a very rigidly delimited hierarchy of functions in the overall pattern of social labour. This is the social structure of the social collective worker, which differs from that of capitalism and yet in every respect strikingly resembles it. For he sees class structure as being in the throes of complete dissolution on a world scale, 'and not least in the classical capitalist countries themselves'. There the class structure too is being replaced by a rigorous system of stratification, he believes, and to this extent Bahro may be regarded as a theorist of convergence in social structure between socialist and non-socialist societies, a belief that has its adherents also in the United States and Western European countries among writers who, in their way, would regard themselves as Marxists.

As far as relates to the construction of socialist society, Bahro believes that leaders such as Lenin were not, in fact, wrong. They took the course which was necessary to secure the aim that they had immediately in sight. The long-term consequences of their actions they could not forsee. The results have not been as they expected, however. Workers' councils have not been effective organs of commitment for the proletariat, and the industrial proletariat has not achieved the self-consciousness which Marx predicted for it.

Today, the official theory and propaganda that maintains the 'leading role of the working class' serves the sole purpose of justifying the domination of the apparatus. The idea of working-class power is used to conceal a reality that is diametrically opposed to it. The working class as a whole, and the worker members of the party in particular, are allocated the political role of ballast when this is needed to reinforce the weight of the party–state machine against any attempt of effective correction. It was not by chance that Novotny tried to appeal to the workers before his overthrow, even if to no avail! Nor that the organisational apparatus of the party is careful to reinforce the 'workers' quota', the only section of the membership needing such artificial stimulation! For the workers are in no hurry to take on the kind of 'leading role' that the system ascribes to them. It has rather been shown, in Czechoslovakia as in Poland, that they play a progressive role in society precisely when they emancipate themselves from the tutelage of the party apparatus. [ibid., p. 191]

What has happened, Bahro asserts, is that, freed from its dialectical opposition with the bourgeoisie, the proletariat as a class has failed to achieve true class-consciousness; it retains merely trade union consciousness. And behind this lies a far, far worse possibility:

Marx and Engels recognised the historical possibility of the *common ruin of the contending classes* in a particular society. We now have a similar danger in the overall human situation. Communism only remains possible if this danger can be banished.

Under these conditions, the communist movement can no longer take up the standpoint of exclusive and particular class interests, which moreover transcend less than ever the limits of the national and supernational economic complexes. [ibid., p. 259]

In recent years such criticisms have been heard even within the Soviet Union itself. The same themes reappear, for example, in Roy Medvedev's *On Social Democracy*, first published in the West in 1972.

While I do not believe that the bureaucracy can be described as some kind of new class, I am forced to agree that those in charge of Soviet society now constitute a definite stratum sharing certain customs and rules of conduct .... That senior administrators should form a separate and clearly defined estate is not in itself an ominous development – the problem is that, having grown arrogant and out of touch with other strata classes, this estate has passed beyond the control of society. [Medvedev 1975, p. 299]

In his focus on the role of the intelligentsia in Soviet society, Medvedev highlights (as have writers from other East European countries, though perhaps in less tellingly forcible circumstances) the curious paradox of an egalitarian society in which those in charge remain most strenuously concerned to prove that they belong to a separate stratum from the others. The certainty with which a member of the Soviet intelligentsia firmly declares his membership of that stratum, implicitly or explicitly making it quite clear that he is not a member of the proletarian class, stands in striking and painful distinction to such historical observations as that of the biographer of Rosa Luxemburg that she 'more than any other Marxist, succeeded in transposing her loyalties from *nation* to *class* – intact'. Her loyalties – as indeed, perhaps, those of Marx himself – were to the proletariat, not to the intelligentsia (Nettl 1969, p. 518).

It is only fair to point out that Bahro's interpretation of Trotsky flies in the face of the evidence of Trotsky's own writings, and in particular his *Revolution Betrayed* (1936). There Trotsky reaffirmed his view that the October Revolution and Lenin's policy were both correct, and that throughout this period the working class was able to operate to create socialism through the Party. It was Stalin himself whom he saw then as the governing force in contemporary Soviet society. It was certainly not a 'new class' in the form of the bureaucracy. His rejection of the class nature of the bureaucracy, moreover, took an entirely Marxist form.

The bureaucracy has neither stocks nor bonds. It is recruited, supplemented and renewed in the manner of an administrative hierarchy, independently of any special property relations of its own. The individual bureaucrat cannot transmit to his heirs any rights in the exploitation of the state apparatus. The bureaucracy enjoys its privileges under the form of the abuse of power. [Trotsky 1972, pp. 249–50; see also Knei-Paz 1978, p. 392]

The bureaucracy, therefore, can be a clique but not a class (a view consistently maintained by Trotsky's later followers). Thus Mandel, for example, still sees the Soviet Union as a state halfway, but only halfway, on the road to socialism. Its failure to achieve socialism is the result, indeed, of the ascendancy of the bureaucracy, but it was the failure of class-consciousness among the Soviet proletariat that made it possible for the clique to monopolize power (Mandel 1975). An alternative formulation adopted by the International Socialist group, in total contrast to Soviet orthodoxy, sees the Soviet Union as the extreme form of capitalism, namely, 'state capitalism' (Cliff 1974), and thus converted into the antithesis of a true workers' state by the economic imperatives driving the bureaucracy that professed in 1947 to be still working for its realization and still does so today.

The Soviet Union today

The Eastern European critique began too early. Detailed access to sources of information about Soviet society was not possible for the majority of the writers concerned, either from the East or from the West, and at that stage the practice of sociology in the Soviet Union was still under a cloud. During the 1960s, however, pressure from Soviet scholars for the development of a sociology of socialist societies was met with a friendlier, if still guarded, reception by the political authorities, who, like their Western counterparts of the same period, came to believe that the sociologists might be useful for telling them what to do about their more intractable social problems, such as divorce, vandalism and drunkenness. Western scholars who had long been piecing together evidence from secondary sources and official statistics about the nature of Soviet society were now able to draw on information collected over a much wider range of sources and to supplement official figures and information with interviews. The resulting picture remains irritatingly incomplete just where it should be most interesting, but it does mean that now we can speak with at least some degree of confidence about empirical evidence of the nature of stratification in the Soviet Union itself.

David Lane agrees that the Russian Revolution had a profound influence on social structure in the Soviet Union and rejects the view of Bendix and Lipset that it did not (Lane 1971, p. 30; Lipset and Bendix 1959, p. 282). But he contends that the changes introduced, since they occurred in far from favourable conditions, do not indicate either that socialism is impracticable or that Marx's belief in egalitarian social organization was wrong.

Rather than introducing a socialist society qualitatively superior to capitalism, the Soviet regime in practice was faced with the construction of a technological basis similar to that of capitalist societies and it would be Utopian to imagine that a socialist form of social relations could be constructed on it. [Lane 1971, p. 33]

He regards it as neither correct nor consistent with the Marxist dialectic to term the resulting conflicts in Soviet society 'non-antagonistic contradictions', preferring to regard them rather as 'incongruities' or 'dysfunctions'.

Soviet sociologists themselves regard four forms of inequality within Soviet society as resulting in 'contradictions', namely, 'inequalities between the collective-farm peasantry and the working class, between town and country, between manual and non-manual labour, and finally those arising from the division of labour which transcends the groups of worker, intelligentsia and peasant' (ibid., p. 39).

Collective farmers, who in 1969 constituted over 21 per cent of the working population of the Soviet Union, work collectively to produce food and to market it from land which is leased to them 'in perpetuity' by the state. They are not state employees, though the workers on state farms are and are counted by the Soviet authorities as part of the proletariat. They are, however, guided by the state, in the name of the proletariat, by the enforcement of norms of production and the presence of Party officials in their administration.

Country dwellers generally, in a very large and sparsely populated country, still enjoy markedly fewer material advantages than dwellers in towns, and proportionately many more of them are manual workers. Although there is not a rigid hierarchy of income in the Soviet Union (any more, as we shall see, than there is in Western countries), the division between manual and non-manual work is still of crucial significance in terms of income and resources, since the direction of others is still regarded in the Soviet Union as rightly deserving higher remuneration. In most industries there are six or seven grades of pay. And some 12.1 million people who have had access to higher education are regarded as constituting a separate and distinct stratum, the 'intelligentsia', including the leaders of government departments, directors of state enterprises, teachers in higher education and members of press and artistic organizations.

There is general consensus that considerable income differentials exist in the Soviet Union, but there are technical problems associated with determining just what they are, since official statistics concentrate on average incomes for each sector and have to be amplified by survey evidence for individual incomes in specific areas. However, in 1965 Bottomore estimated the differential between the income of a factory manager and an ordinary worker in the Soviet Union as about 25:1 (Bottomore 1965, p. 47; cf. Lane 1971, p. 74). The evidence too is that top incomes in the Soviet Union range very much higher. Such differentials are often excused, as Lane excuses them, on the grounds that the differentials are much greater in the United States, and that the Soviet Union, unlike Western countries, has no 'structural unemployment'. The second point, however, is not relevant (even if it were true) to the question of income differentials. It seems clear that these income differentials do, in fact, tend to stratify the society into three groups, non-manual workers (especially members of the intelligentsia), manual workers in towns and collective farmers, with the same sorts of uncertainties and overlaps that are found in other societies. What a Soviet citizen *can* do is to find a privileged position in which he can enjoy high income, status, power and even considerable independence from the power of others. (Contrary to popular belief in the West, private medicine does exist in the Soviet Union and is, indeed, very popular; see Matthews 1978, p. 29.) What he *cannot* do is to use his high income to form capitalist enterprises employing others, nor may he, even if he wants to do so, live in the Soviet Union without being required to work at a job designated for him. If the Soviet Union does not have 'structural unemployment', it does have labour camps, and the press repeatedly provides evidence of people being sentenced to periods of work in them for under-employment, absenteeism and drunkenness at work.

In fact, cross-national research by Inkeles and Rossi showed that the esteem accorded to occupational groups in the Soviet Union displayed a high degree of congruence with that accorded in the other countries surveyed: the United States, Japan, Britain, New Zealand and West Germany. Not surprisingly, the designation 'worker' was accorded higher esteem than in Britain and the United States; the term 'farmer', equally significantly, was rated lower. With Veblen in mind, it is ironic to see that 'engineer' rated higher in the USSR, 'scientist' in the United States, but this may reflect only semantic differences (Inkeles 1968, p. 184). Not all workers, however, were rated highest in the Soviet Union, and the unskilled manual workers were clustered at the bottom of the prestige hierarchy (Lane 1976, p. 182). 'It seems to me,' Lane writes,

that the really significant difference in the systems of social stratification compared to Western industrial societies is the absence of a private propertied class possessing great concentrations of wealth. Otherwise, the USSR is not dramatically unlike Western societies. There is a system of inequality closely related to occupation. Workers who have skills requiring training and education and who are in short supply tend to receive a greater financial reward than those who have little or no skill. It would therefore seem to be true that the USSR is entering an epoch of classlessness only if one defines class in terms of private individual ownership of productive means. [Lane 1971, p. 69]

But, as we have seen, the USSR does have a stratum, the intelligentsia, which controls state property. How far does empirical evidence support the belief of Medvedev that the state bureaucracy is thus coming to constitute a class?

In his *Class, Inequality and Political Order* Parkin says that there is little evidence of the emergence among the bureaucracy of a distinctive culture, accent or mode of dress. He suggests, therefore, that though in a sense, seen at a single moment in time, the Soviet bureaucracy may resemble a class, in the longer term it is not. He points to the evidence that it is, or has been, possible for a worker's son in a single generation to reach the highest governing strata of Soviet society in a way that has not latterly appeared to be common in either Britain or France (Parkin 1971).

This argument would be more telling both if it were not contradicted by Medvedev and if Soviet society had been in existence rather longer than it has. It may well not yet be possible to tell if in the next generation people from disadvantaged backgrounds will reach the highest levels of the Soviet apparatus. The ossified nature of the Politburo and the higher political leadership and the increasingly advanced age of its members suggest that structural obstacles will become more pronounced. 'The conditions needed for a high rate of upward social mobility have long existed in Soviet society,' Matthews concludes, 'but in recent years there have been signs of increasing stabilization.' Perhaps the most important of these signs is the evidence that over 95 per cent of factory managers retained their posts in a sampled area between 1950 and 1970. But there are also rather more fragmentary signs that the children of the elite are retaining high social status, if not actual political power (Matthews 1978, pp. 163, 58).

As Parkin himself recognizes, we cannot assume that the present-day members of the Soviet bureaucracy will *not* wish to pass on their advantages to their children. The laws of inheritance, with the top rate of death duties standing at only 10 per cent and absolute secrecy maintained on that part of the remuneration of all top officials represented by privileges and unaccounted payments, certainly do not appear to make the transmission of privilege particularly difficult. If, as Matthews estimates, the members of the Soviet elite enjoy a standard of living 'roughly equal to, or perhaps somewhat below, that of an average American household' (Matthews 1978, p. 177), further accumulation of wealth seems only too probable as a goal for many of their families. More important, the distinguishing attribute of that distinctive stratum of the intelligentsia, education, is one which Western experience suggests is likely to be closely related to the level of education attained by the parental generation. The first generation of Soviet leaders rose in an almost totally uneducated society; subsequent generations start with differentials of opportunity already established.

Recently Ivan Szelenyi has argued from Marxist premises that

the power to which intellectuals aspire in a state-socialist redistributive economy derives from the basic institutions of social reproduction, and more specifically from the institutions which guarantee the expropriation of surplus from the direct producers, and that consequently it is of a class nature. [Szelenyi 1978–9, p. 51]

It is difficult not to agree that, granted the premises, the conclusion is uncomfortably likely to be true. Differentials must be paid for by somebody, and on the evidence it appears that the foundation and essential support of the Soviet economy is the agricultural worker, exactly as the Physiocrats saw it in the context of late eighteenth-century peasant economy in France. The important point about the bureaucratic 'class' in the Soviet Union, however, is that if it is a 'class', it must by definition be a 'ruling class' (cf. Nove 1975), for it is from its power to rule that the Soviet bureaucracy gains both its privilege and its relationship to the forces of production.

7   Making sense of class

The time has now come to try to understand in what ways various writers have sought to give these different concepts of class some real meaning in the rest of the world. It is a problem, the full difficulty of which should now be becoming clear. For the Physiocrats no doubt at all existed about whether a man was a farmer or a manufacturer. For us, in a more complex society, a man who owns an estate growing coffee and at the same time operates a plant which turns it into instant coffee powder fulfils both functions. And in his own time Marx already showed an awareness that class extended beyond the limits within which he chose to work. The bourgeoisie and the proletariat were two of the classes, and on these two he concentrated because philosophically they were to be regarded as dialectical opposites and hence formed the foundation, in his view, of the society of the future. About the landowners, which he clearly designates as a third class, he was much less definite. He did not ignore them completely, but he tended to dismiss them as the relics of a social order that was disappearing. Yet, as we have seen, it is not at all clear that even in Marxian times could one have described class as existing in the forms of the feudalism of which his landowners would have been particularly characteristic. Moreover, throughout Marx's discussion of classes runs continually the notion of class-consciousness, without which classes as such do not become fully real. To this extent, therefore, we cannot regard the Marxist criteria as forming a satisfactory empirical basis for the delimitation of class membership.

Furthermore, as we have seen, from the very birth of the modern concept of class there was a certain vagueness about its application. The economic basis of class, even where it was agreed, was not uniformly seen as being delimited in the same terms, and it was natural perhaps that with their classical heritage the writers of the nineteenth century should have tended to assimilate the economic concept of class in modern society to the writings of the ancients. Treating class, as they did, as a measure of relative wealth offered the possibility of a clear-cut criterion by which to delimit the classes. It is not surprising, therefore, that a scale of relative income or of relative wealth has continued to be favoured by sociologists as the principal indicator of class membership.

It raises, equally clearly, a serious conceptual problem. Wealth, in terms of simple monetary value, is a continuum in most societies; its distribution may vary from society to society, but though the peaks and troughs may occur in different places in different societies, the graph of wealth tends to be smooth and uninterrupted. Even where it displays two or more humps, there is no clear dividing line distinguishing two or more classes along the continuous spectrum of wealth.

In terms of employment, secondly, the distinction traditionally used by sociologists between white-collar and blue-collar jobs appears to be one of status rather than of class in the economic sense. Not only do the two categories overlap along the continuum of wealth, but such distinction as may have been drawn in the past between the possession and non-possession of capital no longer applies in advanced Western democracies. It is doubtful, indeed, whether it applies even in the Eastern Bloc. There no form of investment is permitted except that in government bonds, but investment in government bonds puts one in the position of having an interest in the maintenance of the system by which the state exploits the labour of its citizens. In neither case is it at all easy for the investigator to discover what sort of wealth a person actually has. Lacking such information, it is impossible to divide people into classes according to certain economic criteria of any kind, and such information, if it is known to anyone, is known only to the state.

In Europe, therefore, class continues to be assessed, as it was at the end of the eighteenth century, by means of criteria which are essentially those of status. Among other modern writers, Galtung (1974) regards class and status as essentially equivalent. Yet the estimation of status is fraught with difficulties. Two methods exist for placing people in status categories. One is the estimation of a person's status position by the investigator in terms of generally recognized indicators of status. Thus in Central America it is possible to determine divisions between classes by indicators such as the language spoken, the consumption of wheaten bread as against the consumption of maize and the wearing of shoes rather than the traditional Indian sandals. Such criteria are, unfortunately, much more difficult to establish in Europe and very difficult indeed to establish in the United States. They apply differently in important subcultural groups, such as that of youth in both America and Europe.

The alternative is what is known as the 'reputational method', that is to say, the assessment of a person's status position by reference to his reputation among other members of the same society. This should give a clear-cut result, assuming the establishment of definite criteria, but in practice there are a number of difficulties with it. First and foremost is the uncertainty in the minds of other members of the society about how many categories they have available to them. Research has shown considerable differences between communities in the United States in the number of classes recognized by the inhabitants, and if such variations exist, the classification of people by the reputational method is correspondingly more difficult. If, on the other hand, the investigator supplies the names of the criteria, then he introduces an element of distortion, and the results are correspondingly in doubt. Secondly, there is the important question of how far a reputational position is established by the subject himself. How far do people accept a person's own assessment of his position in society at face value, and how far do they modify it in practice?

In the popular mind, moreover, class is associated not only with high status but also with the attribute of political power. It may well be that power is not directly related to status. Nevertheless, sociologists agree that in most societies power is related to status, so that one may be traded off against the other. They also agree to a large extent that each may be traded off against one's class position. The empirical assessment of political power is in practice quite as difficult as the assessment of status, the methods being essentially the same. In the case of the former too observers have generally concluded that the best results are attained by a combination of the observational and reputational methods, though there is no certain validity in this that can be explained in terms of theoretical underpinnings. Power is important as a variable, however, for a quite different reason, that the distribution of power within a society determines the extent to which the criteria applied to class in that society are effective. The ancients recognized this when they stated that the division of their societies into classes had been determined by specific law-givers, whether or not those law-givers had actually a real historical existence. In modern times we are aware that class is not determined in such a fashion, as indeed it does not appear to be in modern primitive societies. In both modern and primitive societies it is evident that one's position in society is determined by the extent to which the criteria asserted by individuals are accepted or rejected by the group. Class, therefore, remains a very fluid concept. Attribution to one or other class category may be established by office holders, by aspirants to positions or by some third party or parties (for example, by academic observers). Indeed, it is possible to argue that a belief in class would not exist at all in society were it not for the work of academics in maintaining and extending it and using it to explain movements within society which would otherwise, or perhaps in any case, remain obscure.

The assertion of class has, of course, traditionally been couched in terms of an assertion of superiority: certain criteria are suggested by those who conform to them in order that they may be entitled to a differential share and easier access to power, wealth or respect. To the extent that these claims are accepted by society, it follows that other members of that society must be prepared to accept a lesser position, and their acceptance of that position constitutes recognition of themselves as members of the 'inferior' class. It is a paradox of socialist states that as the members of the 'inferior' class assert, by virtue of that fact, their authority to rule in society, this process of assertion and acceptance technically has no end, and a further paradox follows that if this state continues the determination of class will be truly absolute and unchangeable.

Most political scientists and sociologists, quite naturally, study class in societies in order to understand those societies better. Their focus, therefore, is on the individuals who are allocated to classes. The key question, however, is who allocates? Who, in short, gives the authority to the criteria used to delimit the classes? This is something more than merely a technical question. It has at many times in the past been believed that racial attributions must necessarily be fixed and unchangeable, and a great deal of ink has been spilt in attempts to prove that this is the case. Yet, as the society of eighteenth-century Peru demonstrates, race too can be subject to negotiation, for there it was possible for a monetary consideration to buy a certificate of high racial status which was effective regardless of one's ethnic origins. The same kind of phenomenon has been observed in our own time in periods of severe social stresses associated with class allocation. In this sense, Marx's intelligentsia become honorary members of the proletariat.

This, therefore, raises the question of how far class can be regarded as a permanent attribute. The majority of writers on class have assumed that in some sense one's class position is fixed at birth by one's origin. Class origins have been consistently cited as evidence of present class membership by members of the aristocratic, landed or commercial classes. Those individuals known to American sociologists as 'skidders', who move *down* the social scale from the middle class to the lower class, continue to carry with them an assessment of their class origins which may be belied by their present work status. Conversely, in socialist societies the political power of defined individuals (such as, for example, Nikita Khrushchev) has been strengthened by emphasis on his early origins. American sociologists generally agree that movement between classes takes place over a relatively narrow band, and that those moving from one generation to another between one class and another do so only to the class immediately adjacent to their own. This does not rule out the possibility of wider and more dramatic movements, such as that of the dairyman's daughter who marries the peer, but it does mean that such instances of rapid movement between classes separated by a long distance on the social scale must be regarded as distinctly exceptional.

What makes these assumptions particularly difficult, however, is the fact that in general those criteria cited as evidence of the rarity of long-distance movements on the social scale are essentially those of status rather than of class. The self-made man who rises from humble origins to become a millionaire is likely to be rejected in the higher reaches of society on the grounds that his wealth, being new, is in some way inferior to the older wealth and the longer-term status which members of the upper classes themselves possess, and in this we see a clue to the most intractable problem of class: the fact that its very fluidity leads to its being used as a defensive tactic in the game of status in life. Thus those who hold a 'high' position on the social scale as it is currently understood attempt to maintain the criteria by which they themselves retain their position. Conversely, those who suffer from 'low' status hope to modify those criteria, not merely so that the mighty may be cut down to size but also so that they can be recognized as meriting the esteem of their fellows.

The attempt to win esteem among one's fellows is very basic to human beings. Psychologists have observed that the child in the playground who possesses the talent of being able to waggle his ears enjoys on that account a prestige which is not only satisfying to him but pleasing to his fellows in a way that cannot be understood except through the assertion that any rare quality or talent is accepted as a criterion of distinction independent of other ranking orders, such as ability in games, social situations or even academic work. When we turn, therefore, to the work of political scientists and sociologists on the nature of the class structure of actual societies, we find an incredible degree of complexity in their findings.

Britain

It is widely believed in Britain that the British class structure is uniquely important in the public's view of its own political process. There is an obvious reason for this: since 1923 power has alternated between two political parties each of which regards both itself and its opponent as embodying the interests of a specified class. Like most political statements, however, this turns out on closer examination to be one that needs a great deal of qualification.

To begin with, the term 'class' here does not mean class in the Marxist sense but what we could call 'social class', though 'social status' would be much less misleading. The Labour Party regards itself as the party of the 'working class', and a majority of voters who regard themselves as 'working-class' do consistently support it. But a substantial fraction do not: between a quarter and a third of 'working-class' voters equally consistently support the Conservatives (McKenzie and Silver 1968), despite the fact that the party is generally regarded as the party of the 'middle class' or even the 'upper class'. A third party, the Liberals, cultivating a deliberately 'classless' image, were able to acquire a substantial share of the votes in the 1960s and 1970s, but these were distributed in such a way that the Liberal Party was able to secure no more than a handful of seats in Parliament on the single-member, single-ballot system still maintained in Britain.

The Liberal party, like the Conservative Party, was once one of the two major parties in Britain and able to command a majority in Parliament throughout the nineteenth century, when it was identified with the drive for successive extensions of the franchise (see Clarke 1978). The party's catastrophic decline in the twelve years after 1923 is generally explained by the assumption that the Labour Party formed the natural home for the larger number of 'working-class' voters that had been provided by the successive enlargements of the franchise. Since the last enlargement, in 1918, had been the extension of the vote to women, however, this is an explanation that needs to be treated with some care, since all studies undertaken since have shown that women tend to vote for parties in substantially the same proportions as men. Other factors of importance were the identification of the Liberals with the First World War; their wartime coalition with the Conservatives, the 'first-past-the-post' voting system and the independence of the Irish Free State, removing from Parliament the Irish party whose representatives had previously formed an important bloc of support for the Liberal Party.

One consequence of this change was that the Conservatives for many years appeared to be the 'party with the majority tendency', providing the natural leaders of state and nation. In a time of war, social tension and loss of power and prestige in the world the party therefore attracted the votes of many who did not feel themselves to be socially confident enough to speak for themselves, the phenomenon termed by British sociologists 'deferential voting' (see Shils 1968). Conservatives also emphasized in their appeal to the nation the symbols of nationalism and patriotism, the monarchy and the flag, implying (perhaps at times unconsciously) that their political opponents were less loyal than they.

In practice the role of the monarchy in Britain has for political purposes been reduced to a symbolic one. Britain has retained its old Upper House of Parliament, the House of Lords, in which sit representatives of the medieval First Estate, the nobility, and of the Second, the Church. But since 1948 this body has served a largely deliberative function as a revising chamber for legislation and the formal embodiment of the highest court of justice. In the latter role it is represented only by specially appointed Law Lords; other life peers and hereditary peers play no part. The House of Lords as a legislative body, therefore, makes only a small contribution, if a useful one, to the governmental process. And, unlike Continental models, the hereditary membership of the House is composed only of heads of families; the younger sons of younger sons in Britain have ceased to be noble and have joined once more the endless process of social circulation.

The 'upper class' in Britain, therefore, cannot be identified with membership of the House of Lords. It might be regarded for some purposes as synonymous with the possession of a title, office or dignity that entails inclusion in the Court-authorized Table of Precedence which governs people's official rank on ceremonial occasions. But though this is a definite criterion, in that it can be established by a simple act of reference, it bears little or no relation to the process of political or economic power, or even of social standing, to those who are not aware of its existence. So small is the 'upper class', by any criterion, that it is often regarded as a minute ingredient in the otherwise inexplicably named 'middle class'.

The 'middle class' is even less determinate (Lewis and Maude 1949) but is so large that even its members discern distinctions, the broadest of which are often referred to as the 'upper-middle', 'middle' and 'lower-middle' classes. The 'working class' – *never* called the 'lower class' – is widely regarded as having a distinctive culture (Hoggart 1957; cf. Wright 1867, 1873) but similarly has its subdivisions in the eyes both of its own members and of observers. Since 1911 sociologists wishing to identify a pattern among these have been able to do so with the aid of the Office of Population, Censuses and Surveys *Classification of Occupations* issued by the Registrar General (1970) and hence generally known for short as 'the Registrar General's classification'. In doing so, they concur on a definition of class as a socioeconomic categorization based on the occupation of the 'head of the household' (though, confusingly, the Census independently classifies families under seventeen socio-economic groups). 'Social class', therefore, is defined by two things: occupation (for a head of household) and marriage (for his wife), other dependants sharing, at least in the eyes of the Registrar General, in the position in society thus established.

The Registrar General's classification does not recognize the separate existence of an 'upper class', and thus is at one with many sociologists and perhaps much of the British population. Many of the members of a putative 'upper class' who are engaged in agriculture will turn up, rather engagingly, in Social Class 2, 'Intermediate occupations', as farmers, together with school-masters, artists, journalists and company directors. In order the five classes used by the Census are:

Social Class 1, 'Professional', accounting for some 4 per cent of the population and including doctors, lawyers and other professional groups;
Social Class 2, 'Intermediate occupations' (18 per cent);

Social Class 3 (N), 'Skilled occupations: non-manual' (21 per cent),
  including sales representatives, shop assistants, cashiers and
  policemen, and (M), 'Skilled occupations: manual' (28 per cent),
  including such occupations as bus drivers, cooks and printers;
Social Class 4, 'Partly skilled' (21 per cent), comprises the rest of the
  working-class population, except for:
Social Class 5, 'Unskilled' (8 per cent).

For coding purposes, particularly in the advertising and marketing industries, the same categories are often referred to as 'A', 'B',
'C1', 'C2', 'D' and 'E', the first two and the last two often being
considered together as the potential targets of a specified marketing
strategy.

Giving the classes letters rather than numbers for the purposes of
identification, nevertheless, does not eliminate what to some critics
is the fundamentally objectionable feature of the Registrar
General's classification, namely its rank ordering. This ordering
appears roughly to coincide with a scale of incomes, so that to some
extent it serves as a rough-and-ready indicator of economic
position. But it is specifically declared not to relate directly to
'average remuneration', and if a rank ordering of economic position
is required, why should it not be an accurate one? More seriously,
are the anomalies in the classification such as to amount to
artificially imposed distinctions?

Of these anomalies, the most striking, as well as the most
controversial, is that division between manual and non-manual
work which splits Social Class 3 into two parts corresponding to the
line usually believed to separate the lower 'middle class' from the
upper 'working class' (except, perhaps, by those immediately
'below' it).

The first point to be made about this division is that it has little or
nothing to do with current income levels. Many, though certainly
not all, of those 'below the line' are earning more, and in some
cases substantially more, than many of those 'above the line'.
Naturally, part of the reason for this is that a classification by
occupation will not accurately reflect income distribution, insofar as
the returns from any occupation for any given individual vary with
his age and degree of skill. An occupational classification, therefore, gives at best an indication of potential rather than actual
income. But the source of the anomaly is still clearly largely
artificial, in that imposed on the general scale of income is a

criterion, the division between manual and non-manual work, which is only in part reflected in income terms.

The part that is so reflected is that which historically reflected greater returns for non-manual than for manual work. Those occupations defined as non-manual typically involved an element of direction or control, as well as being relatively free from the most unpleasant features of nineteenth-century industrialization, such as dirt, the risk of industrial accident or disease and the probability that increasing wear and tear on the body would restrict a man's capacity for further earnings, even possibly deprive him of the ability to work altogether. Hence the distinction between manual and non-manual did, historically, have real meaning in terms of gross economic reward; it was not simply a matter of ascribed status.

Today, however, the changing nature of industry and work has altered the picture. As we have seen, the distinction between manual and non-manual has never had any secure theoretical foundation, since a pen is as much a manual tool as a chisel, a typewriter as much as a lathe. The distinction was a purely technical one, but one which gained its social significance not from its technical significance alone but also from the values attached to those technical features by those seeking to evaluate their own or another's role in the social system. The distinction is one, moreover, that would have no significance if the assumption had not been made, first of all, that society should be viewed as a hierarchy and hence that a rank ordering of occupations was a reasonable way of rendering that hierarchy in descriptive terms. Dismiss the notion of a rank ordering and replace it by the concept of a multi-dimensional society in which there are many paths to greater economic reward, and the problem of evaluating manual as against non-manual occupations simply disappears. But we are, unhappily, left to cope with the legacy of the status assumptions and discriminatory practices of the past in circumstances in which they have become largely irrelevant.

Nowhere is this more clearly the case than in the area of domestic work, which, unless performed for monetary reward, does not enter into the Registrar General's classification at all and yet forms the fundamental basis on which all other forms of work depend (cf. Middleton 1974). Work outside the home, which in the past was always for members of the 'working class' *additional* to domestic work, has in the past fifty years in Britain become almost universally so, as the progress of feminine emancipation has had the ironic effect of driving more and more women into paid employment and hence into the 'class structure' in their own right (but cf. Rex 1974, p. 17; see also Acker 1973). The use of the 'head of household' criterion for the determination of class membership thus creates continual uncertainties, uncertainties which are felt not only by sociologists but also by the individuals themselves, as they seek to adjust their expectations between their public and private lives.

A third point which has become of increasing importance in Britain since 1945 is the spread of secondary employment, a fact which the classification, being based on principal employment, cannot take into account. Secondary employment is, of course, likely to resemble primary employment closely, and usually does, but the fact that it is secondary makes for important differences. Especially it gives the individual a degree of choice and control which the classical Marxist and non-Marxist views of class failed alike to envisage. A further complicating factor has been the spread of the 'do-it-yourself' movement. Its economic significance in terms of its contribution to the national economy is difficult to gauge, but in individual terms it makes possible a lifestyle that would otherwise be more socially restricted, while acting powerfully to eradicate the old social snobberies about the impropriety of manual work. The same technological developments that have facilitated this, especially the spread of power tools, have made much more uncertain the once equally sharp distinction between 'skilled' and 'unskilled' occupations, which again the classification still reflects. The last point to note is that although the classification generally reflects the standing of occupations in the community, it does not do so on a secure foundation of response to survey questions. Its socioeconomic categories have been reworked by Goldthorpe and Hope (1974) to supply such an ordering.

It can be said, therefore, that in Britain the use of the Registrar General's concept of social class is at best confusing, in that it mingles criteria of status and economic reward, and at worst socially harmful, in that it tends to preserve the values of a social order that has largely ceased to exist.

It is entirely understandable that as a result of these sorts of uncertainties, class in Britain appears to be a topic of absorbing, and even overwhelming, interest. Unaware of the futility of the exercise, members of the public devote enormous amounts of time and attention to their relationship with others in society. Newspapers, radio and television programmes, advertisements and public pronouncements of all kinds strengthen the belief in an objectively determined social order in which at any one moment the individual can hope to determine his or her position and at the same time strive to enhance it. The public and private lives of the prominent and the notorious, past and present, are eagerly scanned for information which contributes to the seeker's private map of the social universe.

The complex definition of a class given by a well-known journalist in 1979 seems accurately to reflect the assumptions of current British society. For Cooper a class is 'a group of people with certain common traits: descent, education, accent, similarity of occupation, wealth, moral attitudes, friends, hobbies, accommodation, and with generally similar ideas, who meet each other on equal terms, and regard themselves as belonging to one group' (Cooper 1979, p. 14). No sociologist or political scientist could say that this definition is 'wrong'. On the contrary, it is as succinct an expression of what the ordinary Briton means by the term as one could reasonably wish. The problem is how to use it. Here the principal significance attaches, inevitably, to the role of education in Britain in establishing or maintaining the links between the other criteria mentioned, as well as in generating that sense of self-consciousness to which Marx himself attached particular importance.

The principle of universal primary education was first established in Britain in 1871. The 1944 Education Act, passed by the wartime coalition Government, extended the principle to the provision of free state education at all levels, up to and including the universities. It was assumed that this would in time result in a society in which each child had the full opportunity to develop his or her talents; that advancement within such a society alone would depend on 'merit'; and that consequently in time the traditional boundaries of 'class' would disappear altogether through a process of gradual and peaceful assimilation (Floud 1950), a view persuasively supported in the very influential statement of the democratic socialist philosophy of reform, *The Future of Socialism*, by Antony Crosland (Crosland 1956).

Yet when invited to give the BBC's Reith Lectures in 1978, Professor A. H. Halsey described Britain as still 'a class-ridden society'. In a society divided in three ways, by class, status and party, it was the classes that formed and continue to form the fundamental division in society (Halsey 1978). Though he quoted approvingly the view of Colin Crouch that class should be 'treated here as an analytical relationship rather than as an identification of empirical groups of persons', he subsequently used as his own definition a much more concrete formula, 'those occupational groups and their families which share similar work and market conditions', and discussed the changes in British class structure since 1900 in terms of the changes in occupational structure as defined in terms of the Registrar General's classification. His conclusion that the class structure had remained fundamentally unaltered throughout the period was, it appeared, supported by the results of the Nuffield Social Mobility Survey published early in 1980.

The results of this survey of more than 10,000 men aged between 20 and 64 interviewed in 1972 were presented in two parts. The work of Dr John Goldthorpe on social mobility between classes on a seven-class model based on occupational criteria concluded that although the degree of upward mobility in Britain had increased overall, the relative disadvantages of those born into the lower social classes remained consistent (Goldthorpe 1980). That of Professor Halsey and other colleagues on the educational data collected by the survey concluded that access to secondary and higher education for the children of the different classes had similarly remained consistent and unequal, though more members of all social classes had had educational opportunities opened up to them because of the general increase in prosperity of the country as a whole (Halsey *et al.* 1980). They concluded sadly that social policy designed to promote greater equality of opportunity since 1944, particularly in the field of education, had simply failed to meet the expectations attached to it. That failure did not, of course, mean that the policy was wrong or misguided – the inequalities, after all, could have become worse (but cf. Urry and Wakeford 1973). Both works concurred in wondering if, in a time of recession, inequality was not likely to increase again.

It is not possible to measure by these forms of statistical treatment the opportunities offered to a boy or girl to achieve higher social status; the most that can be said is that if the opportunities were there, they were not taken. Though many factors could tend towards the preservation of differentiation (such as attitudes of home and family, peer groups in school and fellow workers in the workplace), criticism of the apparent failure of the educational system to 'deliver the goods' had, in fact, been rising since the 1960s. It was natural that this should be so, since the realm of education, being the concern of governmental policy, was the one most open to pressure groups and legislation.

Criticism tended to be levelled at two features of the British educational system, one predating the 1944 Act and the other created by it. The former was the survival, in parallel with the state system, of independent schools supported by fees paid by parents. The latter was the principle of selection between different forms of secondary education, and hence opportunities for advancement to higher education, made at the age of 11–12 (hence the Eleven-Plus examination) through the administration of an objective test of intelligence within the state system.

Independent schools exist in all non-communist countries and private education in specific subjects even in the Soviet Union. Their peculiar significance in Britain stemmed from a combination of circumstances. They were often, though wrongly, identified with a smaller group of schools, known rather curiously as 'public schools', which had been consolidated out of earlier foundations in the nineteenth century as boarding establishments to cater for the children of a self-consciously Empire-building elite (Kalton 1966; Gardner 1973; Gathorne-Hardy 1977). Some of these establishments not only produced a disproportionately large number of those who held high office in Church and State, but their prestige was compounded by their domination of the entry into the universities, and in particular the ancient universities of Oxford and Cambridge. The existence of these institutions, some critics said, presented an impenetrable barrier to advancement through the state system, however intelligent a pupil might be. Others argued that it was unfair that parents should be able to pay for educational opportunities for their children if they were not bright enough to succeed on their own merits. Spokesmen of the Labour Governments of Mr Wilson (1964–70, 1974–6) and Mr Callaghan (1976–9) often spoke out in criticism of the public schools but were unable or unwilling to do anything about them.

Instead they made their target the methods of selection for different sorts of schooling in the state system. The 1944 Act had established two sorts of schools: grammar schools for those children who had passed the Eleven-Plus, and secondary modern schools for those who had not. The former were to lead on to an education in one of the universities whose numbers rapidly expanded after 1952, with a climax in new foundations in the mid 1960s. The latter were more technically and vocationally orientated, with the result that a late developer who was placed in a secondary modern school found it difficult, if not impossible, to get back into a more academic environment (Jackson and Marsden 1962, pp. 211–13). The remedy, adopted as official policy by the Labour Party and enforced by government action, was to compel the local authorities to reorganize all schools under their charge as 'comprehensive schools' catering for pupils of all abilities. Some educational theorists even went so far as to try to educate all people of an age group in 'mixed-ability' groups, but in practice most systems put limits to the range permitted in order to make the teacher's task a practicable proposition in the generally oversized classes.

Some of the most important grammar schools – generally, the older foundations that had accepted entry into the state system in 1944 under the terms then agreed – refused to take part in the new reorganization and joined the ranks of the independent schools. Labour policy towards one aspect of the educational system had thus had the unexpected effect of strengthening the other aspect that they had most frequently criticized. Significantly, the newly independent schools appeared to have no difficulty in recruiting pupils whose parents were prepared to pay the very considerable fees involved, and among these there were no doubt some who were motivated less by a zeal for intellectual achievement than by the prospect of the social and economic advantages to be gained. But from the point of view of the class structure, the most interesting feature was that the enlarged number of independent schools and the general increase in prosperity during the 1960s had put the possibility of private education for their children within the reach of many members of the so-called 'working class'.

This was but one aspect of the consequence of prosperity which sociologists had earlier termed 'embourgeoisement', namely, the tendency for the improvement in material conditions of members of the working class to be accompanied by the assumption of middle-class values, habits and ways of doing things (Zweig 1961). The embourgeoisement thesis meant in Britain that these changes should in turn be associated with a change in political allegiances tending away from the Labour Party and towards the Conservatives. The growing success of the Conservatives at the General Elections of 1951, 1955 and 1959 appeared to be a certain proof of it in the eyes of the majority of publicists and writers of the period and even of Labour Party advisors (Abrams and Rose 1960, p. 119). It concurred with the belief that the key to the satisfactory management of a capitalist economy had finally been discovered; the consequences were set out in the widely read and elegantly argued work of the Canadian-born American economist J. K. Galbraith, the key theme of which was not 'social class' but 'social balance':

In the advanced country ... increased production is an alternative to redistribution. And, as indicated, it has been the great solvent of the tensions associated with inequality. Even though the latter persists, the awkward conflict which its correction implies can be avoided. How much better to concentrate on increasing output, a programme on which both rich and poor can agree, since it benefits both. [Galbraith 1958, p. 74; cf. Smith 1925, vol. I, p. 12]

In consequence, Galbraith pointed out, the pursuit of equality had disappeared from the liberal agenda, and as it had done so, the assumption that inequality, especially in wealth and income, was disappearing was belied by the facts (see also Titmuss 1962, p. 199). And, in fact, that constant proportion of the male population which over the preceding seventy years had been employed in industry continued to work primarily for money in conditions which fell far short of what might be attainable in terms of comfort, convenience and pleasure.

If the class structure as a whole is stable, however, individuals may still be able to move upward freely within it, especially those who move easily to a new environment where they can take up a new lifestyle (Watson 1964; see also Bell 1969). In 1962 a team from the University of Cambridge picked the town of Luton, a nearby growing and prosperous industrial centre containing a highly socially mobile labour force living in the main in recently constructed housing and removed from the traditions of nineteenth-century industrial development, as the ideal place to test the embourgeoisement thesis. Their findings, published between 1967 and 1969, fell naturally into two parts: those relating to conditions of work and those dealing with the political and social consequences.

Goldthorpe, Lockwood, Bechhofer and Platt (1967, 1969) found that the 'affluent worker', for all his affluence, continued to share the typical life experiences and life chances of wage workers in large-scale manufacturing enterprises. Not only did the large majority of them find their work boring and monotonous in itself, but in order to gain high material rewards they also had to work a substantial amount of overtime, while shift working, and in particular night work, was regarded as a deprivation, since it curtailed social and leisure opportunities. Certainly, they did not gain a perception of their greater ability to 'get on' in life, other than by increasing their returns through membership of powerful trade union organizations.

Politically the Luton sample proved, if anything, more pronouncedly pro-Labour in its sympathies than might have been expected, with no indication of a shift towards the Conservatives in the course of the 1950s. The authors of the study wrote:

Thus, while the data we are able to produce from our sample may be insufficient in themselves to refute conclusively the thesis which links working-class affluence with a political shift to the right, they are at all events conspicuously at odds with this and show, at least, that such a shift does not occur in any necessary and automatic way. [Goldthorpe *et al*. 1967, p. 24]

There was evidence, moreover, that those workers who voted Conservative did so not because they regarded it as socially the acceptable thing to do but largely because they believed that they personally were better off.

By the time the 'affluent worker' studies were published the Labour Party had won the 1964 General Election and was to win the 1966 election with the impetus of the same sorts of short-term economic management policies that had previously brought success to the Conservatives. The Labour Government of 1966–70 failed to hold its support at least in part because of its attempt to curb the growing power of the trade unions (Lapping 1970, pp. 37–53). The succeeding Conservative Government enacted very similar legislation at a time when inflation was already beginning to rise steeply and, when faced by the combination of the oil crisis of 1973 and a miners' strike, very unwisely decided to go to the country prematurely. Thus the theme of the rest of the 1970s became the opposition among organized labour to what were castigated as 'socially divisive' policies.

It was at this point that the voices from the left began to get louder. In Perry Anderson's and Robin Blackburn's *Towards Socialism* (1965), J. H. Westergaard had denounced as 'a contemporary myth' the notion of 'the withering away of class', citing as evidence a very wide range of sources. Anderson's claim that Britain's 'present crisis' offered a real chance for 'an authentic socialist movement' did not at that stage attract a wide following. After the oil crisis of 1973 had given way to the depression of 1974 'the crisis of late capitalism' became a much more plausible scenario than it had appeared in the afterglow of the age of affluence, and this growing pessimism has been reflected in the most diverse parts of the most recent British literature (cf. Westergaard and Resler 1975; Crompton and Gubbay 1977; Reid 1977). It seems unlikely, however, in the light of the empirical evidence suggesting that the British class structure is highly resistant to change, that it is in serious danger of immediate collapse, especially as it is not, in fact, a class structure at all.

The United States

The use of a concept of class to analyse American society was virtually unknown before the Great Depression of 1929. It had, as we have already seen, been employed by Thorstein Veblen in the early years of the century but in an idiosyncratic way which, though fruitful in calling attention to the absurdities of conspicuous waste and expenditure which were even then apparent, did not develop these ideas within a context of social structure. The members of the ecological school of sociologists centred upon the University of Chicago used the term in the 1920s but without much precision, as they saw class considerations as peripheral to the nature of urban neighbourhoods in shaping the lifestyles of their residents (Gordon 1958). It was only with Robert S. and Helen M. Lynd's first study of *Middletown* (1929) that American writers began to use the term 'class' to describe what they saw as major subdivisions of the society they were studying, though they specifically rejected the traditional European division into lower, middle and upper classes in favour of a twofold division into 'working class' and 'business class' (Lynd and Lynd 1929). By 1935 they had extended this basic categorization into one of five groups, ranging from the top group of the old 'middle class' to the 'poor whites' at the bottom of three layers of the 'working class' (Lynd and Lynd, 1937).

Then in the early 1930s W. L. Warner at Harvard instituted the series of studies of 'Yankee City' which under his direction was to make the social anthropological analysis of class structure and behaviour a regular foundation of sociological research in the United States. The first volume appeared in 1941 and was followed by many more, both by Warner himself and by his many col-laborators (Warner and Lunt 1941; see also esp. Warner and Low 1947; Warner 1964). Warner not only published details of his methodology for the study of class (Warner 1963) and status (Warner, Meeker and Weckler 1949) but also set it out in his *Social Class in America* (Warner, Meeker and Eells 1949). *Democracy in Jonesville* (Warner 1964) formed the basis on which he established the study of social stratification as an important sector of socio-logical enquiry in the United States, taking this Mid-Western town as the epitome, in miniature, of the country at large. From a similar town Hollingshead published his study *Elmtown's Youth* (Hollings-head 1967).

Warner defined class as 'two or more orders of people who are believed to be, and are accordingly ranked by the members of the community, in socially superior and inferior positions' (Warner and Lunt 1941, p. 82). The six classes or, more correctly, status groups which he determined by the reputational method from interaction with members of the community in his selected New England and Mid-Western communities formed a continuum from 'upper-upper' to 'lower-lower' and demonstrated only partial ecological separa-tion by area. They did, nevertheless, appear to form reasonably stable groupings over time in the local community, with all the implications that fact has for the distribution of wealth and, consequently, for the distribution of power.

Unfortunately, scaling up the results of such local surveys to the national level, especially in the case of a country as large as the United States, is methodologically invalid, and the view of 'class-as-status' so powerfully propagated by the Warner school as applicable to the whole United States introduced the maximum of uncertainty into the study of stratification there, just as it was getting under way. Later community studies gave widely differing impressions of the number of classes in the communities concerned. Hollingshead found five 'prestige groups' in Elmtown; he demon-strated, even more strikingly, how the groups he identified were perpetuated in the structure of adolescent life, thus denting, if not destroying, traditional assumptions about the fluidity of American society. On the other hand, different observers elsewhere identified a greater or lesser number of strata in the communities they studied, suggesting either that the methods employed were not very reliable or that movement between one town and another, relatively commonplace in the American context, was indispensable to ease of social mobility.

So general was the view of 'class-as-status' in American society that few empirical studies of the immediate post-war period were conducted on any other basis, an important exception being the attempt, not widely accepted, of the psychologist Richard Centers to identify awareness of 'class-consciousness' in his respondents (Centers 1949). Major sociology textbooks accepted the identification of class and status (MacIver and Page 1949). And though no less an authority than Talcott Parsons stressed the importance of occupational criteria among the factors determining status and prestige (Parsons 1954), it was, rather, his prestige as the prophet of functionalism that influenced a distinct tendency to derive from the discovery that classes existed in American society the proposition that they must therefore perform some useful function. This view, stated categorically as one universally applicable to all societies by Davis and Moore (1945), was contested by Melvin M. Tumin (1953), who stressed that in a number of respects, particularly where based on inherited criteria, social stratification could manifestly be dysfunctional (see also Davis 1966). At the same time Gerhard Lenski pointed out that status, because of its various sources, was itself liable to perceptions of inconsistency or lack of congruence between the different elements of which it was made up (Lenski 1952, 1954; cf. Lenski and Lenski 1974).

Though the view of 'class-as-status' was by no means wholly displaced by it, the 1950s saw the emergence of a rival school of interpretation focusing on occupational structure as the basis of class. In part this stemmed from a new awareness of social mobility, the study of which had been established as early as the 1920s by the Russian émigré Pitrim Sorokin, but it now gained in popularity as well as elaboration under the influence of Seymour Martin Lipset and Reinhard Bendix (Lipset and Bendix 1951, 1952a, 1952b, 1953, 1959). In turn this reflected the arrival on the scene of English translations of Max Weber and of critical awareness of his distinction between class, status and party (Gerth and Mills 1948).

Lipset and Bendix (1959) grounded their study of social mobility on the objective basis of occupation, without at all ignoring the subjective basis of status and prestige which occupation brings with it. Their cross-national material was drawn from studies made previously by other researchers in ten industrialized countries: the United States, Germany, Sweden, Japan, France, Switzerland, Denmark, Britain and Italy. The main thesis which they sought to test was the traditional assumption that social mobility was much easier in the United States than in the older European countries, an assumption which goes back to long before the days of Alexis de

Tocqueville (Tocqueville 1961). To test this assumption, however, they had to found their cross-national comparisons, which were based on widely differing systems of listing occupations, on one further assumption, 'that a move from manual to non-manual employment constitutes upward mobility among males'. It was among men that their comparisons were made, and the principal groups into which their occupations were gathered were standardized as 'manual', 'non-manual' and 'farm'.

They concluded not only that social mobility in the United States was very similar to that in other industrialized societies but also that it was wholly compatible with a well defined class structure and even with a general tendency towards the inheritance of social status. In this connection they quoted with approval the simile used by Schumpeter: 'For the duration of its collective life, or the time during which its identity may be assumed, each class resembles a hotel or an omnibus, always full, but always of different people' (Schumpeter 1951, p. 165).

Other studies made during the same period were perhaps no less influential in communicating a new confidence about the use of the word 'class' in the American context. C. Wright Mills, in his *White Collar*, the first major sociological study of the American middle class, accepted the view of class as occupationally based while specifically rejecting the applicability of the Marxist concept of class-consciousness to the American case. For those substantial sectors not in touch with the centres of power in society or with each other he coined the attractive neologism 'the Lumpen-Bourgeoisie' (Mills 1951, pp. 28, 326). But within five years he was to have an even more striking impact on public opinion through the publication of *The Power Elite* (1956), in which the concept of class was again relegated to the background in favour of a concept which was in some ways as far removed from the accepted view of an elite as it was from any prevailing view of a class.

The thesis of *The Power Elite* has enjoyed an amazing popularity and, in an attenuated form, is known to millions of people who have never read it and have never been near the United States. It was, briefly, that the 'command posts' of American politics were in the hands of a relatively small number of people in each of the government, military and business sectors, who, though without self-conscious awareness of their unity of action, acted together to direct the political process. Their ability to do so, and to push local and regional elites into a secondary position, stems, according to

Mills, to a considerable extent from their control of the media in 'mass society' (Mills 1956). This last phrase, to which he seems to have been the first to give general currency, was given a more detailed and far-reaching exposition by Kornhauser (1960). But it was the reference to the 'military-industrial complex' in President Eisenhower's so-called 'Farewell Address' that gave the President- ial seal of approval, so to speak, to the Mills view of the American political system (Eisenhower 1965, vol. II, p. 616). And in the course of the Vietnam War (1965–73) this view in turn underwent a strange modification in the writings of the New Left: instead of being regarded as confuting the class basis of American politics, it became a key text in anti-imperialistic denunciations of the American bourgeoisie.

All these views had one thing in common. They did not attempt to devise tests for the existence of the 'power elite', and, of course, given the nature of the concept, they could not have been expected to do so. It was left to Talcott Parsons, in his careful critical review of the book (Parsons 1957), to demonstrate that where Mills had gone wrong was in forgetting that power and status did not necessarily go together, any more than did status and class. Physicians, he pointed out, enjoyed very high status in American society but little political power. Lawyers, through their control of the processes of power, controlled power itself. They were not, as Mills seemed to assume, simply the lackeys of businessmen. And among academic sociolog- ists and political scientists, as opposed to the general public, it was, as we have already seen, the Parsonian view that prevailed almost unchallenged until the development of the new radical critiques of the 1970s, some of which were very traditionally Marxist (Ander- son 1974).

As the history of Presidential elections during this period demonstrates, occupation – from 1936 a key factor in American national politics – continued to play a crucial part in determining outcomes. The application of stratification data (among other data relating to voting behaviour) to the construction of a computer model designed to predict or 'project' the result of a Presidential contest became a reality in the mid 1950s; 'indicator precincts' were chosen carefully to reflect regional social composition and voting behaviour as early and as accurately as possible. In the Presidential election of 1960 competition between the television networks to demonstrate their accuracy and efficiency did, indeed, give convinc- ing proof of both, though the narrowness of the popular-vote margin, coupled with the peculiar effects of the Electoral College system in distorting the result, made the task intrinsically a very difficult one. For the same reason, the projections failed to give a wholly reliable picture of the results until counting was largely complete in the elections of 1968 and 1976 (White 1969; anon. 1976).

The alternation of the parties in the Presidency tends to distract attention from the fundamental aspect of American politics during the period, the control of Congress by the Democratic Party and the continuing strength, manifested by Carter's election in 1976, of the Roosevelt coalition of the Democratic South, northern liberal intellectuals and, above all, blue-collar support in the big cities.

The emphasis on 'classlessness' in American political ideology has led many European and American political commentators to conclude that party divisions in America are less related to class cleavages than they are in other Western countries. Polling studies, however, belie this conclusion, showing that in every American election since 1936 (studies of the question were not made before then), the proportion voting Democratic increases sharply as one moves down the occupational or income ladder. In 1948 almost 80 per cent of the workers voted Democratic, a percentage which is higher than has ever been reported for left-wing parties in such countries as Britain, France, Italy, and Germany. Each year the lower-paid and less skilled workers are the most Democratic; even in 1952, two-thirds of the unskilled workers were for Stevenson, though the proportion of all manual workers backing the Democrats dropped to 55 per cent in that year – a drop-off which was in large measure a result of Eisenhower's personal, 'above the parties' appeal rather than a basic swing away from the Democratic party by the lower strata. [Lipset 1964a, p. 285]

It was the strength of the urban workers vote in 1968 that – despite the tensions and hostilities generated by the Vietnam War – almost saved the election for Hubert Humphrey, and Nixon's victory was achieved in spite of the loss to the Republicans of several urban strongholds previously considered essential, in particular the State of New York.

It would be wrong to conclude from this victory, or even from Nixon's overwhelming popular and Electoral College vote triumph in 1972 over a weak candidate, a divided party and a flawed strategy, that working-class support for the Democrats implies middle-class support for the Republicans. Even in the débâcle of 1972 both houses of Congress, State governorships and State Houses remained in Democratic hands. It was the 'Southern strategy' of combining the support of the urban middle class in the North, alarmed by the race riots and insurgency among youth generated by the civil rights and anti-war movements of the 1960s and early 1970s, with the temporary support of the still essentially Democratic but decreasingly rural South that brought the Conservative Nixon victory – that and, in an issue-orientated election, Nixon's visit to China and his promise at last to end the Vietnam War.

For, as we have already seen in the pioneering studies of Lipset and Bendix (1951) and Blau and Duncan (1967), urban and rural in the United States are not merely distinctive social groups; they are also ecologically separated by the facts of American geography. Hence what may by one observer be attributed to class motives, in the occupational sense, may by another, with no less validity, be attributed to sectionalism. This same period was marked in the United States by two profound demographic changes: the expansion of the great conurbations and the flight to the suburbs of the urban middle classes. There remained the decaying inner city areas. There the problems of poverty, which in a European context would have been regarded as issues of class, were in the American context typically identified as problems of race. For black Americans had been flocking northwards in search of work both during and after the Second World War. As they did so, bringing their own traditional sense of relative deprivation, they came into conflict with the established values and prejudices of urban whites, further accelerating their drift to the suburbs.

The civil rights movement which gained speed after 1954 at first took an essentially non-violent form, but at Little Rock in 1957 there occurred the first signs of the trouble to come in the South itself. Thereafter Northerners tended to blame all the trouble, in North and South, on Southern resistance to civil rights, and under Presidents Kennedy and Johnson the determination of the North to eliminate further trouble by enforcing integration by Federal authority has aptly been termed 'the Second Reconstruction'. In the 1960s white diehards found their first champion in Governor George Wallace of Alabama; it was Nixon's successful mission in 1972 to convince them that he could do all that Wallace could do for them and, in addition, win. This resistance has been seen, with some reason, as a native variant of the fascism of the European middle classes, but to see it in those sorts of class terms is to ignore the extent to which the growing working class in the newly industrializing South found itself too torn by the anxieties of the period. Wallace's brand of conservatism stirred echoes in urban areas well into the North, and the lesson was not lost on Republican political managers.

In the Northern inner cities the issue was that of power. Were blacks to have the same access to power and influence as other ethnic groups had gained before them? The question lay at the foundation of the correctness of the view of the United States as a 'pluralist' society, a view stemming from the important study of New Haven, Connecticut, by Robert A. Dahl (1961). Dahl and his associates used six different methods to assess the distribution of power and influence in the city over a century and a half. They studied the history of the incumbency of offices, the current participation in politics of identifiable groups of 'notables', the process of decision-making in selected 'issue areas', the sampling both of subleaders in issue areas and of registered voters to determine the extent of their participation and the analysis of actual voting patterns at elections. They concluded that although the city was not run by a secret oligarchy, nor indeed by the mass of the voters, its stability was explicable in terms of a relatively small number of professional politicians with access to a relatively high level of power having to solicit support from a diffuse mass of individuals and groups with varying degrees, but lesser ones, of power or influence (cf. Riesman, Glazer and Denney 1961).

Dahl subsequently put forward a view of the American political system which attached positive value to the maximum possible amount of interaction by the greatest number of organized groups. Thus recognizing the importance of interest groups in the actual workings of 'Madisonian democracy', the pluralists offered a seemingly satisfactory explanation of American democracy as a democracy despite the evident unimportance and powerlessness of individuals as individuals in 'mass society'.

It was the unspoken assumption that all Americans *could* thus combine effectively to mobilize influence in favour of their demands that the resistance to the civil rights movement for blacks seemed to deny. Among the pluralists David Riesman, who described himself as 'a romantic pluralist', had, it was true, offered a slightly different interpretation of American society, based on the role of 'veto groups'. 'These groups are too many and diverse to be led by moralizing,' he suggested; 'what they want is too various to be moralised and too intangible to be bought off for cash alone; and what is called political leadership consists, as we could see in Roosevelt's case, in the tolerant ability to manipulate coalitions' (Riesman, Glazer and Denney 1961, p. 211). Such an interpretation seemed to fit the facts of the civil rights controversy closely, though in the indignation caused by the assassinations first of John F. Kennedy and subsequently, in 1968, of Martin Luther King both legislation spurred by moral outrage and the money to make it effective were made available by Congress. Characteristically, it took the form not of a single, carefully worked out and directed pattern of action but of a multiplicity of programmes designed to deal with each and every aspect of a problem separately. Under Lyndon Johnson there arose more than 400 programmes to tackle the problems of poverty.

It was E. E. Schattschneider who expressed the view that the defects of the pluralist view amounted to a consistent bias in the favour of one class: 'The flaw in the pluralist heaven is that the heavenly chorus sings with a strong upper class accent' (Schattschneider 1961, p. 35). The interest group system was biased, in that membership of voluntary organizations was closely related to upper social and economic status; non-voting was 'a characteristic of the poorest, least well-established, least educated stratum of the community' (ibid., p. 105), and the propensity to vote was generally skewed on class lines.

It was on access to education that the public collision had come in the civil rights controversy. What, then, were the findings of empirical research on the relationship of education to social mobility? The principle of universal public education had been enshrined in legislation in the United States as early as 1787; around 1830, not without opposition, its implementation had become general, and the establishment of the land grant colleges had at least in theory realized the dream of universal education to the highest level. Among academics in the United States in the 1960s there were many, moreover, who had benefited from the educational opportunities made available to veterans of the Second World War and Korean War (1950–3) under the GI Bill. They did not need to be reminded that educational policy was virtually the only area in which government in the United States could foster equality through direct administrative or legislative action. The advantages of the American system were its completeness, its universality (private schooling was extremely rare) and its efficiency. Its disadvantage was its particularism: there were 3164 directly elected school boards with responsibility for education in the United States and over 4000 universities.

The Equality of Educational Opportunity (EEO) survey carried out in 1965 under the Civil Rights Act of 1964 covered 600,000 students in Grades One, Three, Six, Nine and Twelve. It was designed primarily to ascertain whether and where racial bias occurred, not to determine the influence of socioeconomic status or class; but its report, which confirmed that the nation's school system was, in fact, almost wholly segregated in terms of race, concluded that socioeconomic status was the main factor determining educational differentials when individual factors had been excluded.

schools bring little influence to bear on a child's achievement that is independent of his background and general social context ... this very lack of an independent effect means that the inequalities imposed on children by their home, neighborhood, and peer environment are carried along to become the inequalities with which they confront adult life at the end of school. For equality of educational opportunity through the schools must imply a strong effect of schools that is independent of the child's immediate social environment, and that strong independent effect is not present in American schools. [Coleman, Campbell et al. 1966, p. 325]

On the other hand, the retrospective cohort data utilized in the 1960 survey Project Talent indicated that schools, far from functioning as structures maintaining inequality among students, as surveys of enrolled students such as the EEO survey seem to indicate, function as important channels of both upward and (as should also be expected) downward mobility (Hauser 1970, p. 124). The conclusions, therefore, remain prisoners of the methodology employed, for in the nature of things cohort analyses, if they are to be effective, take persistent effort over a long period. But the extreme pessimism expressed by some of the more radical critics of American society would appear to be premature.

Certainly, the American school system, being neighbourhood-based, does not inculcate specifically status-linked attitudes, and though there are (contrary to European belief) very pronounced regional differences of accent in the United States, neither accent nor education in itself is automatically interpreted as an indicator of social status. There is no distinctive 'working-class culture' in the United States, such as appears to exist in European societies (Sennett and Cobb 1977, preface). As many observers have pointed out, beginning perhaps with Vance Packard (1961), so many of the gradations of social status in the United States depend on evidence of material success, as it is a geographically mobile society replenished by immigration, that economic resources are habitually exchanged for social status in a way that in a European society would be very difficult. On the other hand, as Sennett and Cobb point out, if all are equal in the eyes of society, then an individual who does *not* succeed suffers from an unreasonable amount of personal guilt (Sennett and Cobb 1977, p. 256).

France

It seems particularly appropriate to conclude this discussion of the applications of the concept of class in different countries with France, the country in which the concept originated.

The country of Quesnay and Turgot experienced, after the First World War, a period of static population growth and low industrial output interestingly similar to that upon which Britain entered in the 1970s. The consequence was that it failed to match the rising industrial might of Germany and was easily invaded and occupied in 1940. The depredations of the Occupation and the Liberation left France in 1945 a depressed nation and still a country dominated by an agriculture of small peasant proprietors. With approximately the same population and twice the area of the United Kingdom, it remains today, except in the area around Paris, around Lille in the north and, to a much lesser extent, around Lyon and Marseilles, a largely rural country. France has, however, entered upon a period of very rapid industrialization initiated by the wartime nationalization of large sectors of industry and accelerated by massive investment after the end of the Indo-China War in 1954 (Ardagh 1970). The labour for this expansion has been supplied not only by the agricultural areas but also by large numbers of immigrants, especially those from Algeria and the former French colonies in Africa. As the productivity rather than the size of the workforce has increased, employment for skilled workers has risen, but to date not to the extent that it has displaced a very large number of unskilled posts.

The principal class divisions in France reflect assumptions noticeably different from those made in either Britain or the United States. The government Statistical Institute (INSEE) uses a sevenfold categorization by occupation with two residual groups, which, unlike that in Britain, reflects the distinct role of agriculture in the social scene. The categories are:

Exploitants agricoles (farmers),
Salariés agricoles (farm workers),
Patrons de l'industrie et du commerce (employers),
Professions libérales et cadres supérieurs (members of the liberal professions and senior executives),
Cadres moyens (middle and lower management),
Employés et artisans (white-collar workers and artisans),
Ouvriers (manual workers, divided into *qualifiés, specialisés et manoeuvres*).

No work has yet been done on how French people themselves rank occupations, so it cannot be assumed that these categories also form a continuum of status, still less that they can be assimilated to the popular threefold division of French society into *classes supérieures*, *classes moyennes* and *classes populaires*, as many French observers do (Marceau 1977, p. 9; cf. Marceau 1974, p. 208), for INSEE lists the two agricultural categories first.

Three points, pending further investigation, appear to be reasonably certain. The distinctive position of agricultural owners and employees is no accident. It reflects a feature of French society which goes back to the upheavals of the French Revolution and the consequent ruin of many of the French aristocratic families. Their descendants, like their ancestors, have typically neglected agriculture in favour of work in government (cf. Joussain 1949).

In France, unlike Britain, the upper class has not been assimilated to the middle class, but – more logically – those who hold authority in industry, commerce, government or the professions are popularly regarded as forming the upper class, or upper classes, of a Republican society. The position of the middle classes is correspondingly different. Those occupations considered to be middle-class are less well rewarded and stand lower in popular esteem than their equivalents in Britain, and the line of division between manual and non-manual work runs through this class, and not between classes, other than in the statistical sense.

The divide between non-manual and manual labour does, as in other countries, have social significance in terms of esteem. The expansion of technician and cadre posts resulting from industrialization, on the other hand, does not in this case imply a net shift of occupational structure, in view of the fact that the workforce as a whole has expanded so much. Samples taken in the 1960s showed 73 per cent of respondents in the non-manual sector and 71 per cent in the farm sector following their fathers' occupation. The corresponding figure for the manual sector was 55 per cent, with 35 per cent joining the non-manual sector and 10 per cent the farm sector (Hamilton 1967) – this last figure being higher than that for any other industrial society surveyed (Lipset and Bendix 1959, p. 19). So it seems as if the movement from manual to non-manual work was already well established by that time. Certainly, linguistic usage implies that non-manual work confers significantly higher social status: the French word *salaire*, for example, means 'wage'; the word for 'salary' is *les appointements*.

Advancement into and within the ranks of the upper classes depends on the possession of certain specified qualifications, the range of which is much wider and the definition in each case more precise than that found in Britain or the United States. As in the United States, private education is rare, but this does not mean that the elaborate state system of education facilitates social mobility. On the contrary, the system is highly selective from the age of 11 onwards, with all classes other then the highest ones of the *lycée* or its post-1959 'comprehensive' equivalent, the Collège d'Enseignement Secondaire (CES), leading out of the system and into lower grades of employment at the earliest appropriate age. The bias in the system in favour of the children of the upper classes becomes even more pronounced in the universities and reaches its peak in the case of entry to the Grandes Ecoles, the unique institutions which stand at the peak of the French educational system and whose graduates command the highest positions in French government, industry, commerce and society.

The French educational system, therefore, acts to a much greater extent to conserve the social position of the leading strata than the educational systems of either Britain or the United States, while still admitting new members to the privileged circle. As Marceau puts it:

An upper-class son in the Paris region is virtually sure of educational and occupational success and of maintaining the position in society held by his family of origin. He will acquire the right diplomas, the right connections, the right capital, and the right position despite the massive economic changes of the last twenty-five years. At the other end of the scale, the son of a farmer or of a small provincial town manual worker will be virtually sure of maintaining his. . . . In France as elsewhere there is most movement in the middle levels – it is these strata which have benefited most from the basic economic transformations and whose members are able to use the school system to some extent to acquire 'cultural capital' in the form of diplomas. On the whole, however, they also acquire middle-range qualifications which do not allow long-distance movements. [Marceau 1974, pp. 230–1]

In fact, of the three countries it is France in which the upper classes come nearest to constituting a ruling class, in the sense that at their head there stands a self-conscious, directing elite using its possession of a shared culture as a claim to rule as well as a badge of membership. For this group, which Mosca called the 'political class' and Pareto the 'elite', Raymond Aron prefers the term 'leading strata' (used above), and although he is writing in this respect in a cross-national context (Aron 1967), his term appears especially appropriate here.

As Aron had earlier pointed out in the context of post-Liberation French society (Aron 1950), a distinctive feature of French leadership in that period was the combination of stability, in the sense of continuity with the men of the Third Republic, and challenge, in that a quarter of the electorate habitually voted Communist. This, with only minor fluctuations, it has continued to do until 1981. In contrast with the other great Communist Party of Western Europe, the Italian Communist Party, though, the French Communist Party maintained a rigorously Stalinist line long after it had ceased to be fashionable to do so, and after only a brief flirtation with Eurocommunism M. Marchais returned to unconditional support for the Soviet Union at a time when many of his colleagues were continuing to edge away from it.

There could, therefore, as long as this situation lasted, be no accommodation within the structure of a mixed capitalist society with the ultimate ends of the party which represents the votes of the majority of the French industrial working class. Yet the situation lasted. The control of the elite survived the trauma of the revolution of 1958 which brought de Gaulle back to power and initiated the Fifth Republic, but the Party had worked with de Gaulle down to 1947 and at that time no doubt expected to do so again. In any case, his prestige as the liberator of France was still intact.

It was shaken by the student uprising of June 1968, but not destroyed, and the new political order survived the challenge, though de Gaulle succumbed to his mistake of judgement on the referendum the following year. In the end what turned out to be really significant about the events of 1968 was the fact that the workers of the great state enterprises rejected the call to man the barricades (Seale and McConville 1968; Gretton 1969; Posner 1970).

As early as 1956 survey data had suggested that French workers who voted Communist might not necessarily be as hostile to existing institutions as that act might seem in theory to imply. Over half of those interviewed (53 per cent) thought there was 'confidence' between employees and management in their firms, and over four-fifths felt that their employers were doing their jobs well. On the other hand, only 12 per cent expressed much interest in politics, and their view of the world was most tellingly shown by the fact that 54 per cent considered that the country where workers were best off was the United States (Lipset 1964b).

About the impact of affluence on the lifestyle of French workers there could be no doubt. They shared in the suddenly expanding wealth of their societies, as did the workers of Britain or the United States, shopping at the *supermarché*, buying new cars and an expanding range of household goods and equipping themselves with greater comfort for their substantial annual holidays, which, however, they continued to take mainly, and for preference, in France itself. Most important, they bought a range of food comparable with that bought by other social groups; in this respect the gap between rich and poor was especially narrow. Yet the embourgeoisement of lifestyles was not, it seems, accompanied by a change of political allegiances; rather, at most, by a muting of them, a turning away from politics, which Gaullism, facilitated by de Gaulle's neutralist stand, even-handed posture towards the Soviet Union and emphasis on French tradition and nationalism.

The study of changing political attitudes in France marked in itself a dramatic departure from the traditions of the past. Before 1958 French political parties, keyed as they were to a traditional multi-party system depending on the generation-long dominance of key *notables* in the provinces, had virtually no national electoral organization. Reticence about politics was such that canvassing for votes from door to door, as in Britain, was unknown and would have been considered impolite. In any case, the *concierge* knew the political opinion of all the residents in her apartment block, as she did their personal habits and way of life. With rents frozen since 1914, patterns of residence and land use had been frozen also (Hamilton 1967, p. 280). Gaullism introduced into French politics mass political organization, facilitated by the state control of the radio and television services (ORTF), and at the same time made mass-attitude surveys an essential tool of the new generation of political organizers. That this development is not more closely reflected in the literature of French political science is in itself an indication not only of the difficulty of the task in a country with a fluid multi-party system regionally divided but also of the fact that in France political science has traditionally been a subject leading – and directly – to a career post in the Civil Service (*fonction publique*). The new technocratic *fonctionnaires* of the Pompidou years seemed at times to be almost indifferent to public opinion, and indeed to regard themselves as the creators of it. Paris itself bore the brunt of their technological confidence – witness the *Périphérique*, the motorway through the *quais*, the Centre Georges Pompidou, the cliffs of the Défense, all symbols of the self-assurance of the planners' zeal to embrace the future and a continuity of planning which the system guaranteed regardless of changes in personnel or even of regime.

Less spectacular but no less eloquent evidence of the continuity of French policy was the prosperous state of French agriculture, fostered by the French role in the creation of the European Economic Community and the establishment of its Common Agricultural Policy, which particularly benefited French smaller farmers and gave the rural sectors a share in the general prosperity such as they had never known before. The electrification and mechanization of the French countryside brought about the same transformation of actual living standards there as had occurred in Britain or the United States a generation previously, and with the same result: traditional allegiances were transferred to the parties symbolizing the new age in government. The results of all these changes were most dramatically shown in 1974. In the Presidential election of that year brought about by the death of M. Pompidou the Socialists led by M. Mitterand, who with Communist support were mounting their strongest challenge for control of the system since the Second World War, were defeated by the candidate of the Centre-Right, M. Valéry Giscard d'Estaing, by a margin of less than 1 per cent.

Hamilton in 1967 explained the radicalism of French voters in terms of the rural origins of large sectors of the working class. Having come in the first generation from the countryside, with its clear and visible signs of demarcation, he believed that the French workers with this background tended to be correspondingly more militant than their opposite numbers in Britain or in other countries with a longer-established traditional urban working class (Hamilton 1967, p. 275). Militancy in social terms was most strikingly shown by the refusal of the affluent French worker to move up the social scale in terms of lifestyles. It would indeed be ironic if the conservatism of the French political system had also to be explained by the rural origins of so many of its electors, yet this does indeed seem to be the only possible conclusion. The implications are, however, that class as an explanatory factor serves to complicate rather than to elucidate the distinction between conservatism and radicalism in French politics. Indeed, the distinctions that seem to matter most are not those between the working class and the rest, but those within the working class itself (Touraine 1966).

Since 1974 there have been numerous predictions that the effects of the oil crisis, the world recession and specifically the ending of France's period of post-war growth could accentuate the continuing inequalities in French society to the point at which they become unbearable (Fabius 1975). The elections for the National Assembly in 1979 showed, however, that if this was the case, it was not as yet having any marked effect on the balance of political forces measured in terms of votes or seats. Only in the field of women's rights – an area in which France had long lagged behind either Britain or the United States (Silver 1973) – had the Giscard administration presented a programme of dynamic reform, and government-sponsored changes in the educational system, far from acting to eliminate the element of selection in the system, had actually extended it backwards to the primary-school level (Marceau 1977, p. 190). French education therefore remained highly selective and geared to the supply of vocationally trained personnel for industry in a way that, seen from Britain or the United States, appeared rather to resemble the provision of education in the Soviet Union rather than their own. Most important of all, the process of selection provided for striking continuity among the 'leading strata' at the central governmental level. Yet the evidence supplied by the electorate in 1981 was that it accepted, and indeed welcomed, a governmental system which acted independently and with self-confidence in a divided world, and that the structure of French society was at last able to accommodate to a Socialist Government.

Some comparisons

As these three examples will have shown, there are considerable technical difficulties in applying concepts of social class to cross-national studies of actual societies. The basic criteria of occupation and wealth may be simple enough to ascertain. But each has snags: the definition of occupations varies substantially from country to country; the boundary line between manual and non-manual is generally regarded as significant but is differently regarded in different countries; and the gap between urban and rural occupations may be seen as a matter of class, or region, or both. Wealth too is divided between the possessors of capital and the receivers of income, between the employer and the employee, and according to various grades of assurance in the continued receipt of it such as may be guaranteed by terms of contract, pension schemes or the backing of powerful trade unions. It should also be noted that in the period since 1945 the prevalence of inflation and the artificial effects on exchange rates of the relationships of world trade make what look like deceptively simple statistics on wealth or income distribution treacherously misleading. According to official statistics, a Bolivian peasant does not earn enough to live on, but Bolivian peasants do survive and the Bolivian population is, in fact, increasing at the rate of about 3 per cent per year.

Together wealth and occupation interact with one another in a complex fashion to give a picture of a complex social structure which certainly bears little or no resemblance to Marx's predicted antithesis between proletariat and bourgeoisie. But the embourgeoisement of the proletariat has not, on the other hand, led to significant changes in working-class voting habits, even where it has been accompanied by modifications in the stated positions of the political parties concerned.

Marxist writers, particularly since the depression of 1974, have found it hard to suppress their astonishment that the issue of class conflict in Western societies should not be more prominent, but in reality this is just what we should expect if economic conditions do not affect political allegiances as such. Of course, they may and, as V. O. Key, Jr (1964), was the first to show in the case of the United States, frequently do affect the outcome of individual elections, but this in itself acts as a safety valve, and failure to win elections in apparently favourable conditions, as in France, may deflate a party's pretensions quite as effectively as the experience of actually having to manage a modern economy. In all three countries the fact that their political systems have in recent years been unable to deliver the goods that people have come to expect has led less to the making of an alternative choice than to a strong feeling that governments may not be able to do as much to regulate economic conditions as they have been encouraged to believe. Significantly, the country least affected by this tendency at the moment appears to be France, protected by a favourable international regime and, unlike Britain, not dependent for basic subsistence on imported foodstuffs. British Governments, even Conservative ones, receive only a small proportion of their support from farmers, and to encourage farming they have to make their urban supporters of all social strata pay for it. The urban–rural divide, therefore, remains everywhere of more than incidental importance.

The three countries, however, exhibit the most striking differences in the way in which education acts to form the 'leading strata' of society. The element of education appears to be of greatest importance in France and of least in the United States, where the ability to win elections at local level is the most useful qualification for higher candidature. But in each case the significance of education is not so much that it fails to facilitate the rise of the 'lower classes' as much as it might but that it tends to conserve the social position of the descendants of those initially advantaged. In each case, however, the evidence has to be handled with more care than the summary here presented may indicate. For if the individual exception does not necessarily refute the existence of a general trend, the general trend is, in the last resort, made up only of the sum total of the life experiences of a large number of individuals. The moral is that all general statements about social classes or strata should be regarded as not proven unless accompanied by some empirical evidence and – no less important – by a statement of the concept of class on which it is based.

8   The end of class?

When we look at the present state of the concept of class we find it is
a state of considerable confusion. From the taxonomy of definitions
built up in the earlier chapters we found how the roots of this
confusion are implicit in the growth of the term, and no less in the
constellation of terms that surround it both in political discourse
and in the writings of political scientists. It is true, perhaps, that at
any one time, in any one area, we can reach a definition of class that
is reasonably stable and on which a majority of the inhabitants of
the country concerned would agree. But when we enter the
transnational world we encounter severe difficulties of incompati-
bility between the different measuring instruments employed;
certainly, the internationalization of class is not as straightforward a
matter as it appears to have seemed to Marx and Engels in 1848,
when in retrospect we can see that the unity of Europe had already
been disrupted.

Class as economic standing

The idea of class as a measure of economic resources is fundamental. All else follows from this. It originated as a term for the major
economic divisions of society among the followers of the Physiocrats and Turgot, but by a semantic confusion between the
economic term and its classical roots came to incorporate the
political connotations of the legal divisions of Greek and Roman
society for taxation purposes. Its popularity stemmed from the fact
that in an age when the old boundaries between estates broke down
under the impact of the French Revolution economic distinctions
assumed a new importance for individuals seeking to order their
turbulent societies in terms of a private map of the social universe.

Class is, however, a valueless concept in ordering the economic
universe unless defined in economic terms rather than political

ones. Economic resources in themselves do not form an adequate basis, or these form a continuum and not a series of discrete categories, and in any case conventions of privacy make it difficult to relate studies of individuals to the official statistics of wealth and income, and quite properly so. Conventionally class is equated, therefore, with membership of occupational groupings, even though both the division and the ranking of the divisions of these present very serious conceptual problems.

The ranking of occupational groupings in economic terms alone would be a difficult enough task if everyone in each group received exactly the same rewards. But of course they do not, even in terms of wages or salaries. Younger and less skilled workers receive less than older and more skilled ones. Some receive less when they start: others more. The scales on which they are paid may be longer or shorter, and their rate of progression along them depends not merely on the occupation but also on the individual's good fortune and degree of competence. Benefits may be paid not merely in money but also in kind, and even where they have a calculable equivalent in monetary terms, that equivalent depends on other, outside factors, such as rates of taxation, and not merely on the individual's own income. The assessment of such benefits as pensions, moreover, can only be made in average terms, as a substantial number of people pay for pensions they never live to collect; so that in assessing the relationship of one job to another, the probabilities of benefit depend not only on the quantity of work to be performed during an average lifetime but also on the quality of the working conditions and the extent to which this affects the health and wellbeing of the worker concerned.

The division of occupational groupings, therefore, traditionally followed that divide between manual and non-manual labour which we have repeatedly seen reflected in the status ascribed to individual jobs. But, as we have also seen, even that division of status differs from one society to another, and it does not equate in any way with the differences in status accorded to those who control others and those whose task is simply to carry out instructions. And neither coincides with Marx's division between the possessors of capital and those who lack capital and are therefore forced to sell their labour power. Very few people in modern non-communist societies now fall squarely into either category.

In fact, the division was already invalid in Marx's own time, when he hailed – of all things! – the joint stock company as the possible pattern of the social organization of the egalitarian future, for it was this form of social organization which permitted the separation of ownership and control in the management of industry. On the one hand, managers became, like those they managed, salaried employees, employed on contract for as long as their services might be required. On the other, ownership became increasingly diffused. From the company to the corporation owning many subsidiaries, from the corporation to the holding company, from the holding company to the pension fund or the building or finance company spreading its capital over many enterprises, the ownership of industry, even in the so-called 'capitalist' states, has become increasingly remote from the employees, whatever their position in the structure of management. And by this roundabout route it has eventually come into the hands of the workers themselves, sometimes as savers or insured persons, more often as voters for the Government that manages the affairs of the state.

Again even in the so-called 'socialist' countries there remain substantial numbers of self-employed persons of widely differing incomes and statuses who are tolerated because they are essential and by the dispensation that they do not exploit others. Neither, of course, do their opposite numbers in the 'capitalist' countries. Their right to offer their services on the market is indeed being taken up increasingly by others, who not only work for themselves in ways which, as we have seen, enable them to enjoy a much higher standard of living than their income would once have permitted but also take on second jobs. Who is to say which of their jobs, primary or secondary, gives them the more satisfaction? At least the variety of employment offers them a change, which in any case, over the century since Marx's time, has been supplemented by a varied and substantial range of leisure activities and inactivities.

The question of the rewards for work is certainly closely related to the nature of work itself, yet it is just here that the post-Marxist concept of class is most in need of reconsideration. For work is a word of many meanings. In the simplest form, as the engineer uses it, it refers simply to the conversion of one form of energy into some other form. In this sense all movement is work. Work can also have the overtones of heavy labour, of toil, of strain or of repetition and boredom. Work in this sense, in appalling conditions and for very long hours, was a common feature of the first century of the Industrial Revolution. It has therefore been assumed that such work was the product of capitalism, and it has been deduced from that that the abolition of capitalism would result in the ending of onerous or dangerous working conditions. Through his theory of surplus value Marx indeed sought to prove that the welfare of the rich was produced by the misery of the poor and that the logic of capitalism was to make the working conditions of the masses worse.

The historical experience of the last century is that working conditions in the advanced capitalist countries have, on the contrary, improved. Factories and workshops have become cleaner and safer places. Machines now undertake many of the tasks formerly requiring the effort of men, and in particular heavy lifting jobs have been largely eliminated. Assembly-line working, increasingly mechanized, has been made rather more interesting and tasks have been reorganized to keep interest up. Really dangerous jobs attract very high pay in part-compensation, but the trend of over a century of legislation has been towards the elimination of every avoidable risk, legislation prompted by the relentless interest of strong trade unions and a vocal and watchful public. The many exceptions to each and every one of these points demonstrate that there can be no grounds for complacency, but they do not prove that Marx's prediction was right.

To say this is not, however, to say why it was wrong, and it is not sufficient to say that he made incorrect projections from the data available, though this is certainly true. His mistake was of a different kind: it was to make the assumption that industrial work was fundamentally different from the agricultural work that had preceded it, in that it had necessarily to be performed in unpleasant surroundings and with excessive risk. Today agricultural labour is still performed in the open air, but partly for that reason it is now regarded as among the more dangerous occupations. The nineteenth-century factory, with its drive shafts, unguarded belts and hazardous stairs and catwalks, can be seen as the temporary product of an inadequate technology, the modification of which has occurred regardless of the theoretical nature of the economic system. And, freed from at least a few of the prejudices of the past, we can now recognize that labour formerly exclusively the duty of women – that of grinding corn, preparing food, finding the next meal, washing clothes and so forth – which is even older than the tasks of agriculture which they shared in developing, was in its traditional form boring to a degree that modern man can hardly imagine. Anyone who does not believe this to be true should try grinding enough wheat into flour to feed a family for a day using only a traditional stone quern, a task performed daily by the temporary inhabitants of the Iron Age village reconstituted in Dorset in 1978.

The rich too were there in Iron Age times. Their existence long predates the onset of the Industrial Revolution, as does the concentration of wealth by trade and commerce which helped to finance it. If the rich are the product of capitalism, then capitalism has been around a very long time in human history, and reports of its impending demise are probably premature.

For in modern society the division between rich and poor reflects an obsolete calculus, too unsophisticated to be able to deal adequately with the detailed relationships between the holders of limitless gradations and permutations of social resources. Today's techniques of investigation already enable us to probe much more deeply into the question of what is meant by relative economic standing than was possible even, say, twenty years ago. It is therefore no longer necessary to divide our populations into a few crude categories simply because we could not hope to assess the relationships between more complicated ones, and before assuming that only a few simple categories will do, we have to prove it. Nor is it an excuse that people are unlikely to want to supply us with the information we would need. If they do not, and they are perfectly entitled not to, then we owe it to them to admit that we cannot prove it.

If we still believe, with Marx, that this panorama of economic resources is, despite current evidence, bound to lead in the end to two opposed, conflicting classes, then we have also to resolve the meaning of the point of transition between the two in terms of the transfer of consciousness which it must, under Marx's assumptions, imply. Without the concept of class-consciousness, Marx's view of the evolution and future tendency of classes would lose its principal foundation and motivation. Yet the assessment of consciousness leads us out of the world of economics – which, however complex, still seems ultimately to be capable of exposition in objective, material terms – into the unseeable and insubstantial realm of the mind. It is indeed an irony that Marx's attempt to understand history in materialist terms as the struggle between classes should now depend for its possible justification wholly on the subjective basis of consciousness.

Class-as-status

Certainly, it is this subjective view of class as a membership, a fellow feeling, a sharing of beliefs, assumptions and ways of looking at society, that seems to mean most to ordinary people. They perceive class as something that summarizes their position in relation to their fellows. Mostly this means for them not a simple economic relationship but a set of social ones, and the gradations of relationships expressed in these terms sociologists since Weber have chosen to term 'status'.

In the assessment of relative social position, occupation and economic standing both play important roles. Empirical evidence demonstrates, however, that the precise nature of the role varies from society to society, and that, indeed, there may be very substantial differences in the way that very large sectors of society, typically the agrarian sector, are regarded by different societies, despite the fact that they appear outwardly to be at very similar stages of economic development.

Though there is no prima facie reason to suppose that there must be a general rank ordering of occupations in public esteem in any given society, in practice this does seem to be the case, even in so-called 'primitive societies', where such distinct occupations as arbitrator or medicine man are both recognized and venerated. The division of labour, it seems, has always been accompanied by a ranking of occupations. But it does not follow that the ranking will be along a single continuum. Both branching and parallel hierarchies are to be seen in all complex societies.

The term 'stratification' that is generally applied to the study of such social gradings and rankings is a misleading one. It suggests a degree of permanence and stability that is not found in practice, for social mobility exists in the most rigidly stratified societies and is considerable in all industrial countries, where it is aided by geographical mobility. Social status depends neither on subjective evaluation nor on objective evaluation of position by others, but on the assertion of a claim to status which is accepted, or acceptance of a status which is offered, or both. Far from social stratification being the principal cause of dissension in society, therefore, it appears that most people, most of the time, accept their position in society for what it is worth and, with it, accept the assumptions that govern the ascribing of status to individuals in that society. Indeed 'stratification' acts, according to some writers, to stabilize the social order by enshrining a mutually compatible view of social relationships which avoids too much dissonance on the part of the individual. It does not seem likely, though, that any one individual really needs a picture of the stratification of the entire society to do that – if, indeed, the contention is true. The stratification of society, in this sense, may merely be, and probably is, only the observers' summary of the overall ranking of the microsocieties in which each individual actually dwells and, to that extent, the product of the techniques of investigation that purport to reveal it.

Even if this is not so, if social classes have an objective independent existence as constructs of status, we must take great care not to assume that in thus identifying them we have located the true root and meaning of class in the Marxian sense. Class-as-status cannot simply be substituted for economic class in the way that is common in popular literature both in Britain and in the United States. The concepts are related but not interchangeable.

Class as power

The concept of class as an association of individuals holding a similar relationship to power is something that ultimately we owe to the ancients.

To the Greeks and Romans classes (in so far as their concept of these in any way resembles ours) were based on recognized grades of economic resources, defined in strict legal terms. Economic position in society conferred not only rights but also duties. It was the duty to take part in the running of the state thatt high economic status conferred that was copied in England in the Middle Ages in the various requirements that men of certain position should assume the status and responsibility of knighthood, take on political and military leadership and administer justice either directly or subsequently as a magistrate on behalf of the crown.

The failure of the nobility in France adequately to discharge these or similar duties led, in the French Revolution, to their overthrow in favour of a classical Republic in which all were to be equal. It was at this point that the concept of class emerged to grade the equals, since the concept of estate which had served since the high Middle Ages would no longer serve the new conditions. This did not in itself mean that those who ruled the state now came from different backgrounds. It meant, rather, that instead of being described as an estate, they were now regarded as a class. Where previously they would have been appointed to a formal rank that marked their position now, like anyone else, they had to assert it.

For Marx himself it was natural to assume the equation between economically advantaged class and ruling class. Pareto and, more particularly, Mosca were later to draw a distinction between the two. Lenin asserted that economic status and the right to rule had been sundered by the October Revolution. Mao Tse-tung sought to eliminate, through the device of 'permanent revolution', all trace of class from Chinese society, so that there could never again be any question of the equation of class and rule. But as Stalin recognized, in his cynical way, if wealth does not bring the right to rule, rule has always brought the right to wealth, and every attempt to devise a wholly egalitarian society in modern times has foundered on the inability to restrain the powerful from acquiring a disproportionate share of the society's goods.

The number of these powerful has never been large. Certainly, it has never extended over a grouping of society as wide and comprehensive as a class, in the sense that all the individuals designated as a class in Marxian terms do, or could, hold official positions that entitle them to administer the affairs of others. Indeed, Marx himself seems to have specifically ruled out the equation of power in his ideal state with that in already existing society, and his followers have seen rule in the socialist states as being exercised on behalf of, as opposed to by, the members of the proletariat and peasantry. If we deny the title of 'ruling class' to the proletariat in these circumstances, however, we must be consistent and deny it also to any other class – for instance, the so called 'bourgeoisie' in what the Russians and Chinese (amongst themselves) still persist in regarding as the 'bourgeois states'. It does not help to separate the concept of ruling class from the concept of dominant class, as the revisionist Marxists have tried to do, for what has to be demonstrated is the clear and consistent identification not just of interests but also of action, and this has not been done.

Class as an essentially contested concept

The fact is that however far we stretch our taxonomy of definitions, we will never find a concept of class that is universally acceptable. As a term applicable to a division between human beings, it must require the separation of these beings on each side of the divide. A society with only one class is by definition inconceivable, for a society with only one class is a society with no classes. To have any classes a society must have at least two. As we have seen, even the Soviet Union has two classes, officially recognized as such (the workers and the peasants), which are regarded as 'non-antagonistic'. Classless, therefore, the Soviet Union is not, and the question of the absence of antagonism is one which, as we have seen, has increasingly attracted the attention not only of Western critics but also of the East European revisionists.

At this stage I wish to turn from the practical consequences of the in-built division to the theoretical ones.

If there must always be at least two classes, however they may be composed, it will follow that there will always be two views of what class is, depending on which side of the divide the speaker stands. It does not follow inevitably that they will be very different, still less antagonistic, but they will be different.

There is reason, therefore, to suspect that class might well be what Gallie has called an 'essentially contested concept', one of a family of concepts 'the proper use of which inevitably involves endless disputes about their proper uses on the part of their users' (Gallie 1956). Gallie lists five characteristics of an essentially contested concept:

(i) It must be *appraisive* in the sense that it signifies or accredits some type of valued achievement.

(ii) This achievement must be of an internally complex character, for all that it is worth is attributed to it as a whole.

(iii) Any explanation of its worth must therefore include reference to the respective contributions of its various parts or features; yet prior to experimentation there is nothing absurd or contradictory in any one of a number of possible relevant descriptions of its total worth, one such description setting its component parts or features in one order of importance, a second setting them in a second order, and so on. In fine, the accredited achievement is *initially* variously describable.

(iv) The accredited achievement must be of a kind that admits of considerable modification in the light of changing circumstances and such modification cannot be prescribed or predicted in advance.

|(v)| ... to use an essentially contested concept means to use it both aggressively and defensively. |Gallie 1955-6, pp. 171-2|

Can class be said to be an essentially contested concept in this sense? I think that it can, but, as can be seen from Gallie's conditions, this definition will involve a considerable reappraisal of what we mean when we talk about class.

Certainly, when we talk about class, economic, social or political, we appraise the relative standing of individuals and evaluate statuses. But can class be regarded as an achievement? No doubt there are many who see it in just that light yet would not recognize it as such until the fact was pointed out to them, but insofar as the element of rank ordering has been demonstrated to be inseparable from all concepts of class as commonly used, the point appears to be made. If high standing is esteemed more than low standing, then the achievement of high standing, in the terms in which a society recognizes it, is an achievement and is commonly valued as such. As Blount (1969) pointed out, in Roman society those individuals who were in the first class, *classici*, were regarded as outstanding and as examples to others.

Certainly, too, the achievement must indeed be of 'an internally complex character', for, whichever definition of class we accept, its evaluation can be, and has been shown to be, a complicated one in view of the number of criteria to be applied and the competition between authorities for the special value of their chosen criteria. Even if we accept the notion of class as an economic gradation, the evidence for economic position, as shown by dress, manners, behaviour, display and the rest, is inconclusive.

In the 1950s the writer Nancy Mitford provoked an intense debate in Britain over the meaning and social importance attached to different words in everyday speech. Her contention was that certain words were characteristically used automatically by individuals of high social standing, the 'upper class'; these words were, to use the term invented by Alan Ross, 'U' (Mitford 1956; Ross 1969). The words and phrases for the same articles or actions used normally by people of lower social standing, which were 'non-U', were in themselves irrefutable evidence of this lower status. It was therefore important to avoid the misuse of these words. It was legitimately argued by Miss Mitford's critics that her assessment of which words conferred high social status was in itself subjective, based on her own position within the social system as the daughter of a peer, and the 'U' and 'non-U' controversy tailed off, as such controversies do, into a syllabus of social errors.

The controversy had done much, however, to demonstrate the frailty of the criteria by which many human beings choose to rank themselves and others. These criteria are, characteristically but not exclusively, those set by the established members of the 'upper classes' as the indicators of their exclusiveness. They are, therefore, in a position to change any or all of them, just as soon as they believe that they are no longer fulfilling their function of keeping outsiders out. (To return to our example, it soon became 'non-U' to describe things as 'U' or 'non-U'!)

To this extent, therefore, I would agree with Parkin's contention that we can regard status systems as systems, in Weberian terms, of social closure. 'By social closure Weber means the process by which social collectives seek to maximize rewards by restricting access to resources and opportunities to a limited circle of eligibles' (Parkin 1979, p. 44). He argues that this is done through a combination of property and qualifications (for example, degrees and diplomas), which provide access not only to ascribed status but also, more important, to jobs, money and power. But there are two reservations we should make. Strategies of social closure do exist no doubt, but do they work? Some certainly do – one cannot practise as a doctor or a lawyer without passing the necessary examinations. But access to wealth or political power is a different case altogether; here closure strategies do not have the same effect and may, indeed, fail completely. Moreover, such devices, significantly, work to exclude individuals, not other social collectivities, and it is precisely for this reason that class and status remain fluid and indefinable across time in empirically recognizable ways.

As the Russians and Chinese have so drastically demonstrated, it is possible for any ruling group to enforce the reversal of the criteria that entitle men to power. Since economic and social status follow power, in due course they will do so; but the alteration, or even reversal, of class implied by the transfer of power is not automatically accompanied by a reversal of status. There is no guarantee that popular usage will follow legal definition. Since all three criteria are involved, the consequences of any one decree are not wholly predictable, and in this respect the fourth of Gallie's conditions is undoubtedly fulfilled.

The concept of class has certainly proved to be capable of extensive modification in the light of changing circumstances, and the fact that it has done so stems from the flexibility it has gained from the very variety of criteria on which it can draw, the impossibility of predicting before the event which will be more relevant and the difficulty of arbitrating between different claims based on widely differing criteria (Gallie's third condition). Indeed, its ability to change its basis is to such an extent its most striking feature that we might be forgiven for suspecting that 'class' is not a term that describes things as they are at all. It is rather a term that describes things as people would like them to be, a statement not about fact but about aspiration.

As such it is, inevitably, mobile. Since people's circumstances may at any time change very drastically, for better or for worse, it follows that their picture of class must change too, as it follows their notion of their place in the scheme of things. It is perhaps solely because of this that the concept of class has come so ideally to conform to Gallie's fifth condition: it is used both aggressively and defensively. It is used aggressively to deflate the pretensions of others. It is used defensively *by the same people* to protect their own self-image. There is, in fact, virtually no word in the political vocabulary that is more often used in both these ways, often in the same sentence and invariably in defence of positions which, however obviously they may be repugnant to one's political opponents, are defended in terms that suggest that they are self-evident to all sane and reasonable people. Since this is apparently not so, it must follow that there is something missing in the speaker's understanding of the full complexity of the world or of the word.

So great, in fact, is the aggression attached to the use of the word 'class' that, as with 'race' and 'nation', it has been expressed in our century in the most striking form of all, by the wholesale slaughter of men, women and children as 'class enemies'. Those responsible for the slaughter have, once again, sought to justify the maintenance of their own position on the very same grounds as they have sought the right to destroy their political opponents.

It appears that the concept of class does indeed fulfil the five conditions of 'essential contestedness' suggested by Gallie. It does not necessarily follow that class itself is an 'essentially contested concept'. To prove this beyond doubt we should have to show that it was *impossible* to resolve the meaning of the concept in terms acceptable to everyone. It is not sufficient to demonstrate that the resolution has not been achieved, since we could be dealing with a concept that has just been ill defined or inadequately analysed.

Gallie suggests that to show that a concept cannot be resolved two further conditions are necessary. The first is that there should be an original exemplar of the concept whose authority is acknowledged by all the contestant users of the concept. The second is that the continued use of the concept should enable the original meaning of the exemplar to be developed in such a fashion as to provide a further incentive for a continuous competition between the users of the concept.

It is probably widely believed that the original exemplar of the concept is to be found in Marx's own usage. Such is clearly not the case. The concept of class was in use for some seventy years before it fell into the hands of Marx, and Marx left it, as he found it, with no settled definition. We must seek further for an exemplar if one is to be found.

We find not one but three. First in historical time is the legal concept of class in ancient Greece or Rome. But it is in the highest degree improbable that the classical models of class as conflict and class as co-operation are known directly today to the huge majority of those who are familiar with the modern concepts. In neither of the great super-powers of today, the United States and the Soviet Union, is a knowledge of the classics a natural part of the mental baggage of every educated party member. Second comes the concept of an estate, once the common property of medieval Europe and implanted in the structure of the legal codes in such a way as to make it seem that indeed they embodied the structure of class dominance. Third comes the economic concept of class, developed by the Physiocrats and Turgot and transmitted through Ricardo to Marx and his followers.

We are dealing, then, with not one but three exemplars, whose effect is disjunctive in the sense that each has been severally transmuted by its nineteenth-century reinterpretation and is inseparable from its commentary. The classical concept of class was not formed but transformed by Marx, who attributed to it a meaning in society which was the inverse of that previously ascribed, and it was in this inversion of values, in fact, that his chief claim to originality lay. As Gallie pointed out in his discussion of the concept of art, it is probably not necessary for there to be only one exemplar for the case for 'essential contestedness' to be proved, provided that there is a number of exemplars which are each of a sufficiently wide application to overlap one another in public acceptance. Class thus conforms to his actual examples, if not exactly to the first of his specified conditions. The second of them, that there should be such continuous interaction between the exemplars as to provide incentive for endless competition between users of the concept has been met in full over the past century.

If, then, I would argue, class is an essentially contested concept, it is a waste of time to attempt to establish a meaning for it that will command universal acceptance, for the value of the term lies in the fact that that task is impossible. What we have to do, rather, is to accept that class is an appraisive term designating social achievement, which is used in phrases giving a favourable connotation to those things of which one approves and an unfavourable one to those things of which one does not approve. We can then continue to use it with due caution, provided that we do not seek to evaluate it in its own terms.

Above all, we must beware of the special pitfalls that lie in wait if we attempt to subject it to rationalization in terms of modern political science. Advances in computation have certainly made it possible to test many traditional assumptions about politics and society using empirical data, and this is, in fact, the foundation of any real hope for a fuller and deeper understanding of politics. We cannot, however, simply adapt to this task concepts that are wholly evaluative, unless we can specify the dimension or dimensions along which they are to be measured and can provide the data for evaluation. Hard data about economic processes are certainly available, but they do not measure class itself; they only provide a number of 'indicators' of class standing whose relationship to the evaluation of class is in itself uncertain. The hardness of the data, therefore, cannot make up for the softness of the concept.

This is hard to accept, for we are all familiar with the notion of indicators, and we like to rely upon their objectivity to steer us through our complicated world. If a person has a temperature, for example, this is an indication that the mechanism controlling body temperature is responding to a stimulus, which, experience in the past has shown us, is usually an invasion of the body tissues by bacteria or viruses. We deduce that this is likely to be the case and act accordingly; at least we know that there is something wrong, and this makes everyone, including the patient, feel better. Not all individuals conform to the customarily accepted 'norm' for the temperature of a healthy human being (37°C); there is, in fact, a considerable range of variation in the population, in individual families and in individuals themselves. The reading on the thermometer which may be indicative of a fever in one member of the family may represent bounding good health for another. Nevertheless, to throw the thermometer into the dustbin simply because it cannot be relied upon to give a verdict independently of surrounding conditions in all times and in all circumstances would be patently foolish.

But is this the case with class? The word itself is of little or no value; the indicators are unreliable. Yes, experience has shown that in any given society people who have more money tend to behave with more freedom and effect than people who have less – if only for the obvious reason that their greater resources enable them to do more things. But what is great wealth for one society may be dire poverty for another. In one society we can determine gradations and differences between individuals, and it is tempting therefore to use this simple indicator of wealth, with its limited capacity for reflecting accurately relative standing in the economic sense, as evidence of the existence of the concept of class. Nothing could be more dangerous. The indicator gives a clue to the amount of free, disposable resources the individual is likely to have to spare, but it tells us nothing about how they are actually used, still less how he is going to want to use them. To conclude that all individuals in the same band of income will behave in the same way is to make an unwarranted assumption which common sense tells us is not justified, to judge by actual behaviour in travel agents, gambling casinos or supermarkets. So it must necessarily be with all other indicators of economic resources. And when we turn from the economic to the social we enter that world of subjective assertion and objective response which makes class such a fascinating and such a dangerous concept.

Should we, therefore, abandon the concept of class altogether? The answer is almost certainly yes. As a legal concept, it has had its day. As an economic concept, it has too many snags to be measured. As an evaluation of social status, the use of the word serves only to blur the evaluative use of the word 'status' itself. This, being itself of respectable ancestry, could well serve to represent this curious quirk of the human mind for as long as human beings continue to practise such evaluations.

Whether or not they should be encouraged to make such evaluations about one another and to state them as fact is another matter. Our present century has already seen the elimination of a number of forms of discrimination between religions, between races and between the sexes. Racism is widely regarded as abhorrent. Religious bigotry is undergoing something of a revival, but there are hopeful signs that this revival is far from universally welcomed. Sexism has hardly been touched upon except in the world's most liberal societies, just those, in fact, from which come the majority of complaints about its persistence. But it is probably not too soon to consider tackling 'classism' on the same condition: that we work to eliminate arbitrary distinctions wherever they occur and regardless of the strength of those who give them currency.

Bibliography

ABRAHAMSON, Mark, MIZRUCHI, Ephraim H., and HORNUNG, Carlton A. (1976), *Stratification and Mobility*, London: Collier Macmillan

ABRAMS, Mark, and ROSE, Richard (1960), *Must Labour Lose?*, Harmondsworth: Penguin Books

ACKER, Joan (1973), 'Women and social stratification, a case of intellectual sexism', *American Journal of Sociology*, vol. LXXVIII, no. 4, pp. 936–45

ANDERSON, Charles H. (1974), *The Political Economy of Social Class*, Englewood Cliffs, NJ: Prentice-Hall

ANDERSON, P., and BLACKBURN, R., eds. (1966), *Towards Socialism*, London: Collins

Anon. (1976), 'Carter!', *Time*, 15 November

AQUINAS, St Thomas (1959), *Aquinas Selected Political Writings*, ed. and intro. A. P. d'Entrèves, trans. J. G. Dawson, Oxford: Blackwell

ARATO, Andrew, and GEBHARDT, Eike, eds. (1978), *The Essential Frankfurt School Reader*, Oxford: Blackwell

ARDAGH, John (1970), *The New France*, Harmondsworth: Penguin Books

ARISTOTLE (1950), *Politics*, trans. H. Rackham, London: Heinemann; Cambridge, Mass.: Harvard University Press

ARISTOTLE (1961), *The Athenian Constitution: The Eudemian Ethics of Virtue and Vices*, trans. H. Rackham, London: Heinemann; Cambridge, Mass.: Harvard University Press

ARON, Raymond (1950), 'Social structure and the ruling class', *British Journal of Sociology*, vol. I, no. 1, pp. 1–16; vol. I, no. 2, pp. 126–43

ARON, Raymond (1967), 'Social class, political class, ruling class', in R. Bendix and S. M. Lipset (eds.), *Class, Status and Power*, 2nd edn, Glencoe, Ill.: Free Press

BAHRO, Rudolf (1978), *The Alternative in Eastern Europe*, London: New Left Books

BARKER, Rodney (1978), *Political Ideas in Modern Britain*, London: Methuen

BELL, Colin (1969), *Middle Class Families, Social and Geographical Mobility*, London: Routledge & Kegan Paul

BELOFF, Max, ed. (1948), *The Federalist*, Oxford: Blackwell

BENDIX, Reinhard, and LIPSET, Seymour Martin, eds. (1967), *Class, Status and Power*, 2nd edn, Glencoe, Ill.: Free Press

BLAU, Peter, and DUNCAN, Otis Dudley (1967), *The American Occupational Structure*, New York: John Wiley

BLOCH, Oscar, and WARTBURG, W. von (1964), *Dictionnaire Etymologique de la Langue Française*, Paris: Presses Universitaires de France

BLOUNT, Thomas (1969), *Glossographia* (1656) (facsimile edn), Menston: Scolar Press

BOETHIUS, Anicius Manlius Severinus (n.d.), *The Consolation of Philosophy*, trans. H. R. James, London: Routledge

BOTTOMORE, T. (1965), *Classes in Modern Society*, London: Allen & Unwin

BOTTOMORE, T. (1974), 'Social class', *Encyclopedia Britannica*, 15th edn, vol. 16, pp. 946–53

BUKHARIN, Nikolai (1925), *Historical Materialism: A System of Sociology*, London: Allen & Unwin

BURY, J. B. (1956), *A History of Greece to the Death of Alexander the Great*, 3rd edn, revised by Russell Meiggs, London: Macmillan

BUTLER, David, and STOKES, D. (1971), *Political Change in Britain*, Harmondsworth: Penguin Books

CALVERT, Peter (1970), *Revolution*, London: Pall Mall

CANTILLON, Richard (1931), *Essai sur la Nature du Commerce en Général*, ed. and trans. Henry Higgs, CB, London: Macmillan for the Royal Economic Society

CENTERS, Richard (1949), *The Psychology of Social Classes*, Princeton: Princeton University Press

CLARKE, Peter (1978), *Liberals and Social Democrats*, Cambridge: Cambridge University Press

CLIFF, Tony (1974), *State Capitalism in Russia*, London: Pluto Press (taken from *Stalinist Russia, a Marxist Analysis*, 1955)

COLE, G. D. H. (1950), 'The conception of the middle classes', *British Journal of Sociology*, vol. I, no. 4, pp. 275–90

COLEMAN, James S., CAMPBELL, Ernest Q., *et al.* (1966), *Equality of Educational Opportunity*, Washington, DC: National Center for Educational Statistics

CONDORCET, Marie-Jean-Antoine-Nicolas Caritat, Marquis de (1955), *Sketch for a Historical Picture of the Progress of the Human Mind*, trans. June Barraclough, intro. Stuart Hampshire, London: Weidenfeld & Nicolson

COOLEY, Charles Horton (1956), *Two Major Works: Social Organisation and Human Nature and the Social Order*, Glencoe, Ill.: Free Press

COOPER, Jilly (1979), *Class: A View From Middle England*, London: Eyre Methuen

COTGROVE, S. (1967), *The Science of Society*, London: Allen & Unwin

COWE, James (1799), 'On the advantages which result from Christianity, and on the influence of Christian principles on the mind and conduct', review in *Gentleman's Magazine*, August

COX, Oliver Cromwell (1970), *Caste, Class and Race*, New York: Monthly Review Press

CROMPTON, Rosemary, and GUBBAY, Jon (1977), *Economy and Class Structure*, London: Macmillan

CROSLAND, C. A. R. (1956), *The Future of Socialism*, London: Jonathan Cape

DAHL, Robert A. (1961), *Who Governs? Democracy and Power in an American City*, New Haven, Conn.: Yale University Press

DAHRENDORF, Ralf (1959), *Class and Class Conflict in Industrial Society*, London: Routledge

DANTE, Alighieri (1954), *Monarchy and Three Political Letters*, intro. Donald Nicholl, London: Weidenfeld & Nicolson

DAVIS, Kingsley (1948), *Human Society*, New York: Macmillan

DAVIS, Kingsley (1966), *Human Society*, New York: Macmillan

DAVIS, Kingsley, and MOORE, Wilbert E. (1945), 'Some principles of stratification', *American Sociological Review*, vol. V, no. 2, pp. 242–9

DE GEORGE, Richard T. (1968), *The New Marxism: Soviet and East European Marxism since 1956*, New York: Pegasus

Dictionary of National Biography (1920–80), Oxford University Press

DJILAS, Milovan (1957), *The New Class: An Analysis of the Communist System*, London: Thames & Hudson

DURKHEIM, E. (1964), *The Division of Labour in Society*, London: Collier Macmillan

EISENHOWER, Dwight David (1965), *The White House Years, 1956–1961*, New York: Doubleday

ENGELS, F. (1975), 'The conditions of the working class in England from personal observation and authentic sources', in Karl Marx and Frederick Engels, *Collected Works*, vol. IV, London: Lawrence & Wishart, pp. 295–596

FABIUS, Laurent (1975), *La France Inégale*, Paris: Hachette

FERGUSON, Adam (1966), *An Essay on the History of Civil Society*, Edinburgh: Edinburgh University Press (first published 1767)

FINLEY, M. I. (1971), *The Ancestral Constitution*, Cambridge: Cambridge University Press

FLOUD, Jean (1950), 'Educational opportunity and social mobility', in *The Year Book of Education*, London: Evans Bros. for University of London Institute of Education, pp. 117–35

FRANK, André Gunder (1971), *Capitalism and Underdevelopment in Latin America; Historical Studies of Chile and Brazil*, Harmondsworth: Penguin Books

220   *Bibliography*

FRANK, André Gunder (1977), 'Dependence is dead, long live dependence and the class struggle: an answer to critics', *World Development*, vol. V, no. 4, pp. 355–70

GALBRAITH, John Kenneth (1958), *The Affluent Society*, London: Hamish Hamilton

GALLIE, W. B. (1955–6), 'Essentially-contested concepts', *Proceedings of the Aristotelian Society*, vol. LVI, pp. 167–98

GALTUNG, Johan (1974), *A Structural Theory of Revolutions*, Rotterdam: Rotterdam University Press

GARDNER, Brian (1973), *The Public Schools: An Historical Survey*, London: Hamish Hamilton

GATHORNE-HARDY, Jonathan (1977), *The Public School Phenomenon*, London: Hodder & Stoughton

GEIGER, Theodor (1932), *Die soziale Schichtung des deutschen Volkes; soziographischer Versuch auf statistischer Grundlage*, Stuttgart: Ferdinand Enke Verlag

GEIGER, Theodor (1949), *Die Klassengesellschaft in Schmelztiegel*, Cologne and Hagen: Verlag Gustav Kiepenhauer

GERTH, H. H., and MILLS, C. Wright, eds. (1948), *From Max Weber*, London: Routledge

GIDDENS, Anthony (1973), *The Class Structure of the Advanced Societies*, London: Hutchinson

GIDDINGS, Franklyn Henry (1898), *Elements of Sociology*, New York: Macmillan

GLASS, David Victor, ed. (1954), *Social Mobility in Britain*, London: Routledge & Kegan Paul

GOLDTHORPE, John (1980), *Social Mobility and Class Structure*, Oxford: Oxford University Press

GOLDTHORPE, John H., and HOPE, Keith (1974), *The Social Grading of Occupations*, Oxford: Clarendon Press

GOLDTHORPE, John H., and LOCKWOOD, D. (1963), 'Affluence and the British class structure', *Sociological Review* (n.s.), vol. XI, no. 2, pp. 133–63

GOLDTHORPE, John H., LOCKWOOD, D., BECHHOFER, F., and PLATT, J. (1967), 'The affluent worker and the thesis of *embourgeoisement*: some preliminary research findings', *Sociology*, vol. I, January, pp. 11–31

GOLDTHORPE, J. H., LOCKWOOD, D., BECHHOFER, F., and PLATT, J. (1969), *The Affluent Worker in the Class Structure*, Cambridge: Cambridge University Press

GORDON, Milton Myron (1958), *Social Class in American Sociology*, Durham, NC: Duke University Press; Cambridge: Cambridge University Press

GRETTON, J. (1969), *Students and Workers; An Analytical Account of Dissent in France, May–June 1968*, London: Macdonald

HABERMAS, Jürgen (1976), *Legitimation Crisis*, London: Heinemann

HABERMAS, Jürgen (1979), *Communication and the Evolution of Society*, London: Heinemann

HALLER, William, and DAVIES, Godfrey, eds. (1944), *The Leveller Tracts, 1647–53*, New York: Colombia University Press

HALSEY, A. H. (1978), 'The Reith Lectures', *The Listener*, 12 January–16 February

HALSEY, A. H., HEATH, A. F., and RIDGE, J. M. (1980), *Origins and Destination: Family, Class and Education in Modern Britain*, Oxford: Oxford University Press

HAMILTON, Richard F. (1967), *Affluence and the French Worker in the Fourth Republic*, Princeton: Princeton University Press

HAMPSHER-MONK, Iain (1976), 'The political theory of the Levellers: Putney, property and Professor Macpherson', *Political Studies*, vol. XXIV, no. 4, pp. 397–422

HANWAY, Jonas (1767), *Letters on the Importance of the Rising Generation of the Laboring Part of our Fellow-subjects*, 2 vols., London: A. Millar and T. Cadell

HANWAY, Jonas (1772), *Observations on the Causes of the Dissoluteness which reigns among the Lower Classes of the People; the Propensity of some to Petty Larceny, and the Danger of Gaming, Concubinage, and an excessive Fondness for Amusement in high life, etc.*, London: J. & F. Rivington

HAUSER, Robert M. (1970), 'Educational stratification in the United States', in Edward O. Laumann (ed.), *Social Stratification: Research and Theory*, Indianapolis: Bobbs-Merrill

HAVELOCK, Eric A. (1957), *The Liberal Temper in Greek Politics*, London: Jonathan Cape

HEGEL, Georg Wilhelm Friedrich (1962), *Philosophy of Right*, trans. and notes T. M. Knox, Oxford: Clarendon Press

HELVÉTIUS, Claude Adrien (1909), *De l'esprit* (1758), Paris: Mercure de France

HIGGS, Henry (1968), *The Physiocrats; Six Lectures on the French Economistes of the Eighteenth Century* (1897), New York: Augustus M. Kelley

HOGGART, Richard (1957), *The Uses of Literacy: Aspects of Working Class Life with Special Reference to Publications and Entertainments*, London: Chatto & Windus

HOLBACH, Paul Heinrich Dietrich, Freiherr von (1971), *La Politique Naturelle, ou Discours sur les Vrais Principes du Gouvernement* (1773), facsimile, Hildesheim: Georg Olms Verlag

HOLBACH, Paul Heinrich Dietrich, Freiherr von (1773), *Système Social, ou Principes Naturels de la Morale et de la Politique, avec un Examen de l'influence du Gouvernement sur les Moeurs*, 3 vols., London

HOLLINGSHEAD, August (1967), *Elmtown's Youth: The Impact of Social*

Classes on Adolescents (1949), rpt. edn, New York: Wiley

HORKHEIMER, Max (1978), 'The end of reason', in Andrew Arato and Eike Gebhardt (eds.), *The Essential Frankfurt School Reader*, Oxford: Blackwell

HOROWITZ, Irving Louis (1972), *Three Worlds of Development, the Theory and Practice of International Stratification*, 2nd edn, New York: Oxford University Press

INKELES, Alex (1950), 'Social stratification and mobility in the Soviet Union: 1940–1950', *American Sociological Review*, vol. XV, pp. 465–79

INKELES, Alex (1968), *Social Change in Soviet Russia*, Cambridge, Mass.: Harvard University Press

International Encyclopedia of the Social Sciences (1972) ed. D. L. Sills, London: Collier-Macmillan

JACKSON, B., and MARSDEN, D. (1962), *Education and the Working Class*, London: Routledge & Kegan Paul

JOHNSON, Samuel (1785), *A Dictionary of the English Language ... a History of the Language and an English Grammar*, 2 vols., 6th edn, London: J. F. & C. Rivington

JOLL, James (1977), *Gramsci*, London: Fontana

JOUSSAIN, André (1949), *Les Classes Sociales*, Paris: Presses Universitaires de France

KALTON, Graham (1966), *The Public Schools*, London: Longman

KAUTSKY, Karl (1900a), *The Class Struggle*, trans. Daniel De Leon, New York: Socialist Labor Party

KAUTSKY, Karl (1900b), *The Socialist Republic*, New York: Labor News

KAUTSKY, Karl (1903), *The Social Revolution*, trans. J. B. Askew, London: Twentieth Century Press

KAUTSKY, Karl (1908), *The Capitalist Class*, trans. Florence Baldwin, London: Twentieth Century Press

KAUTSKY, Karl (1964), *The Dictatorship of the Proletariat*, Ann Arbor: University of Michigan Press

KEY, Vladimir Orlando, Jr (1964), *Politics, Parties and Pressure Groups*, 5th edn, New York: Crowell

KNEI-PAZ, Baruch (1978), *The Social and Political Thought of Leon Trotsky*, Oxford: Clarendon Press

KOLAKOWSKI, Leszek (1978), *Main Currents of Marxism*, Oxford: Clarendon Press

KORNHAUSER, William (1960), *The Politics of Mass Society*, London: Routledge & Kegan Paul

LANE, David (1971), *The End of Inequality? Stratification under State Socialism*, Harmondsworth: Penguin Books

LANE, David (1976), *The Socialist Industrial State: Towards a Political Sociology of State Socialism*, London: Allen & Unwin

LAPPING, Brian (1970), *The Labour Government, 1964–70*, Harmondsworth: Penguin Books

LAUMANN, Edward O., ed. (1970), *Social Stratification: Research and Theory*, Indianapolis: Bobbs-Merrill

LEFF, Gordon (1968), *Medieval Thought from Saint Augustine to Ockham*, Harmondsworth: Penguin Books

LEHMANN, William Christian (1960), *John Millar of Glasgow, 1735–1801; His Life and Thought and His Contributions to Sociological Analysis*, Cambridge: University of Glasgow, Department of Social and Economic Research, Publications in Social and Economic Studies, no. 4

LENIN, Vladimir Ilych (1967), *Selected Works*, 3 vols., Moscow: Progress Publishers

LENIN, Vladimir Ilych (1968), *State and Revolution*, New York: International Publishers

LENSKI, Gerhard E. (1952), 'American social classes: statistical strata or social groups?', *American Journal of Sociology*, vol. LVIII, no. 2, pp. 139–44

LENSKI, Gerhard E. (1954), 'Status crystallisation: a non-vertical dimension of social status', *American Sociological Review*, vol. XIX, pp. 405–13

LENSKI, Gerhard, and LENSKI, Jean (1974), *Human Societies: An Introduction to Macro-Sociology*, New York: McGraw-Hill

LEWIS, Roy, and MAUDE, Angus (1949), *The English Middle Classes*, London: Phoenix House

LICHTHEIM, George (1962), *Marxism: An Historical and Critical Study*, London: Routledge & Kegan Paul

LINDGREN, J. Ralph (1973), *The Social Philosophy of Adam Smith*, The Hague: Martinus Nijhoff

LIPSET, Seymour Martin (1964a), *Political Man*, London: Heinemann

LIPSET, Seymour Martin (1964b), 'The changing class structure and contemporary European politics', *Daedalus*, vol. XCIII, pp. 271–303

LIPSET, Seymour Martin, and BENDIX, R. (1951), 'Social status and social structures', *British Journal of Sociology*, vol. V, pp. 150–68, 230–54

LIPSET, Seymour Martin, and BENDIX, R. (1952a), 'Social mobility and occupational career patterns, I: Stability of jobholding', *American Journal of Sociology*, vol. LVII, no. 4, pp. 366–74

LIPSET, Seymour Martin, and BENDIX, R. (1952b), 'Social mobility and occupational career patterns, II: Social mobility', *American Journal of Sociology*, vol. LVII, no. 5, pp. 494–505

LIPSET, Seymour Martin, and BENDIX, Reinhard (1953), *Class, Status and Power*, Glencoe, Ill.: Free Press

LIPSET, Seymour Martin, and BENDIX, Reinhard (1959), *Social Mobility in Industrial Society*, London: Heinemann

LOCKE, John (1960), *Two Treatises of Government*, intro. and ed. Peter Laslett, Cambridge: Cambridge University Press

LUKÁCS, Gyorgy (1971), *History and Class Consciousness: Studies in Marxist Dialectics*, trans. R. Livingstone, London: Merlin

LYND, Robert, and LYND, Helen (1929), *Middletown*, New York: Harcourt, Brace and World

LYND, Robert, and LYND, Helen (1937), *Middletown in Transition: A Study in Cultural Conflicts*, New York: Harcourt, Brace & World

MCCARTHY, Thomas (1978), *The Critical Theory of Jürgen Habermas*, London: Hutchinson

MACIVER, Robert M., and PAGE, Charles H. (1949), *Society: An Introductory Analysis*, New York: Holt, Rinehart & Winston

MCKENZIE, R. T. and SILVER, Allan (1968), *Angels in Marble; Working Class Conservatives in Urban England*, London, Heinemann

MCLELLAN, David (1972), *Marx before Marxism*, Harmondsworth: Penguin Books

MCLELLAN, David (1977), *Engels*, London: Fontana

MADISON James, *et al*. (1948), *The Federalist*, Oxford: Blackwell

MANDEL, Ernest (1975), *Late Capitalism*, trans. Joris De Bris, London: New Left Books

MANDEVILLE, Bernard (1728), *The Fable of the Bees, or, Private Vices, Public Benefits*, 5th edn, London

MARCEAU, Jane (1974), 'Education and social mobility in France', in F. Parkin (ed.), *The Social Analysis of Class Structure*, London: Tavistock

MARCEAU, Jane (1977), *Class and Status in France; Economic Change and Social Immobility, 1945–1975*, Oxford: Clarendon Press

MARCUSE, Herbert (1972), *One Dimensional Man*, London: Sphere Books

MARSHALL, T. H., ed. (1938), *Class Conflict and Social Stratification*, London: Institute of Sociology

MARSHALL T. H. (1950), *Citizenship and Social Class*, Cambridge: Cambridge University Press

MARSHALL, T. H. (1964), *Class, Citizenship and Social Development*, New York: Doubleday

MARX, Karl (1962), *Capital: A Critique of Political Economy*, 3 vols. Moscow: Foreign Languages Publishing House

MARX, Karl (1973), *Grundrisse*, trans. Martin Nicolaus, Harmondsworth: Penguin Books

MARK, Karl, and ENGELS, Friedrich (1962), *Selected Works*, 2 vols., Moscow: Foreign Languages Publishing House

MARX, Karl, and ENGELS, Friedrich (1975, 1976), *Collected Works*, London: Lawrence & Wishart

MATHIAS, Peter (1969), *The First Industrial Nation*, London: Methuen

MATTHEWS, Mervyn (1978), *Privilege in the Soviet Union: A Study of Elite Life-Styles under Communism*, London: Allen & Unwin

MAYO, Henry B. (1960), *Introduction to Marxist Theory*, New York; Oxford University Press

MEDVEDEV, Roy A. (1975), *On Socialist Democracy*, trans. and ed. Ellen de Kadt, London: Macmillan

MEEK, R. L. (1962), *The Economics of Physiocracy*, London: Allen & Unwin

MERTON, Robert K. (1968), *Social Theory and Social Structure*, New York: Free Press

MÉSZÁROS, István (1970), *Marx's Theory of Alienation*, London: Merlin

MÉSZÁROS, István, ed. (1971), *Aspects of History and Class Consciousness*, London: Routledge & Kegan Paul

MIDDLETON, Chris (1974), 'Sexual inequality and stratification theory', in Frank Parkin (ed.), *The Social Analysis of Class Structure*, London; Tavistock

MILLAR, John (1771), *Observations concerning the Distinction of Ranks in Society*, Dublin: T. Ewing

MILLAR, John (1787), *An Historical View of the English Government from the Settlement of the Saxons in England to the Accession of the House of Stewart*, London

MILLS, C. Wright (1951), *White Collar*, New York: Oxford University Press

MILLS, C. Wright (1956), *The Power Elite*, New York: Oxford University Press

MIRABEAU, Honoré Gabriel Raquetti, Comte de (1776), *Essai sur le Despotisme, seconde édition, augmentée & corrigée par l'Editeur de cet ouvrage*, London

MITFORD, Nancy, ed. (1956), *Noblesse Oblige: An Enquiry into the Identifiable Characteristics of the English Aristocracy*, London: Hamish Hamilton

MITRANY, David (1951), *Marx Against the Peasant: A Study in Social Dogmatism*, London: Weidenfeld & Nicolson

MONTESQUIEU, Charles-Louis de Secondat, Baron de (1966), *The Spirit of the Laws*, trans. Thomas Nugent, intro. Franz Neumann, New York: Hafner

MOSCA, Gaetano (1939), *The Ruling Class*, trans., ed. and intro. Arthur Livingstone, New York: McGraw-Hill

MOUSNIER, R. (1973), *Social Hierarchies, 1500 to the Present*, trans. P. Evans, London: Croom Helm

NETTL, Peter (1969), *Rosa Luxemburg*, abr. edn, Oxford: Oxford University Press

NOVE, A. (1975), 'Is there a ruling class in the USSR?' *Soviet Studies*, vol. XXVII, no. 4, pp. 615–38

ONIONS, C. T. ed. (1966), *The Oxford Dictionary of English Etymology*, Oxford: Clarendon Press

OSSOWSKI, S. (1963), *Class Structure in the Social Consciousness*, London: Routledge & Kegan Paul

Oxford English Dictionary (1933), ed. Sir J. A. H. Murray, Oxford: Oxford University Press

PACKARD, Vance (1961), *The Status Seekers*, Harmondsworth: Penguin Books

PAGE, Charles (1940), *Class and American Sociology*, New York: Dial Press

PARKIN, F. (1971), *Class, Inequality and Political Order: Social Stratification in Capitalist and Communist Societies*, London: McGibbon & Kee

PARKIN, F., ed. (1974), *The Social Analysis of Class Structure*, London: Tavistock

PARKIN, F. (1979), *Marxism and Class Theory: A Bourgeois Critique*, London: Tavistock

PARSONS, Talcott (1954), 'A revised analytical approach to the theory of social stratification', *Essays in Sociological Theory*, rev. edn, Glencoe, Ill.: Free Press

PARSONS, Talcott (1957), 'The distribution of power in American society', *World Politics*, vol. X, pp. 123–43

PERNOUD, Régine (1960), *Histoire de la Bourgeoisie en France, des Origines aux Temps Modernes*, Paris: Editions du Seuil

PFAUTZ, H. W. (1952), 'The current literature on social stratification: critique and bibliography', *American Journal of Sociology*, vol. LVIII, pp. 391–418

PLAMENATZ, John Petrov (1954), *German Marxism and Russian Communism*, London: Longman

PLATO, (1926), *Laws*, 2 vols., London: Heinemann; Cambridge, Mass: Harvard University Press

PLATO (1955), *The Republic of Plato*, trans. and intro. F. M. Cornford, Oxford: Clarendon Press

POSNER, C., ed. (1970), *Reflections on the Revolution in France, 1968*, Harmondsworth: Penguin Books

POULANTZAS, Nicos (1973), *Political Power and Social Classes*, London: New Left Books

POULANTZAS, Nicos (1974), *Classes in Contemporary Capitalism*, London: New Left Books

PREVITÉ-ORTON, C. W. (1953), *The Shorter Cambridge Medieval History*, Cambridge: Cambridge University Press

RAYNOR, John (1969), *The Middle Class*, London: Longman

REID, Ivan (1977), *Social Class Differences in Britain*, London: Open Books

REX, John Ardeme (1974), *Approaches to Sociology: An Introduction to Major Trends in British Sociology*, London: Routledge & Kegan Paul

RICARDO, David (1895), *Principles of Political Economy and Taxation*, ed. E. C. K. Ganner, London: George Bell

RIESMAN, David, GLAZER, Nathan, and DENNEY, Reuel (1961), *The Lonely Crowd*, abr. edn with new preface, New Haven, Conn.: Yale University Press

ROBINSON, Joan (1969), *The Cultural Revolution in China*, Harmondsworth: Penguin Books

ROSS, Alan S. C., ed. (1969), *What are U?*, London: André Deutsch

ROSS, Edward Alsworth (1920), *Principles of Sociology*, New York: Appleton

RUDÉ, George (1964), *The Crowd in History; A Study of Popular Disturbances in France and England, 1730–1848*, New York: John Wiley

RUNCIMAN, Walter G. (1966), *Relative Deprivation and Social Justice*, London: Routledge & Kegan Paul

SABINE, George H., and THORSON, T. L. (1973), *A History of Political Thought*, 4th edn, Hinsdale, Ill.: Dryden Press

SCHATTSCHNEIDER, E. E. (1961), *The Semi-Sovereign People*, New York: Holt, Rinehart & Winston

SCHRAM, Stuart R. (1963), *The Political Thought of Mao Tse-tung*, New York: Praeger

SCHUMPETER, Joseph Alois (1943), *Capitalism, Socialism and Democracy*, London: Allen & Unwin

SCHUMPETER, Joseph Alois (1951), *Imperialism and Social Classes*, New York: Augustus M. Kelley

SEALE, P., and MCCONVILLE, M. (1968), *French Revolution 1968*, London: Heinemann; Harmondsworth: Penguin Books

SENNETT, Richard, and COBB, Jonathan (1977), *The Hidden Injuries of Class*, Cambridge: Cambridge University Press

SHILS, Edward (1968), *'Deference' in Social Stratification*, ed. J. Jackson, Cambridge: Cambridge University Press

SILVER, Catherine Bodard (1973), 'Salon, foyer, bureau: women and the professions in France', *American Journal of Sociology*, vol. LXXVIII, no. 4, pp. 836–51

SMALL, Albion Woodbury (1905), *General Sociology*, Chicago: University of Chicago Press

SMITH, Adam (1925), *An Inquiry into the Nature and Causes of the Wealth of Nations*, 2 vols., ed. and intro. E. Cannan, London: Methuen

SOMBART, Werner (1967), *Der Bourgeois, zur Geistesgeschichte des modernen Wirtschaftsmenschen*, Munich: Duncker & Humblot; trans. as *The Quintessence of Capitalism*, New York: Fertig

SOROKIN, Pitrim (1927), *Social Mobility*, New York and London: Harper

SOROKIN, Pitrim (1928), *Contemporary Sociological Theories*, New York: Harper

SUMNER William Graham (1959), *Folkways, a Study of the Sociological Importance of Usages, Manners, Customs, Mores and Morals*, New York: Dover (first published by Ginn 1906)

SZELENYI, Ivan (1978–9), 'The position of the intelligentsia in the class structure of state socialist countries', *Critique*, X–XI, Winter–Spring, pp. 51–76

TAWNEY, R. H. (1931), *Equality*, London: Allen & Unwin

TITMUSS, Richard (1962), *Income Distribution and Social Change: A Study in Criticism*, London: Allen & Unwin

TOCQUEVILLE, Alexis de (1961), *Democracy in America*, trans. Henry Reeve, London: Oxford University Press

TOENNIES, Ferdinand (1967), 'Estates and classes', in R. Bendix and S. M. Lipset (eds.), *Class, Status and Power*, 2nd edn, Glencoe, Ill.: Free Press

TOURAINE, Alain (1966), *La Conscience Ouvrière*, Paris: Editions du Seuil

TROTSKY, Leon (1972), *The Revolution Betrayed: What is the Soviet Union and Where is it Going?*, New York: Pathfinder Press

TUMIN, Melvin M. (1953), 'Some principles of stratification: a critical analysis', *American Sociological Review*, vol.XVIII, pp. 387–93

TURGOT, Anne Robert Jacques, Baron de l'Aulne (1973), *Discours sur les Progrès Successifs de l'esprit Humain*, intro. Ronald L. Meek, Cambridge: Cambridge University Press

ULLMANN, Walter (1965), *A History of Political Thought: The Middle Ages*, Harmondsworth: Penguin Books

United Kingdom Office of Population Censuses and Surveys (1970), *Classification of Occupations, 1970*, London, HMSO

URRY, J. and WAKEFORD, J., eds. (1973), *Power in Britain: Sociological Readings*, London: Heinemann

VEBLEN, Thorstein (1918), *The Theory of the Leisure Class: An Economic Study of Institutions*, London: Allen & Unwin

WARD, Lester Frank (1906), *Applied Sociology*, Boston: Ginn

WARNER, W. Lloyd (1963), 'A methodology for the study of social class', in Meyer Fortes (ed.), *Social Structure*, Oxford: Clarendon Press

WARNER, William Lloyd (1964), *Democracy in Jonesville: A Study in Quality and Inequality*, New York: Harper (first published 1949)

WARNER, W. Lloyd, and LOW, J. O. (1947), *The Social System of the Modern Factory; or, the Strike, a Social Analysis*, New Haven: Yale University Press

WARNER, W. Lloyd, and LUNT, P. S. (1941), *The Social Life of a Modern Community*, New Haven: Yale University Press

WARNER, W. Lloyd, MEEKER, Marchia, and EELLS, Kenneth (1949), *Social Class in America*, Chicago: Science Research Associates Inc.

WARNER, W. Lloyd, MEEKER, Marchia, and WECKLER, N. L. (1949), 'Methods of determining social status', in R. J. Havighurst and Hilda Taba (eds.), *Adolescent Character and Personality*, New York: John Wiley

WARTBURG, Walther von (1940), *Französisches Etymologisches Wörterbuch*, Leipzig: B. G. Teubner

WATSON, W. (1964), 'Social mobility and social class in industrial communities', in M. Gluckman and E. Devons (eds.), *Closed Systems and Open Minds*, London: Oliver & Boyd

WEBER, Max (1922), *Wirtschaft und Gesellschaft*, from H. Gerth and C. W. Mills (eds.), *Max Weber: Essays in Sociology*, New York: J. C. B. Moler

WEBER, Max (1930), *The Protestant Ethic and the Spirit of Capitalism*, trans. Talcott Parsons, London: Allen & Unwin

WEBER Max (1965), *The Theory of Social and Economic Organization*, ed. and intro. Talcott Parsons, New York: Free Press

WESOLOWSKI, W. (1979), *Classes, Strata and Power*, London: Routledge & Kegan Paul

WESTERGAARD, John H., and RESLER, Henrietta (1975), *Class in Capitalist Society: A Study of Contemporary Britain*, London: Heinemann

WHITE, Theodore H. (1969), *The Making of the President, 1968*, New York: Atheneum Publishers

WOLFE, Don M., ed. (1967), *Leveller Manifestoes of the Puritan Revolution*, London: Frank Cass

WRIGHT, Thomas (1867), *The Journeyman Engineer: Some Habits and Customs of the Working Classes*, London

WRIGHT, Thomas (1873), *Our New Masters*, London

ZWEIG, Ferdynand (1961), *The Worker in an Affluent Society: Family life and Industry*, London: Heinemann

Index

individual(s), 111–13, 115,
129, 145, 169, 176, 177,
181, 190, 193, 201, 202,
203, 207, 210, 212, 215,
216
individualism, 101, 106
Indo-China, 145; first
Indo-China War
(1945–54), 193
industrial development, 181
industrial revolution, 18, 149,
204, 206
industrial society, 100, 163,
195
industrial work, 205
industrial workers, 141
industrialists, 74, 77, 123
industrialization, 97, 148, 175,
193, 194
industry, 181, 193, 194, 195,
199, 204
inequality, 114, 140, 161–2,
163, 178, 181, 199
inevitability of history, 136
inflation, 182, 200
influence, 135, 190
inheritance, 164
Inkeles, Alex, 144–7, 163
INSEE, 193
insurrection, 141
intellectuals, 80–1, 97, 116,
117, 129, 134, 136, 165,
188; secession of, 80
intelligentsia, 80, 97, 116, 122,
128, 145, 146, 159, 160,
162, 164–5, 170
interest groups, 190
interests, 114, 156, 171
international relations, 139
International Socialist group,
160
International Working Men's

Association, 79
Ireland, 72
Irish Free State, 172
Iron Age, 206
irrigation, 140
Islam(ic), 44, 144
issue areas, 190
Italy, 44, 185, 188, 196

Jackson, B., 180
Japan, 163, 185; Japanese, 127
Jesuits, 16
Jesus, 41–2
Jew(s), 15, 49, 51, 64, 101
jobs, 212
Johnson, Lyndon B., 189, 191
joint stock company, 203
Joll, James, 155
journalist(s), 173, 177
Joussain, André, 194
justice, 39, 172, 208

Kalton, Graham, 179
Kant, Immanuel, 70
Kautsky, Karl, 82, 116, 119,
131, 135, 137
Kennedy, John F., 189, 191
Key, Vladimer O., Jr, 200
Khrushchev, Nikita S., 128–9,
170
kind, 203
King, Bishop, 13
King, Martin Luther, 191
kings: in Greece, 31; in
medieval world, 44, 51, 62;
in Rome, 40
kingship, 101
kinship, 108–9; system, 140–1
Knei-Paz, Baruch, 160
Kolakowski, Leszek, 115
Korean War (1950–3), 191
Kornhauser, William, 187

242   *Index*

2

Revolution, Russian: (1905),
117; (February 1917), 119;
(October 1917), 83, 117,
120, 121, 130, 144, 157,
160, 161, 209
reward(s), 144–5, 147, 163,
175, 176, 181, 203, 204,
212
Rex, John, 176
Rhineland, 64
Rhone, 88
Ricardo, David, 55, 65–6,
67–8, 214
rich, the, 30, 32, 34, 35, 49, 54,
58–9, 60, 61, 64, 91, 152,
197, 205, 206
Riesman, David, 190–1
rising expectations, revolution
of, 134
risk, 205
robbers, 125
Robinson, Joan, 128
Rockefeller, John D., Sr,
107
Roman law, 52, 149
Romania, 150
Rome, 13, 23, 24–5, 211
Roosevelt, Franklin D., 188
Roosevelt, Theodore, 107–8
Rose, Richard, 180
Ross, Alan S. C., 211
Ross, Edward Alsworth, 114
Rossi, 163
Rousseau, Jean-Jacques, 58,
85, 86
royalists, 76
Rudé, George, 63
ruled, 152
rulers, 151
Runciman, Walter G., 114
rural, 122, 126, 189, 193, 198,
199, 200, 201

Russia, 15, 73, 116–22, 137,
146, 148–9, 209; *see also*
Soviet Union

St Petersburg, 115
salary, 195, 203
sales representatives, 174
Samurai, 144
sandals, 168
Santiago de Compostela, 87
savings, 86
Saxons, 61
Schattschneider, C. E., 191
school boards, 192
schoolmasters, 173
schools, 12, 25, 178–80, 191,
192
schools: independent, 179;
public, 179; state, 179–80
Schram, Stuart R., 123–7
Schumpeter, Joseph A.,
111–12, 186
science, 116
scientist(s), 146, 163
Scotland, 14, 23, 25, 48, 63
Seale, P., 197
Second International, 118
Second World War, 133, 136,
198
secret police, 150
selection, 179, 195, 199
self-awareness, 140
self-employed, 204
self-made man, 170
semi-proletarians/semi-proletariat,
120, 123, 124
senate, 60
Sennett, Richard, 192–3
Senusert III, King of Egypt, 36
servants, 24, 103, 131
Servian Constitution, 13, 24,
40, 85